ASPECTS OF WESTERN SUBANON FORMAL SPEECH

SUMMER INSTITUTE OF LINGUISTICS

PUBLICATIONS IN LINGUISTICS

Publication Number 81

EDITORS

Virgil Poulter
University of Texas
Arlington

Desmond C. Derbyshire
Summer Institute Of
Linguistics

ASSISTANT EDITORS

Alan C. Wares

Iris M. Wares

CONSULTING EDITORS

Doris A. Bartholomew
Pamela M. Bendor-Samuel
Robert A. Dooley
Jerold A. Edmondson
Austin Hale

Robert E. Longacre
Eugene E. Loos
William R. Merrifield
Kenneth L. Pike
Viola G. Waterhouse

ASPECTS OF WESTERN SUBANON FORMAL SPEECH

WILLIAM C. HALL

A Publication of
THE SUMMER INSTITUTE OF LINGUISTICS
and
THE UNIVERSITY OF TEXAS AT ARLINGTON
1987

© 1987 by the Summer Institute of Linguistics, Inc.
Library of Congress Catalog No:
ISBN: 0-88312-093-3

Printed in the United States of America

All Rights Reserved

No part of this publication may be reproduced, stored in a retrieval system, or transmitted in any form or by any means — electronic, mechanical, photocopy, recording or otherwise — without the express permission of the Summer Institute of Linguistics, with the exception of brief excerpts in magazine articles and/or reviews.

Copies of this and other publications of the Summer Institute of Linguistics may be obtained from

Bookstore
Summer Institute of Linguistics
7500 W. Camp Wisdom Rd.
Dallas, TX 75236

CONTENTS

Abbreviations and Symbols ix
Acknowledgements xi
1 Introduction 1
   1.1 Language and Linguistics 1
   1.2 Language and Society 2
   1.3 The Present Study 3
   1.4 The Observer 3
   1.5 Formal Speech 4
   1.6 The Western Subanon 5
2 Formal Situations 7
   2.0 Introduction 7
   2.1 Subanon Speech 7
      2.1.1 Speech Values 7
      2.1.2 Social Requisites 8
   2.2 Etic Units 11
      2.2.1 The Speech Situation 11
      2.2.2 The Speech Event 11
      2.2.3 The Speech Act 12
   2.3 Emic Units 12
      2.3.1 Social and Speech Situations 12
      2.3.2 Speech Events: Dialogue 15
      2.3.3 Speech Events: Monologue 16

Contents

- 2.4 Western Subanon Speech Situations and Events 17
  - 2.4.1 The *polontu* 'death ceremony' 18
    - 2.4.1.1 The *mongimunag* or cleansing ritual 18
    - 2.4.1.2 The feast of *dakul* or offering 19
    - 2.4.1.3 The *mogbonduan* or instruction event 20
  - 2.4.2 The *mogogoka'oy* or explanation event 21
  - 2.4.3 The *bisala* 'litigation' situation 23
  - 2.4.4 The Confrontation Event 26
  - 2.4.5 The *piglimudan* 'caused to gather' 28

3 Interchange Dynamics 32
- 3.0 Introduction 32
- 3.1 Participant Perceptions of the Speech Situation 32
- 3.2 Dynamics of Turn Taking 33
  - 3.2.1 Designated Turns 34
  - 3.2.2 Nondesignated Turns 36
- 3.3 Beginnings and Endings 37
  - 3.3.1 Beginnings 37
    - 3.3.1.1 Opening 37
    - 3.3.1.2 Validation of Claim 39
    - 3.3.1.3 Purpose, Apology, and Disclaimer 39
    - 3.3.1.4 Identification of Audience 41
  - 3.3.2 Endings 43
- 3.4 Back Channel Responses 45
- 3.5 Interruption 52

4 The Patterns of Poetry 55
- 4.0 Introduction 55
- 4.1 Parallel Structures 56
  - 4.1.1 Sung Genre 57
    - 4.1.1.1 The Epic 57
    - 4.1.1.2 The Séance 65
  - 4.1.2 Oral Genre Not Sung 69
    - 4.1.2.1 Prayer 1 69
    - 4.1.2.2 Prayer 2 74
- 4.2 Doublets 80
- 4.3 Conclusion 83

Contents

5 Poetic Patterns in Formal Speech 86
   5.0 Introduction 86
   5.1 Parallel Structure in Speech 86
   5.2 Parallelism and Linguistic Analysis 87
   5.3 Parallels from Formal Speech 88
      5.3.1 Linear Patterns 88
      5.3.2 Chiasmus 99
      5.3.3 Verbatim Repetition 107
      5.3.4 Word Forms 109
   5.4 Conclusion 110
   Appendix A   The *mongimunag* Event Text 113
   Appendix B   The Feast of *dakul* Event Text 125
   Appendix C   The *mogogoka'oy* Event Text 131
   Appendix D   The Confrontation Event Text 162
   Appendix E   A Polite Formal Request Text 184
   References 187

ILLUSTRATIONS

Figure 1.1	Social situations	13
Figure 1.2	Speech events	15
Figure 1.3	Kinds of dialogue activity	16
Figure 1.4	Kinds of monologue activity	17
Figure 2.1	Speech sequencing	23
Figure 3.1	Dialogue embedding	37
Figure 3.2	Back channel summary	49
Figure 4.1	Embedded analogous parallels	60
Figure 4.2	Embedded associative parallels	61
Figure 4.3	Grammatical structure paralleled	61
Figure 4.4	Complex synonymous parallel	63
Figure 4.5a	Simple analogous/grammatical parallels	63
Figure 4.5b	Analogous parallel	63
Figure 4.5c	Associative parallel	64
Figure 4.5d	An integrated parallel complex	64
Figure 4.6	Bidimensional array of Unit A sentence	70
Figure 5.1	Embedded sentence parallels	71
Figure 5.2	Embedded parallels	73
Figure 5.3	Parallels of Unit B, Prayer 2	77
Figure 5.4	Complex parallel	81
Figure 6.1	Parallel embedding	89
Figure 6.2	Clause 1a structure	89
Figure 6.3	Sentence component display	94
Figure 6.4	Display of base sentence	95
Figure 6.5	Display of reason margin	95
Figure 6.6	Display of cause margin	96
Figure 7.1	Repetitive parallel sentences	108

ABBREVIATIONS AND SYMBOLS

ab	ablative
acc	accessory
act	actor
adv	adverb
ana	anaphora
att	attributive marker
ben	beneficiary
Cl	clause
com	complementizer
det	determiner
dir	direction
emp	emphasis
ex	exclusive
exl	existential (there is/are/was/were)
f	focus
fru	frustrative particle
hes	hesitation
hs	hearsay particle
in	inclusive
int	intensifier
loc	locative (or, sometimes, ben)
mis	mistake/false start
mkr	marker
mod	modifier

n/	Nnoun
NP	noun phrase
nt	non-topic
p	plural
P	parallel
p.	page
par	particle
per	person
pity	particle expressing pity
pos	possessive marker
posS	postsentence
Pred	predicate
PredP	predicate phrase
PreS	presentence
pro	pronoun
prp/PrepP	preposition or prepositional phrase
que	question marker
rel	relative clause marker
s	singular
sta	stative particle
t	topic
uc	unreal condition marker
VP	verb phrase

SYMBOLS

:	length
...	time interval within texts
/	interchange in speech, enclosing auditor back channel responses and comments
"	English gloss approximation of the Subanon
( )	sets off editorial comment

Note: Abbreviations that identify pronouns are juxtaposed. For example, the pronoun **ita** will be identified as 1ptin or 1st-person-plural-topic-inclusive.

ACKNOWLEDGEMENTS

This monograph, except for some editorial adjustments, is essentially the doctoral dissertation I submitted to the Graduate Faculties of the University of Pennsylvania, 1983, entitled "Some Aspects of Formal Speech Among the Western Subanon of Mindanao." The data used here were gathered over a period of fourteen years while living in the Philippines and working under the auspices of the Summer Institute of Linguistics. Most of the time was spent among the Western Subanon people of Siocon and Malayal in Zamboanga del Norte on the island of Mindanao. I wish to express my appreciation to those who willingly allowed their speech to be recorded; to Rodrigo Salacao, who taped the proceedings of some ceremonies and who transcribed many hours of texts; to Pepe Iyan, with whom I have worked closely in transcribing and discussing the text materials; to Milanio Limpuson, an education administrator and Subanon leader who has been a great encouragement and help to us through the years; and, to many, many more who are too numerous to mention, who are like mother and father, sister and brother to us; and to the Subanons who have allowed us to enter into a fascinating involvement with them in their language and culture.

My appreciation extends to all those who have contributed to and made our work possible among the Subanon in the Philippines.

With deep appreciation, I want to thank my dissertation committee for their help and encouragement, for their instruction, for their reading and providing stimulating and profitable comments on early drafts of this work; Professor John Fought, for his consistent encouragement as dissertation supervisor; Professor Gillian Sankoff, who, even during times of pressing personal responsibilities, gave of her time in patient and helpful guidance; and, Professor Dell Hymes, for his in-depth comments, especially on Chapters 4 and 5, which stimulated new insights into the patterning of the data. For any faults, errors or inconsistencies herein, I alone am responsible.

Grateful acknowledgement is made to the Graduate School of Arts and Sciences of the University of Pennsylvania for their help by paying a part of the dissertation fee from 1978–1980.

I acknowledge my debt to my colleagues of the Summer Institute of Linguistics. I have gained much from their friendship, from their instruction, and from their encouragement along the way.

My gratitude is great to my family, especially to my wife, Lee, who has faithfully encouraged and sustained a sometimes discouraged and frustrated husband. She is an insightful and understanding companion and has shared in many experiences among the Subanon.

I thank God for His sustaining grace and love.

1 Introduction

1.1 Language and Linguistics

Bloomfield (1933:23) made a dichotomous distinction between the speech event and the practical events that are related to it, viz. the events that precede and follow the act of speech. He stated that " ... students of language are ... concerned precisely with the speech event ...." The speech event, or speech utterance is the form of speech while the *real* or *practical* events are the "meaning" (emphasis is Bloomfield's): " ... we say that speech-utterance, trivial and unimportant in itself, is important because it has a *meaning*: the meaning consists of the important things with which the speech-utterance is connected, namely the practical events" (ibid., 27).

However, because these practical events comprise so many independent variables, including, as he said, the personal background and experience of each interlocutor, he considered them to be imprecise and consequently outside the pale of linguistics as a science. Carroll (1953:2) characterized the linguistic scientist in his day as one who " ... does not immediately concern himself with how linguistic codes are learned by speaker or with how they are used by these speakers in referring to whatever they are communicating about." It is, however, the practical events that give the study of language its real importance and relevance to society.

Descriptive linguists usually do take into account a context of language use in their descriptive procedures. For example, in the development of Tagmemic theory, the principle of context has been included. Pike and Pike (1977:4) state that "the analyst must, for some purposes, turn his focus away from specific units-as-if-they-were-isolatable (or almost isolatable) and focus instead upon the unit-as-necessarily-in-context, since no unit is findable or definable except as a relation to context." A subprinciple under the principle of context is that "speech does not occur in a cultural or conceptual vacuum but is relative to some temporary kind of topic, style, genre, or situation, which may be called a *universe of discourse* (or *frame of reference*)." (Emphasis is Pike's; cf. also, Pike 1967.)

Yet, in day-to-day field analyses, the autonomy of language usually prevails and context is confined largely to linguistic environments. Autonomous linguistics looks for the system of language in formal rules of a norm. This is productive; but, there is more to language than this. Real life interaction between interlocutors reveals language in use. Language in use is very much a social behavior (cf. Goffman 1964, Hymes 1964).

In the tradition of structural descriptive linguistics a great deal of knowledge has been accumulated for comparative purposes in language studies. Along with this much insight has also been gained into the intricacies of the patterns of languages both collectively and individually. This conception that sees language as an autonomous entity, language as a whole "in and of itself" is one of the "two-fronts" of linguistics as a science (Jakobson 1963:219). The other of the two-fronts mentioned by Jakobson is "the interrelation of whole-part aspects," i.e., language as a "constituent part of culture and society" in the tradition of Boas and Sapir.

In the last two decades linguists have looked more and more at language in the social context, the meaning of language. Language as form, i.e., the formal structures of languages and their interrelationships whether on a phonological level, a dialogue, or a textual genre, is, of course, of primary concern to the linguist. Nevertheless, consideration of the social context of language use must not be excluded from a descriptive analysis if the study of language is to be relevant to real-life situations and applications.

1.2 Language and Society

Goffman (1964) has made a distinction between what he calls the correlational and the indicative approaches to analysis of language and society. The first makes a correlation between social variables and linguistic phenomena; the second is interested "in the uncovering of new properties or indicators in speech behavior" (ibid., 133). Both of these approaches necessitate the consideration of the context of the speech situation.

Gumperz makes the same dichotomy between correlational studies and what he calls interactional studies (Gumperz 1967, Gumperz and Hymes 1972 Introduction). He imputes basic assumptions to the two concepts: correlational studies being those which show the relationship between two independent systems, the linguistic and the social. The latter system is considered to be somewhat rule rigid. The interactional studies, on the other hand, are those in which language is perceived as an integral part of the social whole. Social categories are subject to situational constraints and the attendant roles are socially defined rather than individually defined. The emphasis upon context is an important feature.

Introduction

Sankoff (1972), in the same way, discusses the two approaches, correlational and interactional, from the point of view of code switches which occur in multilingual societies. The approaches are discussed in terms of trends: two trends, one being the emphasis on the functions of speech, which involves a more comprehensive ethnographic analysis; and, the other being an emphasis on the factors and components of speech (Hymes 1962; 1972; 1974). These two are the obverse of each other and termed interpretive. A third trend is that of linguistic variation which is exemplified by the work of Labov (1966; 1969; 1970).

1.3 The Present Study

The purpose of the present study is to turn attention towards one type of linguistic behavior found among the Western Subanon of Mindanao. In doing this, I am making a distinction between the study of language as an autonomous entity and studies of language use in culture context. The object of the study is to describe some of the speech behavior within the context of the formal speech situation. A major assumption here is that, along with linguistic structure and social structure, linguistic behavior within the social context is patterned and systematic (Goffman 1964, Gumperz 1964, Hymes 1962, Labov 1972).

Another major assumption in this work is that, in defining a speech situation (e.g., one that is formal within the definition of the speech community), the speech used (e.g., styles or codes) will tend to be under some constraint according to Western Subanon social propriety. Norms are described. Predictions regarding speech behavior can only be made in terms of these norms of expected behavior as they pertain to a designated context.

1.4 The Observer

William Labov (1972:209) has discussed the problem of what he has called the Observer's Paradox. This is the problem that confronts the linguistic researcher when he attempts to document certain kinds of natural casual speech without at the same time influencing that speech as an outsider. For his own purposes Labov devised various means to reduce the speaker's attention on the speech situation.

In one sense the attention placed upon the speech event is not a problem for the kind of speech discussed here. Formal speech is an art form engaged in largely for public purposes. And yet, on the other hand, because I am an "outsider" at Subanon gatherings formal speech could conceivably be stifled if I were the intended audience. However, the fact that no linguistic accommodation presently has to be made for me has helped and allowed me during ceremonies and gatherings to know what was happening, although at times not necessarily why it was happening.[1] Early on in language learning, when I began to record the speech during Subanon gatherings, the Subanons rightly recognized it as part of language learning. I could remain as unobtrusive as possible in the background. Now, when recording the speech at gatherings, I do not enter into any discussions that are being recorded — indeed, most of them do not involve me in any way.[2] There is usually ample opportunity to observe interactions that could later be correlated to the recorded tapes.

By nature, ceremonies are public gatherings and are open to all who wish to attend. In fact, a successful ceremony as a community gathering will be well attended. Having a recorder present at such a function has seemed generally to add to its communality. On occasions when I have not had a tape recorder some have been disappointed that discussion would be missed and hence their "deep" words, words that are more esoteric. I have been invited to certain gatherings as opportunities to record "deep" speech. Occasionally, reference is made during a recording to the fact of its being recorded but neither my presence nor the fact that the proceedings are being recorded has seemed to inhibit unrestrained verbal activity.

During ceremonies such as rituals (see sec. 2.3.1) I have asked if a recording could be made. In this way formal prayers at ritual ceremonies have been obtained (see sec. 4.1.2).

As an observer I have never "directed" a situation. Usually the microphones were simply passed out and the Subanons themselves have put them where the speech was taking place. Only on one occasion that has been recorded and that is included here has speech been possibly directed to me as audience (see sec. 2.4.5). It is my opinion that the nature of formal speech being public speech has allowed for a minimum of observer interference.

1.5 Formal Speech

It is necessary to define the use of the term "formal" here. Irvine (1979) has noted three principal senses of the use of the term in recent literature. Some authors have used the term in referring to discourse that is structured to the point of predictability. Others have used the term in describing the characteristics of a social situation including an increase in politeness and respect. Thirdly, "formal" is sometimes used in the sense of the analyst's statement of rules governing discourse.

Irvine's thesis is that formality should be defined more rigorously. She argues that there are at least four aspects of formality which may be considered as independent variables in a definition. She suggests that the formal situation may be described in terms of the identities of the participants — their positional or public identities. Another aspect of the formal situation is the focus of the gathering — who speaks and who listens, i.e., the focus of attention.

With regard to formal discourse or code, she suggests that there is an increase in structuring and predictability in syntax, including a predictability in

Introduction

turn taking. Also, there is in formal code a consistency in form, something that marks the code as being formal, whether it be pitch, speed, gestures, lexicon or the like.

In the following chapters, formal situations and some aspects of the speech which normally occurs in them, which herein is called formal speech, are described. In chapter 2, ceremonies and other gatherings are social situations that are event-structured according to community convention. Litigation also is structured not only in the events but also in the speech acts that take place. In chapter 2, the ceremonies are described as to their participants and focus or reason for gathering. Some basic Western Subanon speech attitudes are also discussed. In chapter 3 the dynamics of turn taking and listener response is described. Chapter 4 begins the description of the syntax and semantics of Western Subanon poetic forms. These largely consist of pattens of parallelism. Chapter 5 discusses parallelism in formal speech situations and how this poetic patterning helps to mark speech as being formal.

1.6 The Western Subanons

The Western Subanon are located in the provinces of Zamboanga del Norte and Zamboanga del Sur and in Zamboanga City on the island of Mindanao in the Philippines. They are primarily agriculturists and plant rice as their subsistence crop. They also plant corn and coconuts. Traditionally they are hunters. Many along the coasts have learned the fishing trade.

Although, generally speaking, educational opportunities have been limited for them, many have been able to take advantage of those facilities that have been available and have themselves become teachers, government employees, lawyers, and doctors. Education is a growing value among the Subanon.

The population of the Western Subanon numbers around thirty thousand. They largely maintain a traditional indigenous religion which is based upon the belief in and the placating of spirits. For fuller details regarding the Subanon, see Christie (1909), Finley and Churchill (1913), and Frake (1960; 1964a). Although these works center upon the Subanun around Sindangan Bay, the earlier works include the Western Subanon areas as well. Frake describes the Eastern Subanun in terms that, as far as I have seen, are applicable to the Western Subanon as well.

Notes

1. I attended a gathering, a litigation event, at which there were also several Visayans, a lowland majority language group. The Subanon councilor in charge of the litigation event made a statement at the outset that no linguistic accommodation would be made for "outsiders", i.e., there would be no use of the Visayan language in any of the proceedings.

2. The ceremonies and gatherings that were recorded have been done so on one of three tape recorders. One was a Uher 4400 stereo reel-to-reel tape recorder, the power source of which was a 6 volt motorcycle battery. The two microphones were lavaliere type and each had ten feet of cord. The second recorder was more often used, a Superscope C-105 cassette recorder with a lavaliere microphone. A third, a Sony cassette recorder, was given to Subanon friends who attended local ceremonies and recorded them for me in my absence.

2 Formal Situations

2.0 Introduction

The discussion of those linguistic phenomena that include discourse considerations must take into account the wider context of speech which includes the social situation, the participants, and the goals and purposes of speech.

In sections 2.1 through 2.3, Subanon attitudes to and emic notions of verbal behavior will be discussed. The discussion will include some of the major social requisites and community attitudes towards speaking in general and speaking in formal situations in particular. In section 2.4, descriptive accounts of three social situations and the major speech events that occurred in them are presented.

2.1 Subanon Speech

2.1.1 Speech Values. Speech, as it occurs in context, may be described in several different ways by the Subanon. Speech in which the meaning is transparent and well understood is said to be **mologdong nog talu'**[1] or 'straight speech' where **mologdong** = 'straight', **nog** = relation marker,[2] and **talu'** = 'speech'. One may use indirect speech (**poglalag**) in which rhetorical figures are used to perhaps obscure meaning. These figures are called **dalil nog talu'** or simply **dalil** 'figurative speech'.[3] **Dalil** has the effect of excluding some hearers but being well understood by others.

When an argument has been answered correctly and to the point or an issue has been clearly defined, then the issue or argument has been 'struck'[4] (**misugat nog talu'** 'struck speech').

Speech uttered in anger is direct and abrupt. Such speech is generally considered by the Western Subanon to be inconsiderate and harsh. It puts people on the spot, causes them shame, and makes them defensive. Speech of this abrupt manner is said to be **motogas nog talu'** 'hard speech'. In public speech, the valued speech characteristic is that of **molamit nog talu'** 'soft speech' or polite speech. Both polite speech and abrupt speech may be speech that is understood by all (**mologdong** 'straight') or it may be speech the understanding of which is limited to a certain audience (**dalil**). This thesis concerns the use of polite or "soft speech".

2.1.2 Social Requisites. The Western Subanon place a positive value on formal speech. There are several factors which, for the Subanon, exemplify a good speaker. These include social requisites such as sex, age, and the ability to use particular linguistic features recognized as elements of formal speech.

A good speaker (**bolomisala/polomisala** 'one who speaks in litigation') in the Western Subanon context is one who can present an argument in a discussion or story in a step-by-step manner (**piksukpatsukpat** 'attached end to end')[5] so that it may be followed easily as one can follow a trail (**motontul** 'follow a track', **dumalan** 'follow a trail').

To be able to achieve speech that "follows a trail" requires not only a knowledge of the language and a knowledge of how to use "soft speech", but it requires also an intuition of what is anticipated by the hearers and the ability to meet such an anticipation.

The good speaker, and one who upholds the formal speech values of the community, generally is male and at least fifty years old. Although not every male fifty years old or older is necessarily a good speaker in the formal sense, the notably good speakers that have come to my attention are of this group. An older man is a potential wealth of knowledge regarding the traditional customs and litigation decisions made in time past. He has learned the figurative language and verbal art forms which are so important in indirect speech, which is one characteristic of soft speech (cf. Malagasy **kabary** in Keenan 1974; 1975).

Younger men who take an active part in presenting their opinions are sometimes referred to in a slightly pejorative sense as being "prone to talk" (**bakan poktalu'**). If, on occasion, a younger man exhibits verbal ability in formal speech, as well as wisdom in content, he may be said to know how to speak or know how to present an argument (**moto moktalu'/moto misala**). But it would be unusual for him to take a place in discussion groups with the older men unless he has attained a socially recognized political role such as Barrio Councilor or Barrio Captain.

Much like the Malagasy situation described by Keenan (1977), Subanon women are characteristically less inhibited in social situations than are men,

Formal Situations

and older women less so than younger women. Women tend to be much more direct in their speech, in the stories they tell, and the questions they ask. Their general speech activity cannot be construed as being aberrant or unnatural to the culture.

Women will often give disclaimers to their ability to speak in formal situations. The implication of such disclaimers is that they lack expertise in the speech that is associated with male speech roles. There is a corollary to this that women's speech is not often highly regarded in formal situations.[6] An example of just such a disclaimer comes from an old and highly respected woman in the community at the close of her short speech.

```
Dadi o',     akon  koyon
so   (par)   I     that
       og botad    nog    botad   sog...solod   nog    bonua,
       (t)custom   (rel)  custom  (ab) inside   (nt)   land
       migustal   na    kumanak   u     koni
       related    now   cousin    my    this
       bu    gilug    u     konia   migustal   na    dinika
       and   brother  my    this    related    now   to-you(s)
     akon  do     ma
     I     (sta)  (emp)
       mika'an  do     bo     en   doga
       few      (sta)  (emp)  it   other
       po'       og    glibun   kini   mika'an  bo
       because   (t)   female   this   few      (emp)
            en   da     ogog   gan   non.
            it   (sta)  (t)    thing it
Dadi  akon,
so    I
       kitu'   tibua  og    tinalu'  u
       that    just   (t)   said     I
       po'       kalangalang   u   di'   indog   dini
       because   hesitate      I   not   stand   here
       po'       dinondag    u   nog
       because   requested   I   (nt)
            gombata'   u   koni   mokodongog
            children   I   this   listen-to
            do      sop   nog   ginakon   nog   midongog  u.
            (sta)   also  (nt)  mine      (nt)  heard     I
```

'And so, you know, as for me
   as for the custom which is the custom of the land,
   my cousin related it already
   and my brother related it already to you.
   regarding me,
      little has been added
         because regarding women, very little is her thing.
And so, regarding me
   that is all that constitutes my speech
   because I am hesitant to not stand up here
   because I was requested to do so
      by these my children so that they will hear
      my contribution that I have heard'.

The disclaimer belies her expertise. First of all, the structure of this portion of her speech shows several parallels, a major characteristic of formal speech (see chap. 5). She has made three comparisons: 1) between the custom of the land and hearsay, 2) between relating by explanation and merely speaking, and 3) between males and herself.

Women do speak in traditional formal styles; however, the female speech role in the community is contrasted with the role of the male. The male role is that of arbitrator or "speaker" which is a role often associated with responsibility in the maintenance of tradition and customs.

There is a Subanon saying that runs thus: **Bila og glibun, og bosi non og baba' non.** 'As for a woman, her weapon is her mouth'. Strength may be measured in more than one way. A woman cannot contend in a quarrel which becomes physical, but she can speak and often exercises her prerogatives with sharp expertise. During litigation sessions women are the ones more likely to express themselves in a direct manner (cf. Appendix D secs. 2, 4 and 5) which would not exemplify the values of formal speech, viz. to be unemotional, indirect, and use good argument, and to avoid as much as possible a confrontation where one party would be caused shame (see also Keenan 1974). There are, of course, exceptions; but, as a general rule, the woman's predilection for direct speech can be seen from the following recorded example:

```
U ay,  bila akon  gompok o',    posisaya'      u    tua'.
huh    if   I     dislike  (par) all-the-more   I    attend

Moktalu' u   nog   ain       glegan    ku    moktalu'.   (CA029)
speak    I   (nt)  whatever  desire    my    speak
```

'Well now, if it were I who did not want it (to be sanctioned by the council), I would all the more appear (at the council litigation). I would say whatever I wanted to say'.

Formal Situations

Speech values and attitudes may be more readily exemplified in the following sections where several speech situations have been displayed in such a way as to show the components of each speech event within the situation.

2.2 Etic Units

Pike and Pike (1977) make provision for talking about context (not just speech context) in Tagmemic theory by positing a referential tagmeme. "The etics of such a referential hierarchy is whatever any person in the world talks about . . ." (p.363).[7] This referential tagmeme functions as an integrated hierarchy with the grammatical and phonological hierarchies. The tagmeme consists of four functions

slot	class(es)
role	cohesion

slot: identifies where the item comes in its context.

role: asks what the purpose and/or determinants of an action are; what the role identity of the item (or actor) is.

class(es): identifies the form of an action or individual or thing performing it.

cohesion: asks how the item relates to others within the system; what the governing factors in this relationship are.

The feature of cohesion incorporates the considerations of time, space, social interaction, and presupposition.

Hymes (1972; 1974) has proposed heuristic units of speech context and components of acts of speech. In the description of speech interaction or communication these units and components help to segment and/or isolate, within context (i.e., the context is retrievable) the focus of analysis.

2.2.1 The Speech Situation. The speech situation is a discrete context with which speech, or the marked absence of it, is associated. A speech situation may define certain rules that govern aspects of settings or genre (Hymes 1974:51). A religious ceremony defines the kinds of speech events and nonverbal events which may be included in it. The Subanon **bisala** 'litigation' is an example of a Subanon speech situation.

2.2.2 The Speech Event. The speech event is a discrete speech activity that is governed by rules, or norms for the use of speech (Hymes 1974:52). Speech events may be composed of single or multiple speech acts. Speech events may also comprise a speech situation. Conversations, discussions, and epic singing are examples of speech events.

2.2.3 The Speech Act. The interest in speech interaction and the increasing interest in linguistics in whole utterance analysis has focused attention, in the last few years, on several concepts developed by philosophers, e.g., speech act, illocutionary force, and the performative (Austin 1962, Searle 1969, Grice 1975, cf. Searle, et al. 1980, Cole and Morgan 1975, and most recently in a Philippine context, Rosaldo 1982). The speech act as an etic unit is our interest here.

The speech act is the minimal unit of the speech event. It is a level of grammar that is distinct from other levels. Speech act significance may be dependent upon phonology (e.g., intonation), syntax (e.g., particles, sentence order), and the social relationships between interlocutors (Hymes 1974:52f). Hymes has listed sixteen etic components including message form and content, setting and scene, the participants involved in the speech interaction, the purpose or goal intended by a speech act, the tone or manner in which it is given, the channel or medium of the transmission of speech, the forms of speech or language(s) available for use, styles, norms of interaction, and genre or categories of kinds of speech acts.

2.3 Emic Units

The speech situation is similar to the social situation described by Blom and Gumperz (1972). The speech situation is a sociolinguistic rubric focusing upon communication processes and verbal interactions in social settings. The term social situation speaks to a general social description of activities, albeit one in which communicative processes occur. In this section I will present a taxonomy of Subanon speech and social situations, the events which may occur, and some of the speech acts that occur in them.

2.3.1 Social and Speech Situations. The Subanon lexicon contains a number of terms which include the semantic components of verbal behavior and of gathering together. Examples of these terms are found in figure 1.1.

In column A are terms whose primary component is that of gathering together. I have found that these terms are generally interchangeable — they are synonyms; however, individuals do have their preferences for using one term over another.

In column B are terms whose primary component is that of speech interaction between interlocutors. (This list is not intended to be exhaustive.)

The terms listed in columns C and D are grouped here for the sake of display and not necessarily as a Subanon would initially group them. I have talked to some Subanons about this grouping and it is a viable one. They would tend, however, to make groupings according to the specific function or purpose of the ceremony thus emphasizing the distinctness of each ceremony. I have grouped under the one rubric religious those ceremonies

Formal Situations

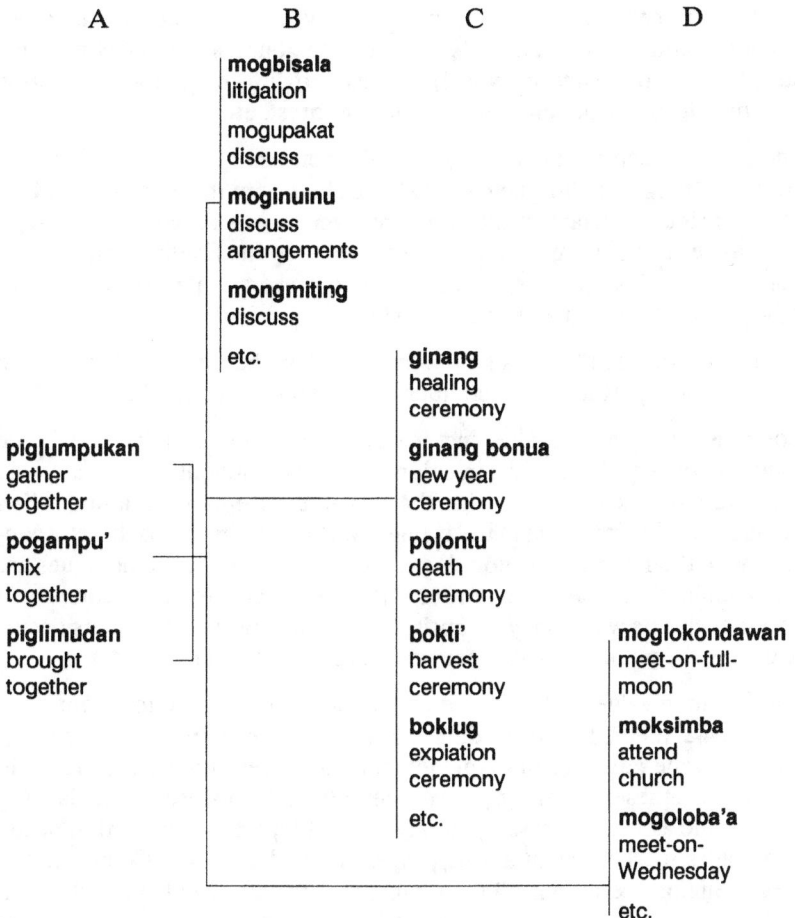

Figure 1.1 Social situations

that are associated with the Subanon "religious" (i.e., a relationship to the spirit world) belief (**tanud**) and their traditions (**solosila**) handed down to them. These involve community gatherings and the concomitant speech activity.

So then, in column C are terms whose primary component is traditional religious belief. For example, **ginang** includes ceremonies performed in order to restore the health of an individual. These ceremonies are conducted by a shaman (**mokosun** 'one who knows') and usually at least one of the council (**bogolal**) present. The religious functions of these activities are the offering and prayers made in the due course of the ceremony. **Ginang bonua** is a yearly ceremony the purpose of which is to take care of past sins committed against the unseen world and to start the new year with peace. Ceremonies like **bokti'**, on the other hand, (described by the Subanon as showing courteous behavior to the unseen world) are made to different deities in relation to planting, harvesting, before going into the forest, etc.

The events in column D are kinds of ritual performance. These might also be termed "religious" but they are distinguished from those in column C in that they primarily relate to the ritual involved as acts of worship (**tamuy**). For example, a whole church service (referred to by the English term "divine worship") provides sermons, instruction, and prayers as part of the normative behavior associated with the gathering.

Columns B through D are a kind of column A in that the people gather to perform or take part in those activities described in columns B through D.

Columns B through D are distinct from each other but each includes some component of verbal behavior: in column B the component is a primary one of dialogue (see sec. 2.3.2), with the possible exception of **mongmiting** 'discuss'.[8] In columns C and D the primary verbal activity that is directly concerned with their contexts is monologue (see sec. 2.3.3). The monologues are seldom planned but there is a norm for the speech events that occur as well as the speech acts which may comprise them. (Several speech events occurring during the **polontu** 'death ceremony' are described in sec. 2.4.)

The Subanon value a situation where conduct is conducive to an outcome of good social feelings.[9] Music, dance, and refreshment (including the ubiquitous rice wine **gasi**) are integral elements in the ceremonies illustrated in column C. At these gatherings, people tend to look forward to the dancing and rice wine as they represent, among other things, the culmination of the preliminary speeches, negotiations, prayers, and other events. Coming at the end of "religious ceremonies" they signal that certain rites have ended and therefore the consequent obligations to the unseen world are fulfilled, at least for the time being.[10]

The use of language within all of the gatherings in figure 1.1 may be diagnostic. Philippine societies are generally multilingual, including the Subanon. The local criterion for language choice is based upon cultural identifications and associations. The recognized gatherings within the Subanon culture are situations where Subanon code is used by Subanons as a norm.[11] As a rule, when Western Subanons are speaking to Western Subanons, the code used is Western Subanon.[12]

The purpose of some gatherings may be contrived, e.g., a gathering called to hear a speech or report. (One such gathering is described in sec. 2.4.5.) Sometimes contrived gatherings for the purpose of monologue become that of dialogue (**gupakat**). The outcome or ends component of the speech act is an important consideration in an analysis of gatherings.

Formal Situations

2.3.2 Speech Events: Dialogue. Dialogue (**bitan**) occurs as the very purpose for meeting in several Subanon speech events. Figure 1.2 illustrates a Subanon's conception of the relationships between the events.

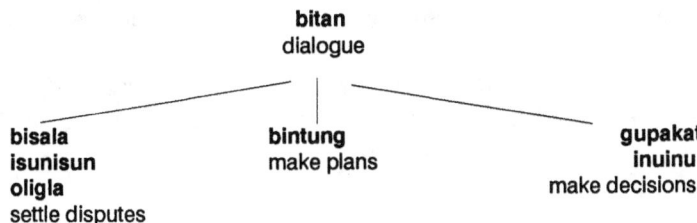

Figure 1.2 Speech events

gupakat is a discussion for the purpose of making decisions or arriving at a solution for a common problem. A P.T.A. meeting could be a **gupakat** if there were specific decisions to be made; or, it may simply be a **miting** 'meeting', a more general gathering for discussion and information.

bintung involves a discussion in which plans are made. The participants are not expected to be of one mind so the purpose here is to come to consensus. **Bintung** is said to be preliminary to a **gupakat**.

inuinu is a meeting held specifically for discussing the details of time and place and other such arrangements for major ceremonies. It may also be a discussion, in preliminary form or preview, of the issue of an impending litigation.

isunisun[13] and **oligla**[14] both refer to a meeting of individuals for the purpose of settling civil disagreements outside of the formal structure of litigation or **bisala**. An idiom refers hyperbolically to such a meeting as a very small speech exchange (**bata'bata' bitan**).

Kinds of speech activities that are characteristically found in the **bitan** 'dialogue' and monologue and are also characteristically "formal" to gatherings, are illustrated in figures 1.3 and 1.4. The terms listed in figure 1.3 are descriptions of speech activity requiring at least two interlocutors or sides. They are primarily descriptions or evaluations of kinds of speech rather than acts in which one is requested to engage in, except **mogabitabit** which is often an invitation to speak or discuss some topic.

mogabitabit 'conversation' (from **abit** 'talk about') is the most general speech activity between individuals. It is not affixed as a goal-oriented activity; there is nothing to be specifically attained through it.[15]

moksinaksakoy literally means "each one asking another" (from **sak** 'ask'). It is a neutral term but it is affixed as a goal-oriented activity.[16] It is

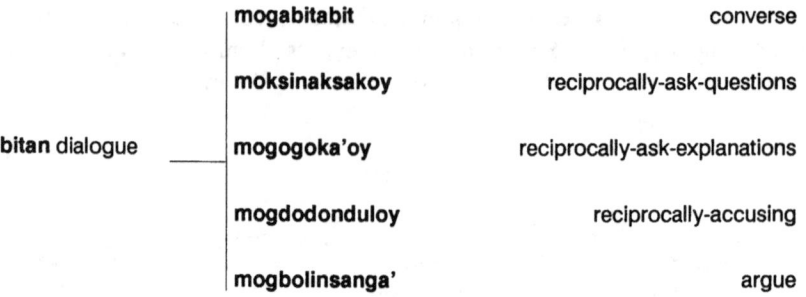

Figure 1.3 Kinds of dialogue activity

nonargumentative. The activity is one of asking questions and giving answers where possible in order to come to some kind of decision or at least to arrive at some community consensus.

mogogoka'oy (from **oka'** 'ask explanation') involves asking for explanation and clarification. It is a goal-oriented, discursory activity that seeks details for correct decision making. This is a kind of speech interchange in which the older men often engage. It is nonneutral in that the activity involves the taking of sides, arguing for certain decisions, or promoting certain issues. There is often a rhetorical implication when one asks for clarification of some action. The goal may be to interrogate someone for litigation purposes.[17] One may find oneself in the awkward position of making excuses rather than giving explanations. I was told that when the old men **mogogoka'oy,** this precludes the use of obstinate noisy arguing or **mogbolinsanga'**. It is in the verbal exchange of **mogogoka'oy** that the social values of speaking are skillfully practiced and exemplified (see sec. 2.4.2, and Appendix C).

mogdodonduloy literally means 'each one shoving the other' (from **dondul** 'push'). It is also a nonneutral speech activity which is slightly argumentative in that it involves making accusations and recriminations.

mogbolinsanga'[18] 'argument' is a speech activity which is not highly regarded because it is often composed of "hard" or abrupt speech. It is argument that is not goal oriented.

2.3.3 Speech Events: Monologue. Gatherings may be called where a monologue (**piktolu'on**) is the primary or characteristic speech activity. These activities may be described by a number of specific terms, examples of which are shown in figure 1.4.[19]

moktalu' 'to speak' is the generic speech act. The kinds of monologue in this taxonomy may be said to be kinds of **talu'** 'speech'.

Formal Situations 17

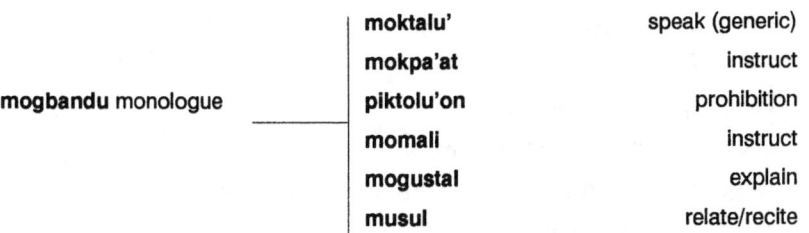

Figure 1.4 Kinds of monologue activity

mogbandu is a kind of proclamation with an implied threat attached. It is prohibition. For example, in the **polontu** ceremony (cf. sec. 2.4.1.3), the topic of the proclamation is instruction in proper customary behavior. The implied threat is litigation for noncompliance.

mokpa'at is also the instruction of proper behavior or coaching, e.g., general instructions concerning particular duties and responsibilities during a ceremony.

momali refers to instructing as to the proper use of an object or the application of some set of rules towards a proper conduct or belief, e.g., a sermon.

mogustal is explaining how or why something is the way it is.

musul is the relating how or why something is the way it is especially as it comes from the distant past, i.e., sources of present custom and traditions. **musul** is also thought of as a kind of **pomali** 'instruction' in that what is custom and tradition is a valued conduct and/or belief.

All of these specific terms have overlapping semantic components. They are all potential lexical candidates for use in parallel constructions (see chaps. 4 and 5).

One speech activity not included in figure 1.4 is that of **gyakin** 'prayer'. **gyakin** refers to speech performed by a human and directed toward a spirit being, imputed or real. There are several kinds of prayer referring to its purpose or function, e.g., making a request (**ngoningoni**) or asking a blessing (**dolangin**). Examples of Subanon prayer will be found in chapter 4.

2.4 Western Subanon Speech Situations, Events, and Acts

The following gatherings are described in some detail. They represent speech situations where formal/ritual speech events occur.[21] The following descriptions are based upon personal observations, field notes, and tape recordings. My purpose is to describe the speech activity that is known to take place in speech situations that are structured social events.

The general format of description of the gatherings will present the following salient features:

1. The purpose of the gathering
2. The participants and the setting
3. The event and structure or structural sequence of events
4. Any supporting events

2.4.1 The polontu 'death ceremony'. The **polontu** is a major Subanon ceremony. It is also known as **pomuas** or **kotopusan**. Its functions and significance directly bear on particular cultural assumptions of the Subanon. When a Subanon dies the soul is destined to another world.[22] The **polontu** is the soul send-off ceremony. It is performed only for those who have died a natural death.[23] The night of its performance is called the night of ghosts (**gobi nog molimatoy**).

The major participants include close kin, a shaman, and members of the **bogolal** 'council'. As with all intercommunity ceremonies, the major events take place in the late afternoon or early evening with the supporting activities following. Dancing and rice wine drinking may go on throughout the night. The dancing and eating may take place outside only if the house is too small to accommodate the crowd; otherwise, it is customary for all activities to take place inside the house. Formal rice wine drinking is done indoors. (See Frake 1964b for a description of the formality of rice wine drinking.)

The kin participants often arrive at least a day or more before the ceremony. The old men and **bogolal** 'council' arrive early on the day of the ceremony. The rest of the people begin arriving in the afternoon. By sundown the social event is usually well attended. The **polontu** ceremony being described here may be divided into three distinct events. The events are referred to by name in the text. They are the **mongimunag** or cleansing ritual, the feast of **dakul** or offering, and the **mogbonduan** or instruction event.[24]

2.4.1.1 The mongimunag or cleansing ritual. This first part of the ceremony involved the sanctifying of the participants and anyone else present. The **mongimunag** ritual was performed by a shaman by sprinkling water on the attendants. This was performed at the conclusion of a prayer given by the shaman. The components for the **mongimunag** event were:

Setting: The setting for all events was the house of the participant kin who initiated the ceremony.

Instrumentalities: The form of speech was the Western Subanon language almost exclusively. Even the use of non-Subanon lexical items would usually prompt comment from the listeners.

Participants: the shaman; the audience.

Formal Situations

Ends: to sanctify the participants and protect them from any adverse spirit activity or retribution.

Key: ritual seriousness.

Genres: prayer, explanation.

Sequence of acts:

1. The shaman formally addressed the audience in which he also included the spirits.
2. He explained (**migustal**) the purpose of the rite to the audience.
3. The shaman made his prayer.
4. The shaman flicked water over the audience, throughout the house, and around outside.

(See Appendix A for the text of the **mongimunag** explanation and prayer.)

2.4.1.2 The feast of dakul or offering. The second part of the death ceremony discussed here was the presenting of the offering to the spirits.

Participants: the **bogolal** 'councilor' (in this case the **timuoy** 'chief councilor'), the ceremony initiator, the shaman, and the audience.

The event was composed of several activities. The first one involved a dialogue between the **timuoy** and the ceremony initiator (see Appendix B1 for the text).

Ends: to formally mention to the **timuoy** those who were being ceremonied, and to give time for the ones preparing the offering to finish.

Key: ritual seriousness.

Norm: turn taking in the form of question and answer.

Genre: dialogue.

The **timuoy** councilor then addressed the crowd but not without the help of the ceremony initiator to first quiet them down so he could be heard (see text in Appendix B2).

Ends: to formally open the present ritual sequence.

Key: ritual seriousness.

Norm of interaction: general background talking by the audience while speaker talked.

Genre: the instruction-explanation form of **momali** (cf. sec. 2.3.3).

The **timuoy** councilor then formally turned the floor over to the shaman.

As the shaman began his speech, his introductory remarks included making sure that he knew who the deceased were. He then made explanation to the audience concerning the rite being performed. While the incense was burning, the shaman addressed the spirits and the prayer was given. (The verbal style of his explanation and prayer in this event was the same as his verbal style in the **mongimunag** event (cf. sec. 2.4.1.1), so the texts are not included here.)

The event was formally closed by the **timuoy** after the prayer was given (see text in Appendix B3).

2.4.1.3 The mogbonduan or instruction event. The third part of the death ceremony illustrated here is the instructions (**mogbonduan**) that were given to the crowd of people in the house. At this point there were between ninety and one-hundred packed into the little house. As part of the ritual of the death ceremony, several "speakers" (**polomisala**) were made carte blanche judges for the night. The number of them corresponded to the number of souls being sent to their destination. The **mogbonduan** event consisted of each "speaker" who had been chosen to be judge for the evening giving advice to the crowd in attendance concerning the proper conduct and behavior which is generally considered proper and expected at such occasions. In their speeches, they declared that anyone who committed a fineable offense during the merrymaking in the remaining hours of the ceremony, they could, as a surrogate council, charge fines in excess of the ordinarily fixed amounts. It was evident by the crowd's reaction that the advice given was expected and probably that which is given at each death ceremony. It was also presented in somewhat stereotyped and familiar expressions.

Participants: the audience, **timuoy**, surrogate council (each one called **timuoy** 'chief councilor' for the night).

Ends: to advise the participants in the remaining merry-making concerning their proper conduct. The advice came with prohibitory threats.

Key: mock seriousness and politeness.

Norm of interaction: turn taking among the surrogate councilors in giving monologues; the use of authoritative tone of voice. Audience responce included shouts of approval, coaching, and some good-natured taunts.

Act sequence: The introduction of the event was made by the **timuoy** 'chief councilor' who asked for the **bonduan** event to take place. Then each one of the four surrogates, in his turn, made a speech. In this particular event, after each had spoken, several had further things to say. Finally, at the conclusion, one of the kin of the deceased rose and spoke. Because he was a member of the organized paramilitary forces, he represented a force outside of the traditional Subanon customs which could be brought to bear on any who would act in an unruly way during the remaining festivities.

This final act contrasted with the previous acts in:

Key: actual seriousness.

Norm of interaction: quietness and lack of good-natured repartee and general gaiety of the audience, authoritarian tone of voice of the speaker.

After the advice had been given, the surrogate council struck a gong as a signal for dancing to begin. At the same time, the rice wine jars were opened and filled with water and the drinking began. Dancing and drinking, the fourth part of the ceremony, extended throughout the night. The next morning the crowd dispersed. The general feeding was an event which took place over an extended time and therefore simultaneously with some of the other events.

2.4.2 The mogogoka'oy or explanation event. During the death ceremony, as has often been observed before ceremonies begin, several old men gathered together to discuss present pertinent tribal issues in relation to old customs. The **mogogoka'oy** is a formal speech encounter which is especially fruitful for speech analysis. During the particular encounter presented here[25] (see Appendix C), verbal strategies were displayed in the maintenance of smooth interpersonal relations. Convincing answers to the questions asked were presented with general purpose of sidestepping any possible culpability on the part of the participants in the several matters discussed. Politeness prevailed in the formal beginnings and endings in turn taking and feedback interaction (see chap. 3), in the free use of friendship names (**glalow**)[26] and conciliatory names, and in the use of politeness markers.

The topic of discussion was in regard to certain customs and procedures involving the dating of the death ceremony in conjunction with another major ceremony. Contrary to custom, there had been no formal meeting (**moginuinu**) for the date setting.[27]

The display found in figure 2.1 representing this particular **mogogoka'oy** speech interaction will set the background for a discussion of some aspects of formal language structure that is used in such speech events (see chap. 3).

Instrumentality: exclusively the Western Subanon language.

Setting: the participants were sitting in a rough circle. A crowd of approximately thirty people were in the house seated along the walls. They consisted largely of women and sleeping children. A number of males were under the house and on the porch listening.

Participants: seven men all in their fifties and sixties. As to their outside roles, two were shamans, one was a councilor, two were "old men" (**mogulang nog gotow**), one was a "speaker" (**polomisala**), and there was one other.

Ends: to inform regarding events surrounding the **polontu** 'death ceremony'; to settle some specific questions regarding possible culpability with regard to specific customs of dating ceremonies.

Key: studied seriousness, politeness.

Norm of interaction: turn taking in delivering monologues, normal feedback responses and attentiveness.[28]

The sequence of acts is illustrated in figure 2.1 (Texts for the speech turns 1-6 are found in Appendix C.)

The columns represent the interlocutors, the rows are the speech turns. The arrows originate at the addressor marked by X and point to the addressee. The solid arrow represents some kind of proposal either in the form of a question or admonition. The broken-line arrow represents the response to that proposal.

Speech events that are conversations or speech exchanges between selected members of a group of participants may be differentiated from those speeches which are addressed specifically to the whole group. In one sense, the distinction may be between dialogue and monologue: dialogue, where there is an answer of exchange between two members (cf. turns 4-6. See also sec. 3.2.2) or between one member and several others (cf. turns 8-11); and monologue, where there is an expression of opinion or assertion directed to the whole. The total speech event or context is, in a larger sense, dialogue activity with the possibility of smaller exchanges or side sequences (see sec. 3.2.2) occurring within the larger. There is a discourse continuity running through the whole of the exchanges. There is an opening or introducing of the topic by speaker A in turn 1 and there is a conclusion as a summation by speaker B in turn 14. The formal taking of turns here is the same that has been observed in formal litigation discussions.

At the conclusion of speech turn 14, speaker B dispersed the group by saying:

B: Dadi   koyon,   midoksu'   dinakon.
   so   that   finished   to-me

A: Di'   ta   na   poksinombagan   ta,   Sopali,
   not   (1pntin) now   exchange-answers (1pntin) Sopali

   po'   bila poksinombagan,   ita   ompayat.
   because   if   exchange-answers (1ptin)   long

Formal Situations 23

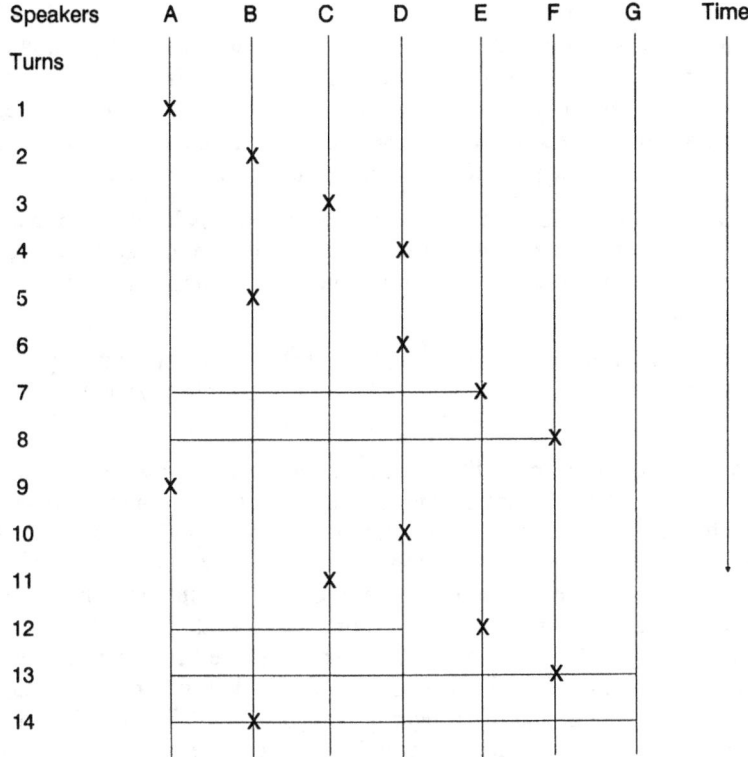

Figure 2.1 Speech sequencing

B: 'O   le.   Loko Sopali, ponogponog u pa.
   yes friend I-say Sopali   going-down I yet

C: 'O'o.
   yes

B: And so, that's it, mine is finished.

A: Let's not exchange our answers, **Sopali**, ('friend') because if we exchange our answers, we'll be a long time.

B: Yes, friend. I say, **Sopali**, ('friend') I will descend to the ground now (polite).

C: Okay.

2.4.3 The bisala 'litigation' situation (elopement case). Frake's (1963) claim that litigation is the cohesive event in Eastern Subanun society is a claim that can also be made for the Western Subanon. The processes of the **bisala** 'litigation' in the Subanon way allow for the preservation of the cultural history. The major basis for decision making and of settling cases is precedence. Precedence means going back to solutions to problems and settlements of cases that the forefathers of the Subanon had made. Often histories are passed on in this way. It is evident in recorded discussions that care is taken against the setting of precedence; however, the contrast between the old and the new, the past and the present, often necessitates compromise.

The qualification of the **bogolal** 'councilor' includes his having a wide experience in the settling of a wide variety of cases or of being able to recall stories and incidents of such and their outcomes, and his ability to make judicial decisions.

Litigation also allows for the preservation of the values of formal speech styles and speech strategies involving a kind of negotiatory verbal duel or bargaining (cf. also, Keenan (1975) regarding Malagasy negotiations).[29]

One very common source of litigation is an elopement (**moksala'** literally "commit a fault"). The elaborate negotiations and ceremony of the Subanon marriage that used to be performed prior to the last two decades are rarely seen today due largely to economic considerations. Ever a viable option for Subanon young people, elopement involves the least amount of monetary expense. At the same time, it also involves a fair amount of shame potential and accusation from kin. Nevertheless, it has been observed that the Subanon community reaction is generally one of tolerance and acceptance towards a couple in an elopement situation regardless of the couple's culpability, for which they are fined. The shame potential from the kin is partially diffused by the community attitude.

When a couple mutually decides that it is time for marriage and they have eloped, they will go (**mogdang** 'climb up stairs') to the house of an elder in the community, who probably is not a close kinsman, and who might represent them fairly in the counting of the fines and charges (**mogbolasi'**). They will present themselves to him (**uakilon glawas nilan dianon** literally "present their bodies to him") in the act of seeking succor.

In the several elopment **bisala** that I have observed,[30] the content of the events that composed the **bisala** were:

1. The **mogustal** 'explanation'

2. The **mogbisala** 'litigation/negotiation'

3. The **mogyakin** 'prayer'

4. The **momali** 'advice'

Each event comprised either a single speech activity (e.g., the **mogustal** 'explanation') or a series of speech acts and interchanges (e.g., the **mogbisala**, the actual negotiations for dowry price).

Formal Situations

The events of the elopement described componentially are:

Setting: the house of the elder where the couple sought refuge and sanctuary from the female's kinsmen.

Instrumentalities: the Subanon language, particularly during the **bisala** section. (Although, in some cases, others were present and had something to say using another language, such as Visayan or Chavacano, interpretations were not made and replies were given in the Subanon language.)

These components hold for all the events of the elopement. The rest of the components help to further differentiate events as they occurred.

1. The **mogustal** 'explanation'.

Participants: the principal speaker of the council, the elder who gave succor to the couple, other council members.

Ends: to relate how and when the couple came to him and what he did about informing the kinsmen of both sides and arranging for the litigation proceedings.

Key: genuine seriousness.

Genre: general narrative (**guksug**).

The explanation is made by the protector to the council. At the end of his narration he turns the couple over to the council.

2. The **mogbisala** 'litigation/negotiation'.

Participants: the council and kin representatives from both families.

Ends: to negotiate the bride payment and any subsequent fines attributable to the incident. The outcome is expected to be in favor of the couple over the protestations of the female's parents (see sec. 2.4.4).

Key: seriousness and at least ritual politeness.

Norms of interaction: within general turn taking there is the give-and-take of lively discussion and argument. There is also much background noise.

Ordinarily, the female's kin would set the price demands within the limits of what is customary while the male's kin would negotiate. However, where an elopement has taken place, the council sets the fines, all of which the male pays.[31] In the elopement **bisala** proceedings, the bride and her kin are the aggrieved party. The major portion of the groom's fine, which is considered the dowry (**sunggud**) or fine, goes to the bride's family. There is a small portion which is also shared among the councilors and those who had a part in the settlement of the case.

Each side is represented on the council by those who are recognized speakers (**polomisala**). The parents, as such, do not officially enter into the actual negotiations except to add information which might bear on the price setting.[32] During this segment of the proceedings, there was witnessed quite a few accusations and arguments, and emotions ran high, particularly among the bride's kinsmen. This venting of feelings, in one case, influenced the council's decision as to the actual price settlement.

3. The **mogyakin** 'prayer'.

Participants: a councilor or shaman, the couple, the whole gathering.

Ends: to pronounce a blessing that they may have many children and that they may have a compatible (**motigdow** literally "cold") relationship.

Key: ritual seriousness.

Norm: general attentiveness; usually loud tone of voice.

Genre: **gyakin** 'prayer' (see chap. 4 for examples of prayer).

When agreement is obtained among the council and tacitly among the parents and kin, the bride and groom are called to sit before the council. Then the one giving the prayer will stand to do so. However, before that happens, and as soon as the young people appear, there is often a renewal of anger and/or verbal display, especially on the part of the female's kin.

4. The momali 'advice'.

Participants: any elder or high status person, the couple, the gathering as a whole.

Ends: to give advice on how to have a compatible marriage.

Key: mock seriousness, jocularity.

Norm: general gaiety, turn taking monologues with good-natured feedback.

Genre: admonition.

By this time the liquor has been passed around and has sufficiently made its effect. After two or three give their advice and well-wishers greet the couple, the people begin to disperse.

2.4.4 The Confrontation Event. Mention has been made in section 2.1.2 regarding women and their role in the community, particularly their role in formal speech situations. An elopement **bisala** provides a context in which discussion or an interchange of speech activity involving women may be found.

As already mentioned, an elopement will be settled (**dodion**) in favor of the couple unless the blood lines are too close resulting in culturally defined

Formal Situations

incest (**sumbang**), or if the male has a record of unsettled faults (see also Keenan (1975) for a similar occurrence among the Malagasy). One strategy of the female's side might be to bring to light (**ukadon** literally "unwrap") unsettled faults involving the male and/or his immediate kin. Several outcomes may result including the annulment of the marriage (**butas**) or possibly its postponement (**sondud**).

During one case, which was recorded (see Appendix D), the mother of the bride was doing all she could to bring the proceedings to annulment. This encounter occurred within the negotiation event of the elopement **bisala**. This conversation or interchange contrasts with the **mogogoka'oy** discussion in section 2.4.2 in its setting, participants, ends, and norm of interaction. It is, nevertheless, just as serious a dialogue as is the **mogogoka'oy**. It is not marked by the polite formality exhibited in the **mogogoka'oy** event.

The components of this event are:

Setting: the house of the elder where the couple sought refuge. The participants were seated in a rough circle. The mat with the small piles of corn kernels, which signify the different fines to be paid, was within the rough circle.

Participants: mother of the female, father of the male, elder, and council representatives for the respective female's kin and male's kin.

Ends: (outcome intended by the council) to convince the mother and female's kin that she had no recourse against the sanctioning of the elopement; (goal of the mother) to try for the annulment of the elopement.

Key: angry desperation on the part of the mother; unyielding tolerance and long suffering on the part of the councilors; studied tolerance giving way to anger and frustration on the part of the groom's father.

Instrumentalities: the Subanon language.

Norm: question (and/or accusation) and answer turn taking; interruptions and insults on the part of the female; patronizing attitude and modulated speech on the part of the council and groom's father.

Event sequence: The council action that actually precipitated the confrontation was its decision not to annul the elopement (see Appendix D1). They called the mother and bride's kin to the mat on which the corn kernels were piled. The mother reacted against the decision and began her argument (Appendix D2). Her questions were answered (Appendix D3). From then on to the finish the council took control again. This confrontation exemplifies much of the male and female roles in formal speech confrontations of this kind.

2.4.5 The piglimudan 'caused to gather together' situation.[33] One instance of a speech situation was purposely set up primarily to get some of the elders together to talk about the customs of the Subanon. In requesting the meeting from the community leader, I asked that the participants be the community elders. A date and time were set. When the time came for the meeting, four elders, chosen through their own influence and roles in the community, showed up. One of the four was female.

Two conditions concerning the meeting are significant: the kinds of information or speech requested were not made explicit beforehand to the participants, but the general topic was; and, the participants spoke in front of an audience of about eighty male Subanon.[34] Presumably, the speakers were addressing me. This is evidenced by the pronouns used; but, pronoun shifts also indicated that in the speaker's minds a versatility existed as to who the audience was and whether to differentiate me from the rest of the audience.

It was not until all had been assembled, except for the absence of two of the principal speakers, that I was asked to formally state what kinds of speeches were desired.

The community leader, who was the one who called the gathering in the first place, acted as the master of ceremonies. After three had spoken, the MC asked for others of the audience who might wish to speak on the subject of customs and traditions of the Subanon. There were no volunteers. However, one male was prevailed upon. He showed much reluctance to speak. He was a middle-aged man in his early forties but was younger by some fifteen years than all of the other speakers; nevertheless, his ability to speak was common knowledge. During his recitation he was noticeably ill at ease. His recitation is significant in that it showed, to a greater extent than the other speeches, the poetic form of verbal art in speech making (see chap. 5, examples 1, 2, 6, 9, and 18).

Regarding topics presented in the speech situation, each related what they interpreted as characteristics of being a Subanon which go beyond simply being able to speak the language. They spoke mostly on the topic of religious beliefs. The monologues were **gusulan**, the relating of stories, customs, and beliefs from of old.

Formal Situations

Notes

1. The Subanon orthography consists of the consonants b, k, d, g, h, l, m, n, p, s, t, w, y, '(glottal stop), and ng. The vowels are i, e, a, o, and u.

The expressions used in this section are Western Subanon descriptions of kinds of speech and speech values. Here and elsewhere in this thesis glosses within single quotes indicate English approximations to the Western Subanon.

The Ilongot of Luzon make a dichotomy between straight and crooked speech. Straight speech is regular conversation and crooked speech is oratory (Rosaldo 1973).

2. Grammatical relation markers include the following:

og which marks the topic of the predicate,
nog which marks what is not topic and not ablative,
sog which marks an ablative, i.e., beneficiary, location and direction.

These markers concord with and have corresponding pronoun sets. The markers and pronoun sets are coordinated with predicate affixes which highlight role relationships of syntactic elements (Hall 1969). Affixes also indicate aspect and mood.

3. A primary purpose of figurative language is to produce an indirectness which would be considered inoffensive speech. Figurative language tends to neutralize a direct meaning and often helps to maintain smooth interpersonal relations between interlocutors, which is a general Philippine value (Lynch 1973). Other purposes for the use of figurative language might be to appear adept in the language (Frake 1963), and to be offensive and insulting in a way the hearer would not understand (see also Rosaldo 1973). Indirect speech between lovers is also called **dalil** 'figurative language'.

4. See Frake (1972) for a similar occurrence of this concept among the Yakan.

5. The convention of hyphenated English words is used to indicate a semantic unit which corresponds to one Subanon word.

6. Frake (1963) describes general attitudes of the Eastern Subanun in a litigation context. The procedures he describes are quite different from those I have witnessed among the Western Subanon but the attitudes expressed regarding the role of women does not appear to be any different.

7. Pike and Pike's use of the term "referential" is reminiscent of Searle's description of reference as a speech act (Searle 1969:26f). "Any expression which serves to identify anything, process, event, action, or any other kind of 'individual' or 'particular' I shall call a referring expression. Referring expressions point to particular things . . . . It is by their function, not always by their surface grammatical form or their manner of performing their function, that referring expressions are to be known."

8. Unlike the Yakan (Frake 1972), the Subanon use of the term **miting** 'meeting' is usually in reference to speech events which are intercultural gatherings and are therefore not necessarily governed by the norms and rules of the Subanon gathering. Frake's description of the categorization of Yakan speech situations, i.e., the functions of speech gatherings, also describes basically the same functions for the Subanon. Much of the same terminology is also used. However, Yakan **ukum** 'litigation' corresponds to the Subanon **bisala** 'litigation'. The Subanon **gukum** (cognate with Yakan **ukum**) is used to designate the role of the jural councilors (**bogolal**) or the decision of culpability rather than the actual speech situation involving their function as is the case for the Yakan.

9. Goffman (1967) has described "face" in terms of feelings. A person may "lose face" or become embarrassed in a social situation; he may "preserve face" or be saved in some way from being embarrassed in a social situation. This concept of "face" is important among the Subanon, as well as generally throughout the Philippines.

10. The Western Subanon do not differ from the Eastern Subanun in this respect. See Frake (1964a) for a description of the Eastern Subanun attitudes.

11. There are occasions, however, when the stylistic use of words from other codes occurs. These are only briefly mentioned, e.g., see chapter 5, note 12.

12. In a strongly literate society or subculture, code shift may be much more prevalant generally. An example of this was reported to me by a colleague working in another language group. When writing a letter by one member of the same family to another, English was used to indicate the degree of education attained. The implication was that if one wrote a letter in his or her own language he or she could not use English, therefore was deficient in education.

13. This term is used by the Kolibugan opposite the Subanon term **gupakat**. The Kolibugan are Subanon who are converts to Islam. In many cases they have intermarried with other Moslem groups, especially the Maguindanao. Their language is mutually intelligible with the Subanon although it is distinctive (see Christie 1909, Finley and Churchill 1913).

14. The etymology of this word reflects not only linguistic but also social change. It probably derives from the Spanish **alegre**. The purpose of **goligla** 'settle a dispute' is to restore peace to a potentially disruptive situation in the community.

15. The duplicated stem **abit** indicates repeated action, i.e., the activity covers a time span. The prefix **mog-** focuses attention on the actor.

16. In this word and the next two, the first syllable of the verb stem (**sak, oka'** and **dondul**) has been duplicated. The affixes are **mog-** focusing on the actor and **-oy** or the combination **-in- -oy** which denotes a goal oriented activity. A combination of the affixes **mog- -in- -oy** and **mog- partial reduplication -oy** indicate a reciprocal action.

17. For a description of similar occasions among the Eastern Subanun, see Frake (1963:220).

18. This activity is sometimes called **mogdiskas**, a marked term (unlike English 'discuss') which designates an argument that has no goal attainment.

19. Other speech activities include teaching (**mokpanad**), relating an incident (**moguksug**), relating or telling a story (**mokigulangoy**), singing (**mogbobat**).

20. All of these activities are verbs which have prefixes that focus attention on the actor performing the activity.

21. Fox (1971:220) takes a different approach regarding speech forms (e.g., riddles, conversation, tales, mockery speech). He says that "What these various speech forms do is signal different standardized social contexts, each with separate conditions and expectations on the use of semantic elements."

22. Hence the name **polontu** 'a lifting/causing to rise'. The normal procedure is to perform a ceremony in order to release or to allow the soul to leave off hovering in the area of the corpse or the general area of the community and to continue on to its destination.

23. It was explained to me that those dying an unnatural death (drowning, falling, murder, suicide) go to another place after death.

24. There is a description of the **polontu** 'death ceremony' in Christie (1909:79) which seemingly bears little resemblance to anything I have seen among the Western Subanon. In discussions with Subanon councilors, it was determined that the actual complexion of the **polontu**

Formal Situations 31

is dependent upon those in charge and modifications do occur in the manner in which other **polontu** are performed in other Subanon areas. All of the **polontu** ceremony discussed here was recorded on a UHER 4400 reel-to-reel stereo tape recorder. The two microphones were passed around to be held by those speaking but usually were held by someone else close to the speaker(s). The speakers as well as the audience were constantly aware of my presence as from time to time reference was made to my being present. Nevertheless, there were none who declined to speak because they were being recorded.

25. One of the participants motioned to me to set the recorder going. I did as he said and just handed the microphones to someone nearby. They were passed from hand to hand with no direction from me. Since it was a stereo recording, the verbal reaction of the audience was also picked up.

26. A friendship name is a single name used reciprocally between as many as four individuals but most often between two. This name is a word which usually recalls some shared experience or knowledge which remains unknown to the general population. These names, although perhaps known and recognized by the community at large, are usually only used by those who own them. Unlike the Malagasy (Keenan 1977), the Subanon penchant for plurality of names is not contingent upon fear of retribution or harassment from enemies, whether living or dead. The purpose of Subanon friendship names, beyond that of solidarity, is not clear.

27. During the previous evening, in fact, one of the councilors was fined because of his part in the way the death ceremony date had been set.

28. A significant factor that points to the formality of the event and its being other than a mere conversation is the attentiveness of the crowd. During this event there was practically no interaction from the nonparticipants. It was an exclusive discussion held between the seven participants.

29. There is a genre of verbal duel singing (**bayuk**) which may be engaged in for fun of obtaining a woman companion (if she loses the duel!).

30. Some of the wedding ceremonies were recorded by a Subanon young man for me in my absence. He used a SONY cassette player with an internal microphone and merely placed it among the participants. During one of these recorded ceremonies mention was made by one old man to its being recorded. He did this apparently as an attempt to stifle some of the arguing. I suspect it did not work!

31. Even this custom is seeing some change. There is an option, usually up to the officiating council, for a lump sum payment as a dowry (**glansal**) or calculating the price on the basis of Subanon custom (**momosita** from **pesita** 'twenty centavos'). In one proceeding it was done both ways so that the bride's family could choose to their advantage.

32. In one such case, for example, the bride's father, who was too feeble to attend the ceremony, had a particular request to be included in the dowry. There was an historical reason for this particular request. One of the old men on the council related that history as a case of individual significance and not one of general precedence.

33. In figure 1.1 in section 2.3.1, there are three terms listed in column A. The **piglimudan** is one of them. This is the term used by the community leader who made the arrangements for the meeting.

34. One indication that this contrived speech situation was not of particular interest was the fact that by the time it was the master of ceremony's turn to speak, only a handful of the original audience was present and they were all past middle age.

3 Introduction Dynamics

3.0 Introduction

Given the social and speech situations and speech events discussed in chapter 2, the question is now asked: What are some of the linguistic features which characterize the different kinds of Western Subanon formal speech events? Are there linguistic features that can be described that, in part, signal the identity of a specific speech event or speech act? In this chapter we proceed with such a query to investigate some features of discourse in the boundaries of interaction in the dialogue events and the beginnings and endings of monologue events within the context of the speech situation. I will also discuss turn taking and feedback or back channel responses (Duncan 1974, Duncan and Fiske 1977) in speech interaction. Reference will be made to text materials found in the Appendices.

3.1 Participant perceptions of the speech situation

Social situations that are culturally definable within the contexts of the shared experience of the community define the kinds of speech activity that is normal to that community. Linguistic variety is inherent in any community whether it be separate language codes, dialects, styles, genre, or jargon. Linguistic variables may be dependent upon social factors such as age, sex, ethnic identity, and socioeconomic status (Labov 1972, Wolfram 1974, Trudgill 1971).

Gumperz (1966, 1967) and Blom and Gumperz (1972) show that linguistic variables, including codes and styles, are (often unconsciously) selected in relation to factors of social situations and the corresponding role relationships and status features obtaining between interlocutors or speaker and audience.

Interchange Dynamics

The conformity to speech norms depends, in large part, on the interpretation by the participants or participant perception of the speech situation (Gumperz 1967). Some situations demand a more constrained speech activity where certain styles, genre, channels, and the like would be considered "out of place" or inappropriate (Hymes 1974).

The intent here is not to discuss the criteria of selection of specific speech activity but to illustrate that there are indeed discrete linguistic genre or styles which are appropriate to certain definable social/speech situations with all of their attendant social relationships.

That the Subanon have such perceptions has already been mentioned in chapter 2. The norms of using the Subanon language, for example, as the form of speech in the litigation proceedings and ceremony situations, even when non-Subanons are present, suggests a relationship between speech context and speech code, e.g., social/linguistic situation precedes codes known by interlocutors. When Subanons are gathered together by one who is not Subanon, i.e., outside of a Subanon cultural context, there is not this restriction on linguistic form. The language code is, or may be, chosen from a different set of criteria.[1]

Similarly, in the **mogbonduan** 'giving instruction' event, (sec. 2.4.1.3), the final speaker somehow changed the whole tenor of the event to that point. The general gaiety and jocularity of the evening was getting underway. The final speaker, with a note of seriousness not present in the other speeches, and accompanied by a short prayer also not present in the other speeches, were cues to the audience that reminded them of the somber purpose for the gathering in the first place. The whole audience shifted their interactive response to conform to the intent of this new speech act.

The shift made by the speaker in the **piglimudan** 'caused to gather together' situation (sec. 2.4.5) from the general relaxed form of speech of the **gusulan** 'explanation of history' to the more ritual style suggests his perception regarding the formality of the situation. Concomitant with that speaker's change in style was the general perception of the audience suggested in their reaction of silence when repeatedly invited to interact in a free manner (or informally) with the speaker (back channels are discussed in sec. 3.4).

3.2 Dynamics of turn taking

Turn taking, to a great extent, is a rule-governed activity. It is rule governed in the broad sense that rules include participant states of readiness, implicature,[2] and signals flashed between auditors and speaker. Turn taking within the context of the speech situations and events where monologue takes place is governed by rules which tend to be more overt and more easily identified than those rules which govern turns in informal conversation.[3] Studies in American society indicate that a number of signals are perceived and interpreted between speaker and auditor during informal conversations (Duncan and Fiske 1977). These signals are not all linguistic in nature. Gestures also play a role and seem to have significant influence in the smooth turn exchanges between interlocutors.[4] Gestures may also play a role in smooth interchanges among the Subanon. In interchanges in formal speech situations, however, it seems that the significant role may be largely linguistic. In this present discussion, then, only the role of linguistic phenomena in the turn taking signal will be treated. The discussion of turn taking begins by contrasting designated and nondesignated turn taking.

3.2.1 Designated turns. Speech situations, viz. litigation and ceremonies, generally have within their organized structure one who is in charge (**tumitonga** 'being in the center' and **gapu** 'owner', respectively). One of his functions is to see that events move along smoothly.[5] In litigation there is also the principal councilor who directs people to speak in their turn in the appropriate events. (See Appendix E for an example of a formal "soft" speech request for further information.)

In the **piglimudan** 'caused to gather together' event (sec. 2.4.5), there was a master of ceremonies who oversaw the speech activities performed. In each case there is some overseer who directs those who are to speak. There is a specified portion of such situations when anyone may have his say. To exercise that prerogative is a strong Subanon value.

A discussion of designated turn taking within these speech situations is only for the record. It does not reflect the dynamics of speech interchange as much as it illustrates the cohesive structure of social situations.

Unlike the informal conversational turn taking which is described as being voluntary (Duncan and Fiske 1977), designated turn taking tends to be coercive in nature. In terms of a theory of speech acts, a designated turn, or rather, designating a turn, would be regarded as an illocutionary act (Seale 1969, Austin 1962) in the form of a command/request to take the floor. This is opposed to an auditor's claim for the floor that is being relinquished by a speaker (see examples 1 through 5). The effect of the illocutionary act of commanding/requesting is the compliance on the part of the addressee to respond with some speech activity.

Examples 1 and 2 illustrate polite designated turn command/requests. They were preceded by an introduction of the speaker. They are characterized by soft, polite speech. The first request is oblique, the second is more straightforward.

```
1. Dadi:::,  potolu'on     ta       ini,   og     solabuk
   so        cause-speak   (1pntin) here   (tdet) single

   gilug    ta       koni  si     Mister Hall, ...
   brother  (1pntin) this  (tper) Mister Hall
```

Interchange Dynamics

mangka ta   potolu'oy... ah::: gilug   ta
then   (1pntin) cause-speak (hes) brother   (1pntin)

koni nog Timuoy.   (CA012A)
this (rel) Timuoy

'Now then, let's have our brother here, Mr. Hall, speak; then, we'll have our, ah,[6] brother here speak, who is the chief'.

2. Dadi ba   LA,... busungbusung dinika,   na,   o'
   so   uncle LA   excuse   to-you(s) now   (par)

   na   pongmaya'maya' a   po mogustal dini.   (CA012B)
   now   carefully   (2st) yet explain   here

'Now then, Uncle LA, if you'll forgive me, now, please now carefully come up here and give explanation to us'.

Within speech events which are characterized by the procedures of litigation or interrogation, the illocutionary acts of commanding/requesting someone to take his speech turn take on a different hue. The difference in the components of the speech act (sec. 2.2.3) determines the contrasts in linguistic expression. Examples 3-5 have the same perlocutionary force (i.e., resultant meaning) that examples 1 and 2 have in getting people to speak, but they differ in their informality and directness.[7] Which being interpreted means, "You are very abrupt (straightforward) in your interrogation!" Examples 3 and 4 are found in Appendix D. Example 5 is from a ceremony situation in which the event is a general invitation for speech. (In this example, the participant, MA, is a **timuoy** 'chief'!)

3. IM: IN, olo   ma' nion? Takun.   (CA022)
       IN   what   like that   give-it-here

   'IN, what is your side of it? Let's have it'.

4. IM: Dan   ku   na.   Ika, inonggat nika   to'
       old   (1snt) now   (2st) invited   (2snt) (que)

   ban   moksuntuk si   LU?   (CA022)
   (emp) box   (tper) LU

   'I don't care about that. You, did you, in fact, challenge LU to fist fight?'

5. AN: Oh... ika   si'oy, moktalu' a.   Sukli   a
       hey (2st) also   speak   (2st) take-turn (2st)

   MA: Akon?
       (1st)

AN: O'o.   (RR012-F)
    yes

AN: 'Hey, you also, you speak. You take a turn.
MA: I?
AN: Yes'.

3.2.2 Nondesignated turns. Speech interaction among the Western Subanon may be described in terms of degree on a continuum of formality or politeness. The range between the poles coincides with the structuredness of the group of people engaged in dialogue. The key or tenor may be serious dialogue in every case but the contrast occurs in the norm of interaction. Other components govern the norm of interaction, e.g., the topic discussed, the purpose for discussing it, i.e., a judgment being made, the scene, the participants, and the like.

At one end of the continuum is the careful dialogue of the **mogogoka'oy** 'seeking explanation' (Appendix C). Here each turn is discrete, being bracketed by well defined beginnings and endings (see sec. 3.3). Although the speech act may be directed to one auditor over another resulting in a "passing on of the floor" (kind of designating), each speaker proceeds in a polite, rule governed manner. If one speaker has not formally relinquished the floor, the next speaker may ask if he has indeed finished speaking. As he begins his turn he may also make a formal claim to the floor (sec. 3.3.2). The discrete character of each turn increases the potential for a smooth turn exchange between dialogue participants. This speech act discreteness in such formal dialogue is very similar in structure to the discrete character of some monologue genre.

In making this observation there is another point to mention about group dynamics. Notwithstanding the discrete linguistic structure of the turns, for the most part, there is evidence that the dialogue event is a cohesive whole of smaller units of dialogue interaction. In figure 3.1, (which is taken from figure 1.4 in chap. 2) turns 1-5 are all discrete in the sense being discussed here, i.e., they have beginnings and endings. Turn 6, however, lacks such formal discreteness and thereby contrasts with the turns that precede it. This suggests that a subsidiary exchange has been going on. A look at the message content indicates that a dialogue between speakers B and D was precipitated from turn 2 (see Appendix C2). Although turn 5 is represented by a dotted line (dotted lines indicate a response to some proposal) responding to turn 4, it functions as a side sequence (Jefferson 1972). It is a request for clarification indirectly (or, a challenge) to speaker D. Speaker D, in turn 6, makes the clarification in terms of a defense or justification for action performed. Turn 7 (not shown here) returns to the main issue and picks up the dialogue from turn 3.

Later in the same (**mogogoka'oy**) dialogue event, turn 8 contains a

Interchange Dynamics 37

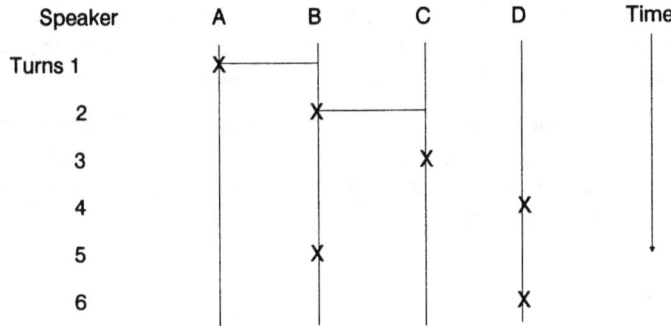

Figure 3.1 Dialogue embedding

proposal, an accusation, really, that is answered in turns 9-11. In terms of Jefferson's (1972) notation of O S R: the ongoing (O) sequence is interrupted by the side (S) sequence, in this case turns 8-11, and then turn 12 provides the return (R) to the ongoing sequence. The whole dialogue, including the side sequences, remains on the general topic and is considered as a formal discourse.

3.3 Beginnings and endings

Certain Western Subanon speech genres have characteristic ritualized or formal beginnings and endings.[8] These beginnings and endings serve as boundaries, in many instances, between turns, or they serve as brackets around a speech event or act (e.g., a folktale). All formal monologues are included in these genres. A formal monologue is one which adheres to traditional discourse structure associated with a particular genre. A typical case is the folktale which has a stereotyped syntactic beginning and ending with consistent discourse strategy of complication and resolution (cf. Walrod 1978). Some discourse characteristics will be discussed in the following sections and more extensively in chapters 4 and 5.

3.3.1 Beginnings. Beginnings may be composed of several components. The absence or presence of any or all tend to place the monologue or speech act along the continuum of formality. These components may be described as being an opening (sec. 3.3.1.1); a validation of claim for the floor (sec. 3.3.1.2); a statement of purpose including the asking for pardon and a disclaimer of malicious intent in speech content (sec. 3.3.1.3); and, the identification of the audience (sec. 3.3.1.4). The components are not optional. Their order generally occurs as just listed. The absence of certain of the components may well mark a speaker's intent to be impolite (e.g., see example 11).

3.3.1.1 Opening. There is a set of words and particles which characterize the polite opening (**bokna**) of monologues and formalized speech turns (usually except in the case of prayers). The words and particles have two general functions that seem to be closely related to how the speaker considers his speech contribution and how it fits in to the dialogue as a whole.

When beginning a monologue, the particle **ati** is most generally used. The particle is difficult to translate but has the force of gaining attention and signalling the formal opening of a speech.[9] Examples of its use are found, for instance, at the beginning of folktales:

6. Ati   dow[10]   ini ...
   (par) (hs)   this

'It has been said ...' (or, 'Once upon a time ...')

It occurs as the opening of monologues:

7. Ati   ma'   nini   (CA012B, RR012B7)
   (par) like this

'It's like this:'

If adding to what someone else has said, answering a question, or giving explanation within an interchange, a number of discourse concatenators might be used in place of **ati**, for example, **dadi** 'and so',[11] **sa'an** 'reason', and **tibua** 'however' as in:

8. Dadi, ma' ninia: (RR012C)
   so   like this

'And so, it's like this:'

9. Sa'an ma' ninia: (RR012C)
   reason like this

'The reason is like this:'

10. Tibua, ma' ninia sop: (RR012B10)
    but   like this   also

'However, it's like this also:'

The deictic **koni** 'this' or 'here' or the pronoun **ginakon** 'mine' also draw attention to the speaker's contribution and marks an opening of a speech.

11. Koni lo'   en ma' ninia: (RR012B3)
    this (par) it like this

'Now then, it's like this:'

12. Ginakon ma' ninia: (RR012B12)
    mine   like this

'Mine is like this:'

The consistent component of the polite opening in dialogue is the statement **ma' nini** 'it's like this'.

3.3.1.2 Validation of claim. The validation of the claim for the floor comes after attention is directed to the speaker and he has made his opening. Such validation, again, is not obligatory, but it is common. The validation is generally a positive assertion that the speaker is in some way entitled to take the floor. The following are examples of the validation.

13. Mama' u   nog   kotubagan bisara ni   OT. (RR012A)
    like (1snt) (rel) proximity speech (ntper) OT

   'I seem to be next after the speech of OT'.

14. Mama' u   nog   mokoponglambul... (RR012B10)
    like (1snt) (rel) able-to-be-near

   'I seem to be next ...'.

There are occasions when a polite opening is dispensed with within a discourse. In example 15, the speaker makes an assertion which indicates the tone of what he will say. (See example 19 in sec. 3.3.1.3 for a statement of his purpose.) Stated explicitly and lacking the polite form opening, his speech may be characterized as being "hard" (**motogas nog talu'**).

15. Ngon do   men ditu' ginakon mika'an;
    (exl) (sta) (emp) there mine   few

    dadi, ngon poktolu'on ku   dun.[12] (RR012B8)
    so   (exl) speech   (1snt) (ana)

   'There are also a few words of mine about that; therefore, I will make a speech about it'.

3.3.1.3 Purpose, apology, and disclaimer. Another component in formal beginnings is the statement of purpose in making the speech. Besides the purpose, the statement may also include the message content as well as the message form, e.g., story telling. The following examples illustrate some of these assertions.

16. Ngon poktolu'on ku   bu bisaraan ku   otagan
    (exl) speech   (1snt) and speech   (1snt) concerning

    sog   polontu.   (RR012D)
    (dir) death ceremony

   'I have something to say to you concerning the death ceremony'.

17. Moleg u   moksak dinika...   (RR012B10)
    desire (1st) query   to-you(s)

    'I want to ask a question ...'.

18. Moguksuguksug u,   ha?   Sa'an moguksuguksug u
    relate   (1st) (par) reason relate   (1st)

    agun   ita   sog   glam ta koni, mod olag
    so-that (1ptin) (dir) all (1pntin) this bright

    dinita.   (RR012B3, also Appendix C3)
    to-us(in)

    'I will relate a story, okay? The reason I will relate a story is so
    that, for us, for all of us here, the issue will be clear to us'.

As was already mentioned in section 3.3.1.3, a speaker's intention may not always be polite. Example 15 in section 3.3.1.2 illustrated the validation of claim for floor of just such a speaker. Example 19 states his purpose. It is a rather unveiled insult and stimulates several responses from the other participants in the dialogue (cf. sec. 2.4.2, figure 2.1, turn 8).

19. Po'   sa'an ngon poktolu'on ku   dun, og   gotow
    (par) reason (exl) speech   (1snt) (ana) (tdet) person

    da' poksolabuk og   sabut   non.
    not agree   (tdet) understand (3snt)   (RR012B8)

    'The reason why I have something to say about it is because, as
    for a person (=the participants) his understanding is not in
    agreement (i.e., with the truth)'.

On the other hand, a speaker may blurt out his purpose in speaking, indicating that he only wants to speak. For example, in example 20, the dialogue was beginning to come to summation and the speaker had not yet been given the floor. He, in fact, had no particular title in the community and was not directly involved in the decision making process of the dialogue; nevertheless, he did have the option to speak. He dispenses with the polite opening and validation of claim for the floor and blurts out his purpose.

20. Akon, kolegan ku...   (RR012B13)
    (1st) desire (1snt)

    'As for me, my desire is that ...'

Occasionally, when speakers are in a context where they have been desig-

Interchange Dynamics 41

nated to speak, they will characteristically begin by a disclaimer or by making statements intimating that the fact that they are speaking was by some amount of coercion on the part of the designator. These assertions are seen in the speeches given during the **piglimudan** 'caused to gather together' (cf. sec. 2.4.5). The participants, without fail, introduced their speech first by the disclaimer to any real knowledge of the topic and/or ability to speak. They attributed what they did know to hearsay rumor.[13]

Along with the disclaimer, or in place of it, some speakers as a rhetorical device will ask pardon from the audience. Presumably this act will absolve them from whatever might be said that would be offensive. The disclaimer is found in the **piglimudan** situation and in the **mogogoka'oy** event. Examples 21 and 22 illustrate it.

21. Sopulu'   tobia'   sog   glam ta   koni . . .   (CA013C)
    one-ten   pardon   (dir) all (1pntin) this

    'Ten pardons to all of us here . . .'

22. Mongoni u   nog   ma'ap   bu   gampun,
    beg   (1st) (ntdet) forgive and pardon

    songibu   gampun dianiu
    one-thousand   pardon to-you(p)

    sog   glam ta . . .   (RR012B14)
    (dir)   all   (1pntin)

    'I beg forgiveness and pardon,
        one thousand pardons to you
            to all of us . . .'

3.3.1.4 Identification of audience. Audience identification is taken as a specific act and is here being differentiated from the speaker requests for auditor feedback (cf. sec. 3.4).

A speaker may direct his speech to a particular auditor in an audience or use one of several reference formulae directed to the whole audience (cf. chap. 4, discussion of doublets).

When a particular auditor is addressed, it is often done by use of a friendship name.[14] Titles, as well as social and kin relationships are also used rhetorically to give deference or to emphasize social relationships. The use of referent or generic terms (e.g., **gotow** 'person') rather than personal names does not have the same conversational implicature of lack of intimacy as in western cultures (cf. Keenan 1977). The following examples are illustrative.

Speech that is directed towards one auditor:

23. Ati le[15] timuoy,... (RR012E)
    now friend chief

    'Now, my friend chief,...'

Speech that is directed towards two auditors:

24. Bamba u,   motud men   ginika;
    uncle (1snt) true (emp) yours(s)

    motud ginika   bolian... (RR012B9)
    true   yours(s) shaman

    'My uncle, your speech is true;
            your speech is true, shaman...'

Speech that is a general reference to a specific audience

25. Ati, ma' nini le,   sog   glam ta... (RR003)
    now like this friend (dir) all   (1pntin)

    'Now, it's like this, friends, to all of us...'

The formulaic addresses including the whole of the auditors have been recorded primarily in traditional ceremony speeches. Like in example 22 in section 3.3.1.3 and example 24 in section 3.3.1.4 the addresses are put into the poetic parallelistic form (cf. chap. 4). Some examples are:

26. ...sog   gilug   guarisgusba u
    (dir) brother kinsman   (1snt)

        moloksang molintok
        large   small

        lupa'   baloy
        ground house

        liu   solod...(RR012D)
        outside inside

    '...to my brothers and kinsmen,
            elders and youth,
            those on the ground and in the house,
            those outside and inside...'

27. ...sog   glam ta   dini
    (dir) all   (1pntin) here

        glibun po   laki
        female yet male

bata' po mogulang... (CA013C)
child yet elder

'...to all of us here,
female and male,
young and old...'

3.3.2 Endings. As with beginnings, endings are also marked along a continuum of formality. The ending provides a discrete boundary to the speech, as well as being an overt relinquishing of the floor to another. The speech situations where discrete endings are the most common are those where there are designated turns, formal turn taking (e.g., in the **mogogoka'oy** discussion), and in speeches during ceremonies (cf. the **mogbonduan**, sec. 2.4.1.3).

Sermons are characteristically ended by the formula **mogyakin ita** 'let us pray'. Prayers, on the other hand, may have rather lengthy endings. They often end with expressions of committing various entities, including individuals, over to the one or ones being addressed.

The components of an ending generally consist of a summary, the intent to end, and the close statement. Often the summary, beginning with an introducing word like **dadi** 'therefore', or **soga'id non** 'instead/rather', signals concluding remarks and thereby the intent to end.

The closing statement often is simply, "it is finished," or "that's it." The following illustrate the close statements:

28. Ma' antu'. (RR012B4)
    like that

    'It's like that'.

29. Dion ku na potomanoy. (RR012B2)
    there (1snt) now put-a-limit

    'That's where I'll end it'.

30. Na putukan ku;
    now sever (1snt)

    di' u dungagan. (CA022–2)
    not (1snt) add

    'Now I'll sever it;

    I'll not add to it'.

Occasionally, a speaker taking a turn in a speech event in which the norm is a discrete speech act will fail to make an ending in an explicit enough manner. The next speaker will, if he is doubtful, inquire of the finished speaker if he, in fact, has finished. The incidence of this kind of exchange in recorded speech is very low but the appropriateness of the query in such cases is documented.

During a speech event, when turns are being taken, speakers may close their speech with an act of relinquishing their turn. In example 31 the floor is made ready for the next speaker in the **bonduan** 'instruction' (cf. sec. 2.4.1.3).

```
31. Soga'id    non     koni,  ma'   nini,  glam  ta,
    rather     (3snt)  this   like  this   all   (1pntin)

               ginakon  koni,
               mine     this

               di'   u       na    popoyaton  poktolu'on  ku
               not   (1snt)  now   lengthen   speech      (1snt)

    po'        modakol  ami      pa   moleg    moktalu'.
    because    many     (1ptex)  yet  desire   speak

    Dadi,  koni  posuklion  ku      duma       u
    so     this  exchange   (1snt)  companion  (1snt)

           po'      modakol  pa   duma       u.    (RR012F3)
           because  many     yet  companion  (1snt)
```

'Instead, it's like this, all of us,
   as for my speech,
   I'll not prolong what I'm saying
because we are many who want to speak.
I'll turn it over to my companions
   because I have many companions waiting to speak.'

The floor is made open to anyone who would like to contribute to the **piglimudan** 'caused to gather together' event (cf. sec. 2.4.5) in example 32.

```
32. Dadi,  ginis     lo'    en     nog    subungan  nog
    so     variety   (par)  (3st)  (rel)  handle    (rel)

           ginami    nog    poktulikan.
           ours(ex)  (rel)  belief

    Dadi,  kun   sug     doda'    o',
    so     this  (tmkr)  indeed   (par)

           ngon  po   mini   do     sop   mogustal,
           (exl) yet  (emp)  (sta)  also  explain
```

```
          poktompungtompungan        ta.     (CA012A)
          use-multipointed-fish-spear  (1pntin)
```

'And so, that is a variety of the
           beginning of our beliefs.
And so, as for those,
     if there are yet here those who want to speak
     we'll add them to those who have already spoken.'

Example 32 is an invitation to present information, but it is also somewhat of a challenge for others to display their ability in the use of oratory.

3.4 Back channel responses

Back channel or feedback plays an important role in the processes of speech interaction. The back channel is the spontaneous response of an auditor that "... is taken to indicate [his] continuing attentiveness of one sort or another to the speaker's message" (Duncan and Fiske 1977:202). Variation in the kinds and occurrence of back channel responses exists according to speech situations, events, and acts. The norms of interaction in each case would dictate the appropriateness of the kinds of feedback. A church situation provides for different participant responses than, say a traditional ceremony. The norm during a sermon is silence while the norm during a ceremony speech allows for background chatter and generally less constraint on auditor response.

Although back channel responses are generally considered as being spontaneous, certain Western Subanon speech genres require, or at least expect, a kind of verbal assistance. Some story tellers, for example, will not recite unless there is one who will give a ritualized **uh huh** response periodically. The Western Subanon epics probably provide the clearest example of this kind of feedback, which is called **tanga'**. When the epics are sung, there is a formal accompaniment by one who systematically repeats a short section of the tune at regular intervals (cf. sec. 4.1.1). This kind of singing verbal response, however, contrasts with the back channel responses being discussed here.

Back channel responses are not considered to be a speech turn by Duncan and Fiske. (They cite a number of works to support their claim.) There is evidence also in the Subanon data that back channels are not turns, that the floor has not been relinquished during a back channel response.

Duncan and Fiske list several manifestations of back channel responses for their English data that are appropriate also to Subanon interaction.[16] The following list corresponds closely to theirs but with Subanon fillers for each item.

   1. Assent. The nasal **mm** or **m'm** indicates assent in Subanon. Also included as assent markers are **o** and **o'o** 'yes', **o ma** 'of course', and

ma' antu' 'it's like that'. Occasionally value statements like **motud** 'it's true' may be heard. They may also be considered as assent markers.

2. Sentence completion.[17]

3. A request for clarification.

4. A brief restatement.

5. Not included in Duncan and Fiske but seen in the Subanon data, is another back channel response of repeating verbatim a word, a phrase, or a sentence which the speaker has just completed.

Back channel responses may or may not be acknowledged by the speaker. They may be ignored and, in some cases, they may even be resented.[18] Two back channel responses in particular characteristically remain unacknowledged by the speaker: the assent class responses and the verbatim repeat. These two tend to communicate affirmation to the speaker. They display conversational etiquette (Hymes 1974).[19] The acknowledgement of the completed sentence back channel consists of the speaker's repeating the sentence completion. For example, in example 33 Auditor B brings to logical conclusion the statement of Speaker A. Speaker A acknowledges B's back channel response by repeating it (see also examples 35 and 36).

33. A Dadi koni posuklion ku   duma   u
       so   this exchange (1snt) companion (1snt)

    B Po'   modakol pa gduma   mu.
      because many   yet companion (2snt)

    A Po'   modakol pa duma   u.
      because many   yet companion (1snt)

    A 'And so, now, I'll cause my companions to take their turn.
    B Because your companions are numerous.
    A Because my companions are numerous.'

A back channel request for clarification is acknowledged when the clarification is given. A restatement as a back channel response may either be acknowledged by an assent response, or a speaker may repeat the restatement, sometimes with a slight modification.

The restatement back channel may include added information or a slight adjustment to a statement that may be acknowledged as though it were a request for clarification.

The choice of which back channel response to use depends, of course, upon the meaning or goal of the response (cf. figure 3.2). There is room for personal choice between the possibilities listed in the assent class. Compared to the assent class, the incidence of the verbatim repeat is scarce. It primarily occurs when the auditor is responding positively to the major point made by the speaker. This and the restatement response particularly convey understanding of what the speaker is saying.

There is an aspect to back channel responses which was not included in the discussion by Duncan and Fiske. Because their analysis was done on data derived only from two-party talk, back channel responses were interpreted as showing attention, and in some cases showing auditor ready state, i.e., that the auditor anticipates taking a turn. In the Western Subanon data, however, a number of interlocutors are involved. Interaction may not only be seen between speaker and auditor but often between speaker and audience, where the audience may be divided regarding the issue under discussion.[20] This was seen, for example, in the **mogogoka'oy** event described in section 2.4.2, figure 2.1 when speaker F spoke. His speech polarized the topic being discussed and clearly delineated those who felt like he did and those who did not. Those who felt like he did were the ones who gave supportive back channel responses. (Actually, there were none that were particularly supportive.) After speaking, he got up and left the circle. Those who spoke in rebuttal were given supportive responses by those who supported them. An element of speaker-hearer solidarity may be evident in such cases. This solidarity with the speaker may be expressed by the use of back channels, particularly the verbatim repeat and the sentence completion. The general effect is an alignment of participants, or the taking of sides in an argument. This alignment may be fluid or changeable within a discussion according as new information is given through the interaction of the speakers.

Back channel responses occur at the ends of sentences. There are two characteristics which signal the end of a sentence or statement: intonation and slight pause. A sample count of three speeches in a discussion consisted of a total of 153 sentences. Four participants contributed ninety-four back channel responses with seventy-eight of these occurring sentence finally. Back channel repetitions and restatements occurred exclusively at sentence boundary. Back channel completions occurred in equal number after hesitation and at sentence boundary. The assent set of responses occurred primarily following sentence boundary but it also occurred during pauses between phrases.[21] This does not imply that back channel responses do not occur elsewhere with different implications. For example, a **mhm** back channel occurring simultaneously with a speech conveys a somewhat bored attitude on the part of the auditor. The percentage ratios of back channel syntactic occurrence and speaker acknowledgement was replicated in other speech samples taken from other events.

The completion back channel occurring after sentence boundary often is begun by a sentence postmargin introducer (cf. Hall 1973), e.g., **saka** 'yet/at the same time', **bagun** 'so that', and **mangka** 'and then' (figure 3.2).

A speaker may employ several different rhetorical means to gain auditor attention and thereby possible auditor responses. For example, he may use contrasting loud and dramatic speech with softer voiciness, the singling out of an individual and calling him by name, the use of the **huh** set of particles,[22] The **huh** set include **huh**, **ha**(h), and **ah**. They occur with a sharp rising intonation indicating the intent of, 'do you understand/follow me?' or a direct question.

Speakers tend to favor one rhetorical device over another in their use of syntax and paralinguistic features. The use of such features does not guarantee a back channel response but it does reestablish attention on what is being said.

In the **mogogoka'oy** text (Appendix C), two questions were asked and received short answers. In neither case was it construed to indicate a relinquishing of the turn. Questions may be asked, however, and remain unanswered. Such cases, in a proper interchange, would be interpreted as rhetorical. A proper interchange in this case is one that has maintained its discrete turns and not become a situation where everyone talks at once.

Figure 3.2 summarizes the discussion on the back channel responses. The columns indicate the form of the back channel response, whether it is acknowledged, what the characteristic answer consists of, where the back channel response occurs, and what its use implies.

The following examples illustrate back channel responses. The asterisk indicates the back channel response in each example.

The Assent set:

34. Speaker: Sa'an   moguksuguksug   u
             reason relate   (1st)

             agun   ita   da:
             so-that (1ptin) (sta)

             sog   glam   ta   koni
             (dir)   all   (1pntin) this

             modolag   dianita.
             bright   to-us(in)

    *Auditor: Ma'   antu'   (RR012B3)
              like that

    Speaker: 'The reason I will relate it
              is so that, all of us,

Interchange Dynamics

Form:	Speaker acknowledgement	Speaker response	Occurence	Meaning
Assent set	no	∅	sentence/ phrase boundry	assent or agreement, positive comment, solidarity
Sentence	yes	repeat	sentence boundary	comment or contribution, solidarity
			after hesitation	assistance
Request for clarification	yes	answer	sentence boundary	unclear statement or confirmation request
Restatement	yes	repeat Assent	sentence boundary	solidarity, comment or contribution
Verbatim repeat	no	∅	sentence boundary	solidarity, assent or agreement, understanding

Figure 3.2 Back channel summary

       to all of us here,
       it will be clear to us.
*Auditor: It's like that.'

The sentence completion following hesitation:

35. Speaker: Ah na,   og   mosala' tanan og..og   guan
             ah   now (tdet) fault   just   (tdet) (hes)

   *Auditor: og   gotow   miginang
              (tdet) person performed

   Speaker: og   gotow   miginang   nog   migunauna
             (tdet) person performed (rel) preceded

        ginang bonua.
        new-year-ceremony

*Auditor: M'm   (RR012B14)
         (assent)

Speaker: 'Well now, the fault just lies at ...
*Auditor: the person who performed
Speaker: the person who went ahead and performed the new year's
         ceremony.'

The sentence completion following a sentence boundary:

36. Speaker: ... ngon   sinama'.
             (exl)   left-over

*Auditor 1: M'm.
            (assent)

*Auditor 2: Saka sop   mologon nog   di'   modunut.
            yet also difficult (com) not   follow

Speaker: 'O'o. Saka sop   mologon nog   di'
         yes   yet also difficult (com) not

         modunut.
         follow

*Auditor 1: M'm, m'm.   (RR012B3)
            (assent)

Speaker: '... there is one already set aside.
*Auditor 1: Yes.
*Auditor 2: Yet, it is difficult not to follow the custom.
Speaker: Yes. Yet, it is difficult not to follow the custom.
*Auditor 1: Yes.'

The request for clarification or confirmation:

37. Speaker: Midongog u: SA, sinosa'an nika ...
             heard   (1snt)   SA   set-date   (2snt)

             og   ginang bonua   nika.
             (tdet) new-year-ceremony   (2snt)

*Auditor: Ika   mikodongog dun?
          (2st) heard   (ana)

Interchange Dynamics

```
Speaker: Akon    mikodongog  dun.
        (1st)    heard       (ana)
```

*Auditor: M'm.   (RR012B11)
         (assent)

Speaker: 'I heard SA, that you had set the date for your new year's
         ceremony.
*Auditor: You heard it?
Speaker: I heard it.
*Auditor: Yes.'

The restatement:

38. Speaker: ...bila   sigisigion   ta   moginang,
             if   continue   (pntin) perform

             otawa   loktodon   moginang,
             or   establish perform

             koponitayan   buan.
             be-bridge   (emp)

*Auditor: Kopononggi'an.
          be-example

Speaker: Og   kopononggi'an   buan.   (RR012B8)
         (tdet) be-example   (emp)

Speaker: 'If we continue to perform it,
         or establish the performance,
         it will become a bridge!
*Auditor: It will become an example.
Speaker: It will become an example!'

The verbatim repetition:

39. Speaker: ...koni   glunsan   gombata';
             this   each-one   children

             da'idun   bogolal   non.
             none   councilor (3snt)

*Auditor: Da'idun   bogolal   non.   (RR012B3)
         none   councilor   (3snt)

Speaker: '... here each one was a youth; there were no councilors.
*Auditor: There were no councilors.'

3.5 Interruption

Interruptions are manifested by simultaneous speech or by a comment which pulls the speaker from his directed topic. In the latter case, a short exchange may ensue in which the speaker may show exasperation in his response or he may elect to ignore the comment. Another option he has is to treat the interruption as an intent of one participant to take the floor. In this case, the formula: **kitu' pa og talu' mu, bamba** 'before you say anything, Uncle', may be used. It is a polite form that is used to maintain the floor.

An auditor may change his state to that of speaker by interrupting a speaker in progress. It is a somewhat aggressive speech action and is usually accomplished along with a softening expression, **sumolopot u pa dinia** 'I'll squeeze in at this point'.

Other interruptions indicating auditor readiness to speak may be ignored as they are signals of intention (cf. sec. 3.3.1.1).

Ordinarily, comments and back channel responses which are forthcoming from those not included as one of the speech participants are treated as interruptions and usually ignored.

Exigencies exist when it is necessary to interrupt as a legitimate action. The role of being a runner who is bringing news of a death, for example, necessitates speed and allows one to interrupt someone speaking. One accomplishes this, however, with the formula:

Solibangga'   u   le   sog   talu'   niu.
knock-against (1st) friend (dir) word   (2pnt)

'Friend, I'm interrupting your speech.'

Interchange Dynamics 53

Notes

1. A Western Subanon may have any or all of the following languages in his repertoire: Visayan (Ilongo, Cebuano), Ilocano, Chavacano, Kolibugan, Maguindanaon, Tausug, Tagalog, and English. Their knowledge of these depends primarily on the Subanon area and the number of speakers of these other languages in those areas. Usually the degree of education of the Subanon will determine how well he will know and use Tagalog and English.

2. Grice (1975) discusses the concept of conversation implicature and the mutual understanding of underlying maxims that govern how implied meaning is to be interpreted. The maxims (be informative as much as is required; do not say what you believe to be false; be relevant; be perspicuous; and, avoid unnecessary prolixity) are culture sensitive and culture dependent (Keenan 1977). The maxims are culture sensitive in relation to attitudes towards men's and women's speech. For example, in Malagasy or Subanon, an identical response by a man and by a woman may have two different implications. Maxims, although they may be a universal in that all cultures have them (I am not making this claim), are culture dependent. Keenan (1977) illustrates that the western European maxim of 'be informative' is not a cooperative principle among the Malagasy (nor, for that matter, among the Subanon).

3. Edelsky (1981) describes two types of "floors", the single floor where boundaries between speakers are overt and well defined, and a joint floor where, especially in discussions where the topic takes precedence over formal social propriety, the matter of who actually has the floor is difficult to determine. In this thesis I will be describing the occurrence of the single floor.

4. The procedure in Duncan and Fiske utilized sophisticated videotape equipment in recording conversations between two individuals. They refused to make claims for universals in turn taking theory but similarities do seem to exist between their findings and my observations of Western Subanon turn taking.

5. He also oversees the litigation process to make sure all functions correctly. In this role he may also be a resource person. It is a very low-key role. Within the elopement **bisala** recorded, the one in charge did not take an active role in discussion although he did make a speech in each case.

6. James (1978) discusses the use of **ah** in marking hesitation within sentences in English. Interestingly, her discussion of **ah** is applicable regarding its use in Western Subanon also. It is beyond the scope of the discussion here, however.

7. An attitude is expressed "softly" regarding a councilor's being too abrupt in interrogating one of the participants in litigation. Following the speech of example 4, a fellow councilor made this statement:

(chuckling) 'O, molokas ma og bolangoy mu koen le (laugh).
    (par) swift (emp) (tdet) canoe (2snt) that friend

'Wow, friend, that canoe of yours sure is fast!'

Which being interpreted means, "You are very abrupt (straightforward) in your interrogation!"

8. A similar marking of Ilongot oratory exists as well (Rosaldo 1973).

9. In a situation where there are multiple claims for the floor, or when asking for quiet with the intent to speak, one can often hear a preliminary "Ati:: . . . ."

The intent to speak is expressed more in a less formally structured discussion where the participants and their roles are not, perhaps, as clearly defined, or functional. For example, one would expect more vying for the floor in a **gupakat** than in the formal **mogogoka'oy** where much emphasis is placed upon oratory. This also reflects the purposes for gathering and for speech, e.g., information, ritual, etc.

10. The **dow** or hearsay marker is generally used as a disclaimer for the veracity or verifiability of a story by the story teller, whether it is a folktale or passing along gossip.

11. This word functions on different levels of discourse in slightly different ways. It is a paragraph conjunction within paragraphs meaning, "and so/therefore". It may be used to introduce an interparagraph summary, "therefore." It may also be used to signal a new paragraph (e.g., a conclusion) with only loose causal relationship to immediately preceding statements.

12. The anaphora **dun** refers back to the immediately cases it refers back to the whole of the previous sentence. The particle not only refers back but also makes a statement about the sentence in which it occurs, that the sentence content is affected in some way by the preceding predicate or sentence.

13. Meiosis or understatement (**topotan**) is a feature that is used widely among the Subanon. This characteristic also seems to occur among the Ilongot (Rosaldo 1973).

14. Cf. note 26, chapter 2 for an explanation of friendship names.

15. The word **le** generally means "friend" and is a term denoting solidarity. However, if two or more occurrences of **le** appear in a sentence, anger and/or frustration with a person or situation is implied.

16. This list is also found in Duncan (1974). Duncan and Fiske include head nods and shakes as back channel responses; however, because gesture phenomena cannot be reproduced from the Subanon data, they will not be treated here.

17. There are instances, in the Western Subanon context, of sentence completions which clearly fall under the category of repairs made by other than speaker (cf. Schegloff, Jefferson, and Sacks 1977). Repairs or not, they are still to be considered as back channel responses in their reflecting auditor attentiveness to the speaker's message.

18. Every interaction includes a background of interpersonal relations and established assumptions that may potentially produce a seemingly aberrant or puzzling response or reaction on the part of any of the participants in a speech situation and which may seem intractable to an analysis.

19. Back channel responses cannot always be taken at face value. Because they are part of conversational etiquette, it would be impolite not to respond in some way. The request for clarification and the brief restatement may be more neutral than the assent, sentence completion or verbatim repeat, all of which tend to be positive.

20. This was seen, for example, in the **mogogoka'oy** event described in section 2.4.2, figure 2.1 when speaker F spoke. His speech polarized the topic being discussed and clearly delineated those who felt like he did and those who did not. Those who felt like he did were the ones who gave supportive back channel responses. (Actually, there were none that were particularly supportive.) After speaking, he got up and left the circle. Those who spoke in rebuttal were given supportive responses by those who supported them.

21. This does not imply that back channel responses do not occur elsewhere with different implications. For example, a **mhm** back channel occurring simultaneously with a speech conveys a somewhat bored attitude on the part of the auditor.

22. The **huh** set include **huh, ha(h),** and **ah.** They occur with a sharp rising intonation indicating the intent of, "do you understand/follow me?"

4 The Patterns of Poetry

4.0 Introduction

Two integral speech events in Subanon society have so far only been mentioned briefly in passing. These are formal singing (**bobat**) and prayers (**gyakin**). Both of these genres have subsumed under them kinds of singing and praying, respectively, as well as kinds of situations appropriate for them.

It is not the purpose here to discuss these kinds of singing or prayer genre as such, but rather to discuss a characteristic patterning of syntax and semantics found in them. It is this patterning of form and meaning that is seen in varying degrees in other formal speech use including that already discussed in chapters 2 and 3. It is apropos, then, that the discussion of this patterning begin with the genres that are characterized by the elaborate syntactic forms, the ritual poetic speech genres of Western Subanon.

Poetry in Western Subanon may be metrical with a definite rhythm, as found in certain word-play rhymes; or, it may be what Hymes (1981) has termed "measured verse." Measured verse is characterized by syntactic and semantic patterned repetition but is not strictly framed in a rhythmic or rhymic meter. Both Subanon metrical and measured forms of poetry are realized by syntactic and/or lexical parallelism. It is this parallelism of structure that is also found in formal situations.

There are two main modes in which Subanon metered and measured verse may be expressed: through song, that is, accompanied by some tune as a rhythmic meter framework, and through regular verbalizing.

The following discussion will cover, first, the patterning characteristics of poetic speech genres that are sung, illustrated by a short section from the

Subanon epic song and by a short section from a séance. Then, the poetic patterning of measured verse will be illustrated in two nonsung examples of prayers. Finally, the chapter will conclude with a short discussion of doublets, or binomials.

4.1 Parallel structures

There is an intriguing quality to parallel structures that has caught the attention and interest of numerous scholars since the 18th Century. The study of parallel structures is of interest in comparative studies in poetics and literature and formal speech genres (Bricker 1974, Fox 1971, 1974, Gossen 1974, Hymes 1981, Jakobson 1966).

Hymes (1981:176) points out the cohesive effect of parallels and uses them to help identify and define measured lines in Chinookan poetic forms. As do the Chamula in Mexico (Gossen 1974), the Subanon may use parallel structures in formal speech making for emphasis or to highlight major points (see chap. 5).

Fox (1971; 1974) describes a situation where parallels characterize a separate poetic or ritual code among the Rotinese. This form of ritual language or **bini**, consists of semantic sets, one element or word forming a pair with more than one other element. For the Rotinese, this formal speech code is highly developed and is utilized in a variety of rites. "The sets are structured in formulaic phrases and their presentation generally consists in compositions of parallel verse" (1974:73). The parallels are between dyadic sets that are semantically associated. These sets may form parallel lines in which the elements paralleled are consecutively ordered, alternating, or unordered. Fox's description of the form of the ritual language of the Rotinese bears a striking resemblance to the form of the Western Subanon ritual speech of the epic and séance. The difference is that the dyadic sets and parallels do not form a separate code in Subanon as they do for the Rotinese.

Jakobson's (1966) discussion of parallelisms includes the historic treatment of Lowth's in which Lowth categorizes, in a gross typology, three kinds of parallel structures: (1) synonymy, (2) antithetical, and (3) synthetic or purely grammatical congruencies.

It was noticed early in the analysis of the Subanon data that the majority of parallels consists of parallels of repeated syntactic form — verbs, nouns, and adjectives matching verbs, nouns, and adjectives in a distich. However, not all parallels are of form; for example, on one line a word may be companioned with a phrase in the next line. The classification of parallels in the Subanon data is based upon the semantic relationships that exist between the parallelism and repetition of syntactic forms. The kinds of parallels posited here are (1) synonymous, (2) analogous, and (3) associative. These three types may be realized by most of the grammatical categories that Jakobson

(1968) lists, including numbers, genders, aspects, moods, voices, animate and inanimate, appelatives and proper names, affirmatives and negatives, definite or indefinite pronouns or articles.

A synonymous parallel is one in which the semantic force of two words or phrases are considered to be virtually identical or synonymous in a particular context. This may involve Subanon phrases like "he did not stray/ he did not leave", or, "he is not Subanon/ he is a foreigner."

An analogous parallel is one in which there is a tight correspondence of semantic associations between the two lines of a parallel where at least one of the lines is used as a figure. There is a semantic resemblance in some particulars between things otherwise unlike. For example, in Subanon, "they gave to us histories/ they passed along to us speech gatherings" where "speech gatherings" is metonymy. The gatherings are where the histories are given.

The associative parallel is one where an associative relationship exists between two or more statements comprising the parallel. The statements themselves are not synonyms nor are they analogues but they are closely connected in function with each other. The associative relationship often is one of being the components or attributes or activities making up or expounding a particular context. For example, from the Subanon, "if we do not obey them, what about our accomplishments/ what about our abilities?".

The uses of parallelism in Western Subanon speech provide, as Fox has put it, a stereoscopic effect to expression and description.

4.1.1 Sung genre. Frake (1964) has described the importance and place of drinking songs (**glombana'**) which occur potentially in every Eastern Subanun and Western Subanon ceremony where rice wine (**gasi**) is served. This singing genre may be either dialogue or monologue. Verbal dueling (**bayuk**) may also be done through singing. Mothers chant lullabies and a number of pieces with metered lines have been recorded. All of these speech forms are characterized by parallelism in syntax.

To illustrate the kinds of parallel structures which exist in ritual forms, sections will be taken, first of all, from two recorded corpora of sung genre: the epic **Goguman**[1] and a séance.

4.1.1.1 The epic. In Western Subanon, the epic is traditionally sung (**bobat**) and in this it is much like those of other Philippine societies, especially on Mindanao (Wrigglesworth 1977; 1979). There are several varieties of production forms for the epic, all of which are sung. The manner of singing, the tune, and the actual participants in the production may all vary to some distinctive degree according to the production. There may also be some variation of the dramatis personae between several of the various productions of the epic. But, however it is performed, it commonly consists of dyadic sets, parallel lines, and formulaic descriptions.

The singing of the epic **Goguman** takes two individuals, the raconteur and one who echoes the tune (**polonanga'**) at prescribed interludes. Three lines are sung with a short interlude in which the **polonanga'** repeats a tune of one line only. After this, two or more lines are sung by the raconteur before another **tanga'** interlude. The story is conveyed by this vehicle of alternating three- and two-line rhythmic stanzas.[2]

The lines are all of seven syllables with the option of six syllables at the beginning of a group of three lines. This option depends upon which tune is being sung. (There were two different ones used in the production excerpts quoted in this section.) In keeping the syllables even, the syntax is necessarily trimmed to its barest elements in this poetry form. The imagery of the figures used, as well as the implied meanings of the phrases, all add to the mystique and enjoyment of the epic.[3]

The two short excerpts of the Western Subanon **Goguman**, which are quoted in this section, illustrate some of the kinds of parallels which can occur in this genre. The first section quoted begins a description of the river and the fiefdom. It continues through and includes a description of the house groups. This section occurs at the outset of the epic and sets the general scene.

9 Tubig dow nog Migogling	The river, they say, Migogling
10 Mologdong dow tokodoy	is, they say, very straight
11 Ma' kinotong tali	like stretched rope
12 Tidu sog minanga non	from its mouth
13 Mabut sog gulu tubig	reach to the river head.
14 Da' dow pikpiku'an non	There is, they say, no crookedness.
15 Niug migloponglopong	Coconuts measured evenly in height
16 Kabun migbatukbatuk	planted exactly the same
17 Sog mogdipag mogdipag	on each side of the river.
18 Bawang dow palanua'	Inhabited area, they say, with crowds of people.
19 Baloy miktubu' ligbos	Houses are mushrooms growing
20 Sog mogdipag mogdipag	on each side of the river.
21 Bukid sog dibaba'	Upstream and downstream

The Patterns of Poetry

22 Dunon ta dunon ta dun	that is the way it is.
23 Tubig dow nog Migogling	The river, they say, Migogling
24 Dolungan Miksigola	the well Miksigola
25 Miksib dow silingan non	Crowded, they say, its neighbors
26 Tugda' le gugdan dun	the foot of ladders, friend, meet because of it
27 Tinulunoyoy nog gapuy	reciprocally handing fire
28 Tinobukoy nog sandok	reciprocally receiving a ladle.
29 Sog bukid sog dibaba'	Upstream and downstream
30 Bo ma le bonua kun	This is some place, friend!

The synonymous parallel.

23 Tubig dow nog Migogling water (hs) (nt) Migogling	The river, they say, Migogling
24 Dolungan Miksigola well Miksigola	the well Miksigola

In this context, the source of water for personal uses, **tubig** 'river' (literally 'water') is synonymous with **dolungan** 'well' (the source of drinking water). The names, **Migogling** and **Miksigola**, are also considered to be synonymous. The structure of this synonymous parallel is an example of a simple or unembedded parallel. The two lines are a straightforward matching of semantic and grammatical elements.

10 Mologdong dow tokodoy straight (hs) (int)	is, they say, very straight

(lines 11–13)

14 Da' dow pikpiku'an non no (hs) crooked (3snt)	There is, they say, no crookedness.

Lines 10 and 14 illustrate a synonymous parallel between a negative and a positive statement, both of which have the same meaning. Line 10 (including lines 11–13) are positive and line 14 is negative.1b Lines 10 and 14 bracket lines 11–13:

11 Ma' kinotong tali like stretched rope	like stretched rope
12 Tidu sog minanga non from (loc) mouth (3snt)	from its mouth

13 Mabut sog   gulu tubig   reach to the river head.
    reach (loc) head water

These lines are a figure expressing the straightness of the river. The beginning words of lines 12 and 13 (**tidu** 'from' and **mabut** 'reach to') illustrate a common way of expressing relationships of extremities and points along a continuum.[4] These lines (12 and 13) also parallel line 10 and expound the straightness of the river. There is also a correspondence between **minanga** 'river mouth' and **gulu tubig** 'river head'.

The structure of the antithetic nature of this parallel is complex. There are four parallels included: Lines 10 and lines 11–13 form an analogous parallel, the one being a figure for the other. Lines 10 and 14 form a synonymous

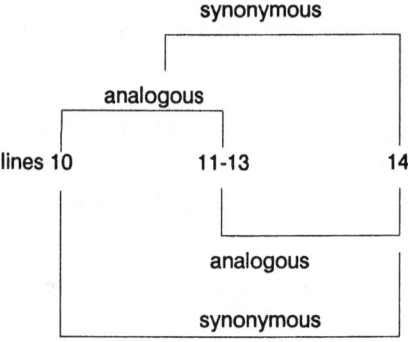

Figure 4.1 Embedded analogous parallels

parallel. By extension then, lines 11–13 and line 14 also comprise an analogous parallel. Likewise, lines 10–13 form a parallel with line 14 as shown in figure 4.1.

The analogous and associative parallels.

The fact of being crowded is a positive value. Noise and merriment are also positive as they evidence activity and good will. Hence, the fairly long section describing the nearness of houses. The analogous parallel will be illustrated by lines 25–28.

25 Miksib dow   silingan   non   Crowded, they say, its
    crowd (hs)   neighbor (3snt)   neighbors

26 Tugda' le   gugdan dun   the foot of ladders,
    foot   friend ladder (ana)   friend, meet because of it

27 Tinulunoyoy[5] nog   gapuy   reciprocally handing fire
    hand-over   (nt) fire

28 Tinobukoy nog sandok   reciprocally receiving a
   receive   (nt) ladle   ladle.

A number of different semantic elements are paralleled in these four lines resulting in a complex parallel structure. Line 25 is a statement of the condition or situation and line 26 is its analogue or corollary. These two lines are in an analogous relationship.

Lines 26, 27, and 28 are all expressions expounding or exemplifying the closeness of houses. In this regard they stand together in an associative parallel relationship to line 25. Likewise, line 26, by expressing the nearness of the houses, allows for the associative actions expressed in lines 27 and 28. Lines 27 and 28 together form an associative parallel. The semantic associations of the two lines express the personal camaraderie of the neighbors who may exchange both fire (**gapuy**) and ladles (**sandok**) just by reaching from house to house. The predicate of line 27 (**tinulunoy**) means to hand over something in a reciprocal manner and in line 28 **tinobukoy** likewise means to receive something reciprocally. The activities themselves are paralleled: fire implies the cooking process while the ladle implies dishing it up or eating what is cooked, i.e., the meal.

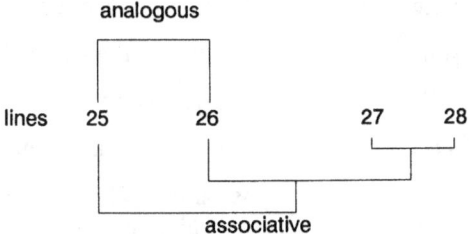

4.2 Embedded associative parallels

The semantic structure in the complex embedding of four parallels is shown in figure 4.2.

The associative parallel consists of the innermost parallel (lines 27 and 28) which forms a parallel with line 26 and they together form a unit parallel with line 25.

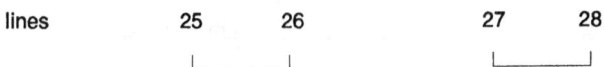

Figure 4.3 Grammatical structure paralleled

y also be seen two different grammatical structures paralleled in figure 4.2. Lines 25 and 26 consist of the grammatical elements: predicate, particle, noun, pronoun. Lines 27 and 28 also match their grammatical elements: predicate, nontopic relation marker, noun, (in that order). The parallels, then, may form a complex of levels or different relationships both grammatical and semantic.

The dyads found in lines 21 and 29 (**bukid sog dibaba'** 'upstream and downstream') and in line 36 (**motud sobonal** 'true truth') are examples of doublets (cf. sec. 4.2).

The following section quoted from the **Goguman** describes the prosperity and the strictness of the law in this fiefdom.

36 Dow motud sobonal	They say, is true, the truth
37 Tubig dow nog Migogling	The river, they say, Migogling
38 Sinu le modonggu' dun	Whoever, friend, comes ashore there
39 Dongogan non na muli'	Is heard he is now home.
40 Sima mokangoy dion	Whoever happens to go there
41 Bantug non mogilong	News is he turns about-face
42 Bogayan ma nog songku'	Is given of the harvest!
43 Bohagi'an nog bandi	Is given share of the wealth
44 Tondu'an nog niugan	Is pointed to a coconut plantation
45 Golalon podotu'on	Is caused to be titled as a chief person.
46 Sondow kosula'an	The day one is cursed
47 Asta sog sampoyumul	Even to the end of his days
48 Sima dow sumula' dun	Whoever, they say, curses it
49 Putukan le nog gulu	Head will be severed, friend.
50 Si sinu momombuy dun	Whoever expels from it
51 Tuaban nog gigdob	Chest will be ripped open.
52 Pogondi' le nog datu'	Prohibited, friend, by the chief.
53 Ba'aba nog kowasa	An awesome chief he is.

Lines 36 to 45 form one section, while lines 46 to 53 form another. Starting with lines 38–45,[6] several parallels are evident. These are made obvious by their being grammatically parallel.

The Patterns of Poetry

38–39 Whoever, friend, comes ashore there, news is he now is home.

40–41 Whoever is able to go there, news is he comes about-face.

The parallel is a complex synonymous parallel. The phrases of lines 38 and 40 are semantically the same as are also lines 39 and 41. Together the phrases of these lines form a synonymous parallel of two sentences.

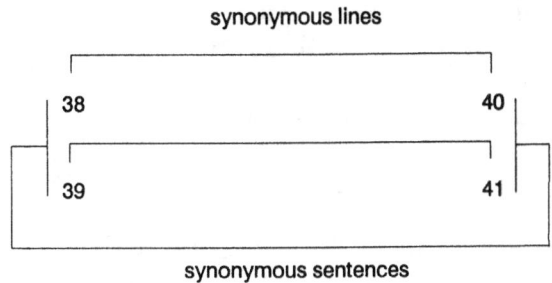

Figure 4.4 Complex synonymous parallel

Analogous parallels may be seen between lines 42, 43, 44, and 45. These lines are also parallels in grammatical form.

42 That one is given of the harvest.

43 That one has a share of the hard wealth.

44 That one is allotted a coconut plantation.

45 That one is made a chief person.

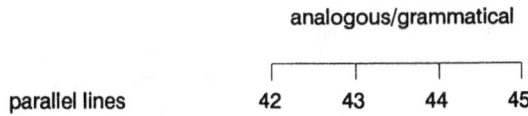

Figure 4.5a Simple analogous/grammatical parallels

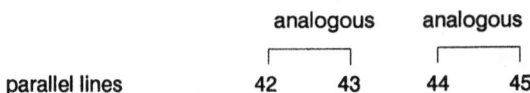

Figure 4.5b Analogous parallel

Not quite so obvious is the parallel in the analogous semantic relationship between lines 42–43 and 44–45, where lines 42–43 imply shared wealth and line 44–45 denote community position/role (i.e., land owner/title holder).

An associative relationship may be seen between lines 42 and 44 and between lines 43 and 45 that produces an associative parallel. The associative parallel exists in the relationship in lines 42 and 44 between harvest and coconut plantation. An association also exists in lines 43 and 45 between hard wealth and chief person where a major semantic component of the word stem for chief person (**datu'**) is 'wealthy person'.

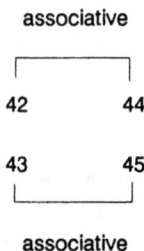

Figure 4.5c Associative parallel

The elaborate syntactic structure of these four lines enhances the semantic relationships which exist. Figure 4.5d illustrates the complex relationships by conflating figures 4.5b and 4.5c. The analogous parallels A and A' are analogous parallel lines 42, 43, 44, and 45. Likewise, the associative parallels B and B' are associative parallel lines 42, 44, 43, and 45.

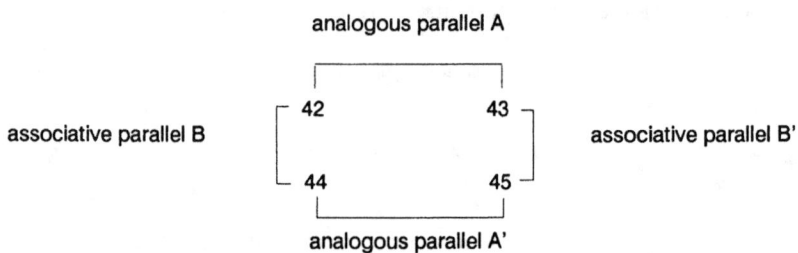

Figure 4.5d An integrated parallel complex

48 Whoever, they say, curses it

49   his head will be severed, friend.

50 Whoever expels someone from it

51   his chest will be ripped open.

The Patterns of Poetry 65

There is a structural parallel between lines 48 and 50 and between lines 49 and 51. These four lines comprise two parallel sentences, lines 48 and 49 and lines 50 and 51. This is the same kind of parallel relationship between lines and sentences that was just pointed out for lines 42–45. This also illustrates the kind of semantic and grammatical pattern that is found extensively throughout the epic song.

4.1.1.2 The séance. The séance is considered to be a communication from the spirit world to the physical world. It is regarded as an interchange between a spirit entity and a human. In this regard it differs from the epic, which is presented to an audience. Also involved in the seance is a human medium. The séance is a fairly common occurrence in certain Western Subanon areas. A recognized shaman is often the medium; however, others who are predisposed to the rigors associated with this practice may also become 'possessed' (**mokpalin**).

The séance may have two oral channel forms: sung and not sung. The ethnic tune that accompanies the séance when sung is usually well known to the community. In the selection quoted in this section, each strophe (numbered consecutively in the transcription) is a repetition of the simple tune.[7] The first line is usually composed of more than three syllables, while the second line is restricted to only three syllables.

The following selection of a séance chant is quoted from one recorded at the request of the shaman medium.[8] The addressees are the council (**bogolal**) who are arranged in a semicircle around the entranced and supine shaman.

1 Na' a polo' ma le[9]	Listen to me, friend
Tumanggung ng:[10]	Tumanggung,
2 Timuoy le dow	Timuoy, friend, (hearsay)
Timuoy	Timuoy.
3 Sakan ku po	I will interrogate
le amu mng:	friend, you all.
4 Migampul no ma	Many are indeed
gbolian	shaman;
5 Migampul ma	Many are indeed
ktimuoy	timuoy
6 Sog bulus[11] nog	the length of
Litoban	the Litoban river.

7 Sakan migondun dun	Asking why it is,
miksabap le	what is the reason, friend,
8 Ain le mi..gu..	where, friend, is
gupu'an	the source,
9 Ain le ginu..	where, friend, did it
munat n::	leave from
10 nog gulaban ma le	the disrespect, friend,
gbotad n::	of custom
11 pobonan ma le	the slowness, friend,
gba'asa n::	of social amenities?
12 Amuyamuy	(Attention, please)
tokodoy	very much
13 Saka kimokosunan	yet, shamans
amu ma m::	you (pl) are
14 kobogolalan	councilors
amu ma n::	you (pl) are.
15 Migondun dun	Why is it
miksabap m::	what is the reason?
16 Ain le dow ng	Who, friend, (hearsay)
miksala' n::	committed a fault?

This ends the first turn.[12] The components of the turn (cf. sec. 3.3.1) begin with the claim for the floor in the first line

```
1 Na'   a     polo'  ma    le
  not  (2st)  yet   (emp) friend
```
'Listen to me, friend.'

then the addressee is mentioned in the second, third, and fourth lines, **Tumanggung** (title), **Timuoy** (title), **le** 'friend', **Timuoy** (title) respectively, and, finally, the validation of the claim in stating the purpose of the turn expressed by the performative in the third strophe, **sakan** 'ask'. The addressee is referred to by his title, (**Tumanggung**), and is considered to be the spokesman for the whole group. There was no one present with the title of **Timuoy**. By implication, the remaining councilors are considered to be the ones referred to by the title **Timuoy**, which then stands in a parallel relationship to the title **Tumanggung**.

Strophes 4 through 6 comprise a syntactic unit. Strophes 4 and 5 are independent clauses; however, strophe 6 indicates that 4 and 5 are parallel clauses within a sentence of which 6 is also a clause. It modifies, grammatically, both 4 and 5. The two clauses (4 and 5) stand in an associative relationship and are grammatical parallels.

    4 Migampul no ma   gbolian
       grouped   now (emp) shaman

                                  6 sog   bulus   nog   Litoban.
                                      (loc) length (pos) Litoban

    5 Migampul ma   ktimuoy
       grouped   (emp) timuoy
    4) Many shaman are, 5) many timuoy are 6) along the
        length of the Litoban river.

Strophe 7 begins the query to the council and extends through to strophe 14. Strophes 8 and 9 are independent parallel clauses that are in a synonymous parallel relationship. Strophes 10 and 11 are likewise paralleled but in an analogous relationship. Strophe 12 is a parenthetical interlude that commands attention. The parallel strophes 13 and 14 end the main query as an analogous parallel. In review, then,

Type	Strophe
P1 (synonymous)	7
P 2 (synonymous)	8–9
P 3 (analogous)	10–11
P 4 (analogous)	13–14

P 1 and P 2 are both parallel question constructions and semantically stand in an analogous parallel relationship. Either P 1 or P 2 are grammatically and semantically appropriate for P 3, although the questions themselves may ask for slightly different information in another context. By a slight shift in labeling, Parallel 1 will be made to include strophe 7 as P 1' and strophes 8 and 9 as P1". The result is three analogous parallels and two embedded synonymous parallels.

P 1 (analogous)   P 1' (synonymous) 7
                             P 1" (synonymous) 8–9
P 2 (analogous)   10–11
P 3 (analogous)   13–14

The syntactic structure of each parallel is grammatically identical (except for P 1), e.g.,

P 1 Sakan	asking
P 1' migondun dun solution (ana)	why is it

miksabap le
        reason   friend
        (Pred) (Pro)
	what is the reason,
	friend

P 1" ain le migupu'an where source	where, friend, is the source

ain le ginumunat
                leave
        (Adv) (Pro) (Pred)
	where, friend, did
	it leave from

P 2 nog	(nt det)
gulaban ma le gbotad disrespect (emp) custom	disrespect, friend, of custom
pobonan ma le gba'asa length custom	prolonging, friend, of social amenities
(Pred) (Emp) (Pro) (Noun)	
P 3 saka	yet
kimokosunan amu ma shaman (2pt) (emp)	you (pl) are shamans
kobogolalan amu ma councilor	you (pl) are councilors
(Noun) (Pro) (Emp)	

The relationship of the semantic and syntactic structure is one of linear series. It tends to be less complex than the parallels found in the epic which are discussed in section 4.1.1.1 where there was sometimes a staggered structure, e.g.,

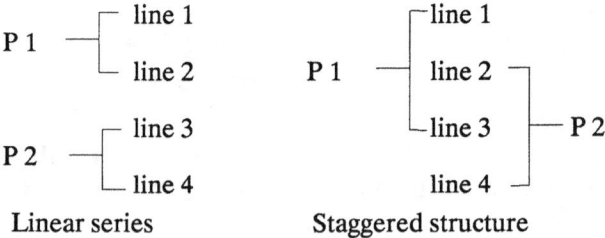

      Linear series   Staggered structure

The Patterns of Poetry 69

This linear series type of structure proceeds throughout the duration of the séance chant.

4.1.2 Oral genre not sung.

4.1.2.1 Prayer 1. To be able to pray publicly in ceremonies constitutes a specific role filled primarily by shaman or their acolytes. These individuals also display an ability to use ritual speech forms.[13]

Formal prayers are characterized by poetic patterns consisting of parallel structures, which are often spoken quite rapidly and loudly. They have a characteristic intonation contour which begins high and ends low in an exaggerated manner. The low ending often is characterized by breathiness. The contour extends over a phonological paragraph. The phonological paragraph includes a total information unit and therefore may also be considered as a grammatical paragraph. The prosodic boundaries of high to low contour correspond, usually, to lexical paragraph discourse markers.

The prayer is a monologue in address form. There is no verbal answer expected. There is no exchange involved.

The prayer that is discussed in this section has been separated into three units (A, B, and C) which correspond to the phonological sentence identified by a high to low intonation contour. The transcription is made by lines identified by the parallelism that exists between the grammatical units of phrases and clauses.

The following three units are from prayers recorded during a religious ceremony.[14]

Unit A

```
1 Dadi  Apu'  Sanag  Apu'  Poktonudan
  so    lord  Sanag  lord  Poktonudan

2       Pongoni  nami      nog    solamat  nika   na
        ask      (1pntex)  (com)  thanks   (2st)  now

3  Bu  pongoni n  ami       nog
   and ask        (1pntex)  (com)

4       Bogayan  nika    na   ilan   nog      bolakat
        give     (2snt)  now  (3pt)  (ntdet)  power

5  Bu  bogayan   nika    na   ilan   nog      pikilan
   and give      (2snt)  now  (3pt)  (ntdet)  mind

6                nog    soupaya  mongon  og       kopongandol  nilan
                 (acc)  so-that  (exl)   (tdet)   faith        (3pnt)
```

7		Bu	mongon	og	kotud	nilan	
		and	(exl)	(tdet)	belief	(3pnt)	
8			sog	diwata	nog	mama'	niu
			(dir) god	(rel)	like	(2pnt)	
9	Apu'	Sanag,	Apu'	Poktonudan.			
	lord	Sanag	lord	Poktonudan			

1 And so, Lord Sanag, Lord Poktonudan

2   we are asking for your blessing now

3   And we are asking that

4   you give them now the spiritual power

5   And you give them now the mind

6 So that, there will exist their faith

7   And there will exist their belief

8   in the gods, who you are

9   Lord Sanag, Lord Poktonudan.

According to the Subanon sentence grammar described in Hall (1973), the structure of Unit A may be defined grammatically as a single sentence with sentence embedding and parallel structures. A bidimensional display will help to differentiate the sentential elements.

	Presentence	Sentence	Postsentence
lines	1	2-8	9
	(1) discourse marker **dadi**	parallels	address form
	(2) address form		

Chart 4.6 Bidimensional array of Unit A sentence

In Unit A are found three associative parallels of the linear series type. They are,

     P 1 lines 2 and 3-7

     P 2 lines 4 and 5

     P 3 lines 6 and 7

Parallels 2 and 3 are embedded in parallel 1. However unlike the linear

The Patterns of Poetry 71

series parallel described in the séance, the parallels here are all connected by a concatenator **bu**, which is sometimes glossed as 'and' (cf. lines 3, 5, and 7). Figure 5.1 displays this sentence.

Unit B

10 Bu   gbata'   nilan   kpitu   kotow   sog   dialom
   and child   (3pnt) seven person (loc) inside

                        nog   gibaan   nilan
                        (nt)   lap   (3pnt)

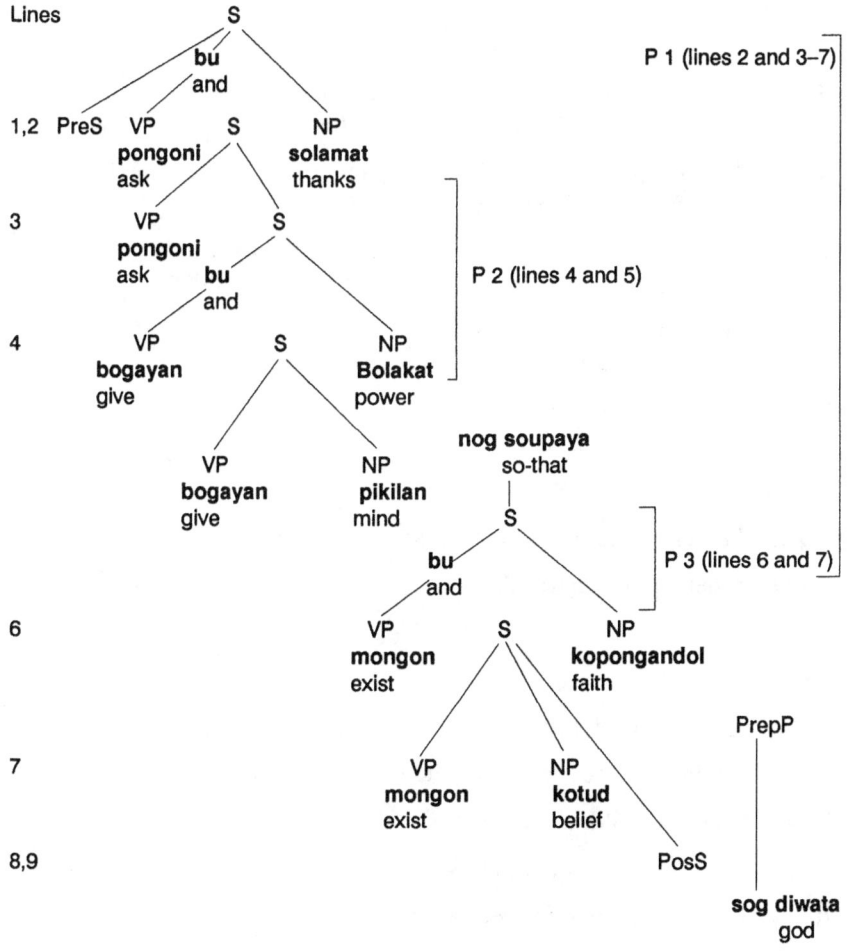

Figure 5.1 Embedded sentence parallels

11 sala kotow na migduoy dun.
   one person now married (ana)

Unit C

12 Dadi, og pitu kotow koyon
   so (t) seven person that

13   sunu'on ku moguakil, Apu', diniu
      include I deliver lord to-you(p)

14 nog bata' nilan koyon
   (rel) child (3pnt) that

15   sog gongkoman nilan ma
          (loc) palm (3snt) (emp)

16   sog dialom gibaan nilan po ma
          (loc) inside lap (3snt) yet (emp)

17   mogunut sog glawas nilan
       follow (loc) body (3snt)

18   Apu' Sanag, Apu' Poktonudan
             lord Sanag lord Poktonudan

19   uakil u dini sog godapan nika
      deliver I here (loc) presence (2snt)

20   gobi kini.
          night this

Unit B

10 And their children, seven persons within their laps

11 one of them is now married.

Unit C

12 And so, those seven persons

13   I am including in delivering them, Lord, to you(pl)

14 who are those children of theirs

15   in their palms

16   within their laps yet

17   including themselves,

18 Lord Sanag, Lord Poktonudan,

The Patterns of Poetry 73

19   I deliver here in your presence

20   this night.

Unit B changes the discourse attention to the children of those being prayed for in Unit A. On the discourse level, lines 10 and 11 introduce new information. In this way Unit B functions as an introduction to Unit C. The discourse connection to the previous unit is signaled by the use of **bu** 'and'.

On the sentence level, the two lines of Unit B comprise a single sentence with preposed sentence topic. It is an equative construction.

10 ...their children, seven persons in their care...

11 one of whom (**dun** anaphora) is now married.

where, "their children" functions as a sentence topic and is in apposition to "seven persons in their care."

Unit C begins with the introducer **dadi** 'so' and with a phrase that parallels line 10 by repeating "Those seven persons."

The construction of Unit C is made complex by the use of a relative construction beginning with line 14. The relative construction modifies the topic (**pitu kotow koyon** 'those seven people') in line 12. The relative clause is an embedded sentence with preposed topic and follows the same syntactic construction as the embedding sentence in lines 12 and 13. In this, the embedded relative clause sentence (lines 14–19) is in a parallel relationship to the embedding sentence (lines 12–13).

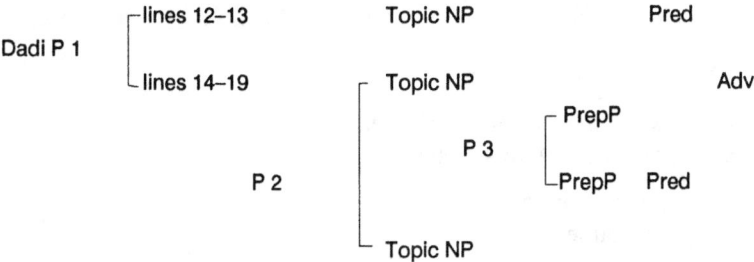

Figure 5.2 Embedded parallels

The sentence elements are identified as a preposed sentence topic NP then a predicate that includes a directional.

Sentence topic NP:

a) 12 og pitu kotow koyon   'those seven people'

b) 14 bata' nilan koyon   'those children of theirs'

17 mogunut sog glawas nilan   'followed by themselves'

where lines 14 and 17 also parallel each other and are shown as parallel 2 in diagram 4.2.

Predicate and directional:

a) 13 sunu'on ku moguakil, Apu', diniu

   'I am including in my delivery to you'

b) 19 uakil u dini sog godapan nika

   'I deliver here into your presence'

Parallel 3 (lines 15 and 16) modifies line 14 **bata'** 'child' and is embedded in the first member of Parallel 2 in the sentence topic NP labeled b) in line 19.

15 sog gongkoman nilan ma   'in their responsibility!'

16 sog dialom gibaan nilan po ma   'in their care yet!'

4.1.2.2 Prayer 2. The two sentence structures of prayer 1 just discussed contrast with prayer 2 in this section. The prosodic features of the two prayers and the parallelism remain the same. The difference is found in the grammatical strategies of the two prayers, e.g., sentence length, embedding, chiasmus, and types of parallels. The following section is quoted from a single prayer recorded during a religious ceremony.[15] The quote is divided into three information units, A, B, and C. The lines are made up of grammatical phrases and clauses which generally correspond to phonological phrases.

Unit A

1 Solamat Inoy, ami   koni   minindog ...
  thanks   Inoy   we(ex) this   stand

2 sumabi sog   ngalan mu,
  call   (dir) name   your

3 tumikang sog   ngalan ni Apu' Sanag,
  step-up   (dir) name   of lord Sanag

4 mangoy ditu'   sog   ngalan ni Apu' Tikulanga,
  go   there   (dir) name   of lord Tikulanga

5 kosolag ni Apu' Ama'   Mikpongon.
  large   of lord father creator

1 Greetings Inoy, we here are standing ...
2 calling on your name,

3 stepping up on the name of Lord Sanag,
4 going there to the name of Lord Tikulanga,
5 ultimately to the Lord Father Creator.

Unit A is the beginning of the prayer. As a monologue it identifies the supplicant, **ami koni** 'we here', the speech act, **sumabi sog ngalan mu** 'call on your name', and the spirit entities who are the addressees. These latter are enumerated in a list and the progression from one to the next is explicit, e.g.,

> line 2 **sumabi** 'call to'
>
> line 3 **tumikang** 'step up a rung'
>
> line 4 **mangoy** 'go'
>
> line 5 **kosolag** 'ultimate/principal'

Unit B

6 sobion nami:
call we(ex)

        mokiipat,
        ask-care

        mokibantoy nog dinami koni nog kohinangan
        ask-watch   (nt) to-us(ex) this (nt) actions

7   po' bagun da'   pongyuba' dinami sog
     (par)   so-that not tempt to-us(ex) (loc)

    buloma'   dinglag
    tomorrow day-after-tomorrow

8 Mokibantoy ami
  ask-watch   we(ex)

        sog gobi bu gondow
        (loc) night and day

              glolabung bu   sisolom
              afternoon and morning

9 nog soupaya da'idun monasat.
  (nt) so-that   nothing cause-illness

10 Mokiipat ami   sog tupus somul non nog da'idun kopus non
   ask-care we(ex) (loc) finish time   it   (rel) none   cease   it

11 nog soupaya di' moksugbak
   (nt) so-that   not pass-on

12		og glolat nog piponog, (t) pity (rel) descend
13		og tunung nog binogoy (t) favor (rel) given
14		dianami, to-us(ex)
15		sog ngalan nog Subanon (loc) name (nt) Subanon
16		milontow buta bongol. being blind deaf
17	Omba'is u kololatan ami tokodoy. good I pitied we(ex) (int)	

6 We are calling:
                requesting care,
                requesting watch-care over our actions,
7   so that nothing will tempt us in the future.
8 We request watch-care
        over night and day,
        afternoon and morning
9   so that nothing will cause us illness.
10 We request care for all the time which never ceases
11   so that there will not go elsewhere
12   the pity that has been caused to descend
13   the favor that has been given
14   to us,
15   to those named Subanon,
16   being blind and deaf.
17 I desire we be very much pitied.

Unit B is composed of four sentences, lines 6–7, 8–9, 10–16, and line 17. The pattern organization of these sentences may first be seen in the recurrence of the pronouns "we X . . . so that . . ." and the final "we" in line 17.[16] Three of these sentences include four parallels. Parallel 1 (lines 6–7) contains a synonymous linear parallel between the predicates **mokiipat** 'request care' and **mokibantoy** 'request watch-care'. Parallel 2 (lines 8–9 and 10–11 (16)) is an analogous parallel with identical sentence elements.

  8–9: Pred - time phrase - postS result clause

  10–11: Pred - time phrase - postS result clause

Parallel 3 (lines 12 and 13) is an associative parallel which matches identi-

The Patterns of Poetry

cal grammatical elements. P 3 is part of and an embedded sentence within the second member of P 2 (line 11).

   det - noun - relation marker - pred
12 **og glolat   nog   piponog**
   'the pity that is descended'
13 **og tunung   nog   binogoy**
   'the favor that is given'

Parallel 4 (lines 14 and 15) is an analogous parallel that identifies the supplicants. The parallel is embedded in the second member of parallel 3 (line 13).

14 **dianami** 'to us'

15 **sog ngalan nog Subanon** 'to those named Subanon'

Figure 5.3 summarizes the description of the parallels of Unit B.

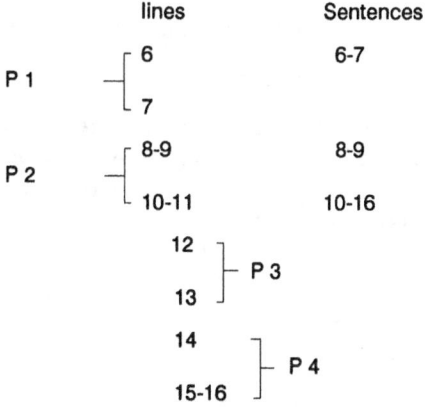

Figure 5.3 Parallels of Unit B, Prayer 2

The whole of Unit B exemplifies a kind of paragraph that has not yet been described. The first sentence (lines 6–7) contains four predicates. The first (**sobion** 'call on') repeats the speech act predicate of Unit A, line 2 as an anaphora. The next two predicates are in parallel, (**mokiipat** 'requesting care' and **mokibantoy** 'requesting watch-care') as already discussed, and are kataphors in that they anticipate the main predicates of the next two sentences. The fourth predicate (**da' pongyuba'** 'not be tempted') is parallel to the negatives in lines 9 and 11. The next two sentences (lines 8–9 and 10–16) both begin with these two predicates, **mokiipat** and **mokibantoy**. They do so, however, in a reversed order which results in a chiasmus.

Aspects of Western Subanon Formal Speech

The first sentence includes a time phrase denoting generality: **sog buloma' dinglag** 'in the future (literally 'tomorrow day-after-tomorrow')'. This time phrase is echoed in the two sentences following it but with more specificity: **sog gobi bu gondow, glolabung bu sisolom** 'in the night and day, afternoon and morning', and in sentence 3: **sog tupus somul non nog da' kopus non** 'for all time which never ceases'.

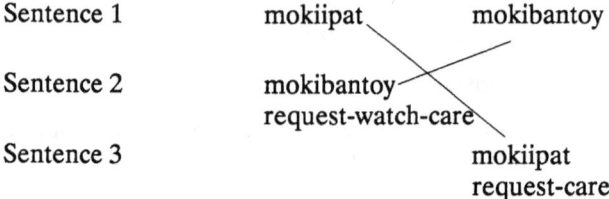

Structurally, the sentences all include a post sentence result clause, each of which is negative. The result-words differ between sentence 1 (line 7) and the two sentences following it (line 9 and line 11).

line 7 po' bagun da'	'so that nothing'
9 soupaya da'idun	'so that nothing'
11 soupaya di'	'so that will not'

Because of these syntactic correspondences and semantic relationships the sentences themselves may be considered as being in associative parallel relationship. Their summation is stated in the last sentence of the paragraph (line 17): "I desire that we are very much pitied."

Unit C

18 Dadi, akon ma   og minindog...
   so   I   (emp) (t) stand

19   Di' u mosipog dun...
   not I shame (ana)

      nog kona' u mikobatuk.
      (rel) not I equal

20   Akon ma og mingatas mogyakin.
     I (emp) (t) spite pray

21 Apu' Sanag, na' a mogbungas
  lord Sanag not you(s) fed-up

22   bu na' a motonop
    and not you(s) bored

The Patterns of Poetry

23 Bogbudoy   mu   ami   sog   glimpulu
   bind   you(s)   us(ex)   (loc) pate

                   nog   pikilan   nog   koba'is
                   (nt)   thought   (rel) good

24 Bu   potosop   nika   sog   gutok   nami
   and   soak-in   you(s)   (loc)   brain   our(ex)

25   mangoy   sog   pusung   nami
          go   (loc)   heart   our(ex)

26   og   kotanud   nog   mologdong
              (t)   belief   (rel)   straight

27   nog   da'idun   kosimoy   non
                    (rel)   none   swerve   it

28   da'idun   kolapang   non
                        none   mistake   it

29 sog   monogmonek   sog   gugdan
   (loc) go-down-go-up   (loc)   ladder

30 sog   gompanow   sog   ainain   nog   kosoksuk   nog   tolunan.
   (loc) travel   (loc)   wherever   (com)   enter   (nt)   forest

18 And so, I am the one standing . . .
19   I am not ashamed of it
           that I am lower than all others
20   I am making prayer in spite of everything.
21 Lord Sanag, don't you become fed up
22   and don't you become bored.
23 You bind us on the pate
     the thought that is good
24 And you soak into our brains
25   going into our hearts
26   the belief that is straight
27   that has no swerving
28   has no mistakes
29 in going down and up the ladder
30 in travelling to wherever is reached in the forest.

Unit C contains several parallels but only those found between lines 23–30 will be discussed here. A complex associative parallel is found in lines 23 and 24–30. The parallel constitutes one concatenated sentence with **bu** 'and' beginning line 24. This kind of construction was also found in prayer 1 (cf. figure 5.1.). The parallel complex involves seven parallels (cf. figure 5.4).

Parallel 1 (lines 23 and 24–30) is composed of a grammatically simple sentence (line 23) and a complex one (lines 24–30). On another level of patterning, there is a parallel, parallel 2, between lines 23 and 24 –25 where the action and location are paralleled:

23   you bind us on the pate . . .
24–25 you soak into our brains and to our hearts . . .

Then, parallel 3, consists of the object of line 23 being paralleled with line 26:

23 . . .the thought that is good
26   the belief that is straight

Parallel 4 (lines 26 and 27–30) is a grammatically simple relative clause modifier (in line 26) and a complex one (lines 27–30). Parallel 5 (lines 27 and 28) is a grammatically simple synonymous parallel. However, they are also parallel to the figure in line 26 and thereby form parallel 6.

26 . . .that is straight
27   that has no swerving
28   has no mistakes

Parallel 7 (lines 29 and 30) is a grammatically simple prepositional phrase (line 29) and a complex one (line 30).

4.2 Doublets

Doublets are combinations of words which share semantic components. Their combination results in an emphasis upon the shared component(s). Doublets often represent a metonymic comparison between the sign and the thing signified or a part for the whole. Three ways in which doublets are used have been observed in Subanon formal speech.

1. The denotation of the doublet combination is wholistic with emphasis upon the most general semantic features as a metonymic comparison. The order of the lexical elements is fixed.[17] Malkiel (1959) has referred to such doublets as being irreversible binomials. For example,

    A **buloma'** 'tomorrow'

    B **dinglag** 'day after tomorrow'

    general denotation: near future

    specific denotation: one day A, two days B in future from today.

buloma'dinglag 'indefinite future' (Prayer 2, line 7)

The Patterns of Poetry

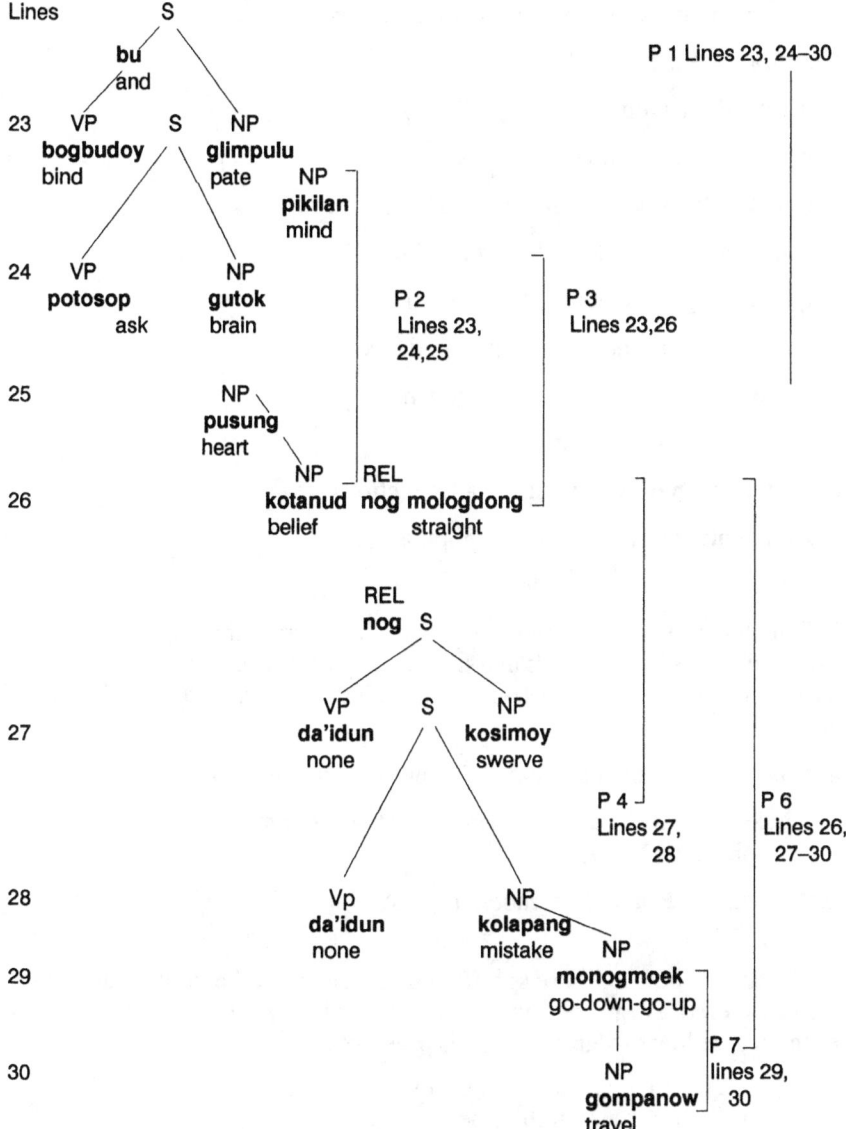

Figure 5.4 Complex parallels

butabongol 'ignorant of surroundings' (Prayer 2, line 16) from **buta** 'blind' and **bongol** 'deaf'.

monogmonek 'daily living around the house' (Prayer 2, line 29 from **monog** 'go down' and **monek** 'go up'.

Other examples from Western Subanon texts include:

glibunlaki (female male) 'all genders'

bata'mogulang (young and old) 'all ages'

gina'ama' (mother father) 'parents'

gusbawaris 'inlaws' (difference is no longer made)

gugatgungud (sinew flesh) 'the whole being'

glupa'baloy (ground house) 'all in attendance'

silungditas (below above) 'all in attendance'

liusolod (outside inside) 'all in attendance'

lintudibang (right left) 'on all sides'

silangansindopan (east west) 'in all directions'

molayu'molani (far near) 'whole population'

saladua' (one two) 'everyone'

2. Doublets may be taken more literally as expressing their specific denotation similarities. The effect is like stating the parts for the whole (not just one part for the whole) or the extremities for all that is included as well. For example,

gobi bu gondow (night and day) 'all day' (Prayer 2, line 8)

sog bukid sog dibaba' (upstream and downstream) 'all along the river' (epic, lines 21, 29)

glolabung bu sisolom (afternoon and morning) 'all daylight hours' (Prayer 2, line 8)

When parts of wholes are specified in this manner, the grammatical form may be altered. The propensity for a certain order is generally preserved. For example, the low to high sequence is preserved in

```
tidu  sog    glupa'  asta   sog    ditas
from  (loc)  ground  until  (loc)  above
```

'from the ground even to above'

Individual speakers have stylistic options in reversing the order. The following examples are from one who reversed the low to high and the young to old orders which are usually found in Subanon speech.

```
tidu  sog    baloy  koni  asta   sog    glupa'
from  (loc)  house  this  until  (loc)  ground
```

The Patterns of Poetry

'from this house even to the ground'

tidu	sog	mogulang	nog	gotow	mangoy	sog
from	(loc)	elder	(nt)	person	go	(loc)

batukbatuk	u	gumobok	sog	gombata'	(DO RR012F)
equal	I	run	(loc)	children	

'from the elders, going to the same as I, running on to the children'

3. Doublets may be combinations of synonyms of synonymous expressions that express emphasis. These doublets are, in fact, parallels.

motud sobonal (true truth) 'it is true'

dasig pagas (strength endurance) 'strength'

somul non da' kopus non (always not cease) 'forever'

These doublets are usually synonymous, including, as in the last example, antithetical synonymity, i.e., the first part (**somul non** 'always') is positive and the second part (**da' kopus non** 'without end') is negative.

4.3 Conclusion

There is a propensity for using dyadic or parallel structure in ritual speech and speech which is found in formally defined situations. This speech tradition is not unique to Subanon as a Philippine language nor as a representative of the Austronesian language family. Parallel structures are found around the world in poetic and ritual speech genres.

Parallel structures are not confined to syntax alone but permeate the semantics in displaying an artistic use of lexical items to produce what has been described as a stereoscopic effect. This is good Subanon poetry.

Binomials or doublets are used in several different stylistic and semantic ways, one of which is the exploiting of figurative language. This is summed up by Malkiel (1968:350).

> "A dynamic speech community cheerfully accepting binomials as a welcome embellishment or a nourishing ingredient of oral and written expression may give tremendous impetus to their spread. Just as certain cultures delight in jokes, especially puns, or spice small talk and day-to-day messages with proverbs, riddles, or songs, so others seem to revel in interlarding with binomials actual utterances or the storehouse of available labels."

Notes

1. This recording was done in 1968, in Barrio Reconella, Siocon, Zamboanga del Norte. The raconteur was Bituy Tomantong, male, about 60 years of age. The singing took twenty-two hours and was accomplished during two consecutive nights.

2. Interestingly, the rhythmic stanzas and the parallels that comprise them do not exactly coincide. The parallel usually overlaps into the next rhythmic stanza.

3. This enjoyment is exhibited in active auditor interaction and feedback (cf. Wrigglesworth 1979 for a description of the Ilianen Manobo singing).

4. These two words are but two of the number of possible terms that may be used in such instances (cf. examples in sec. 4.1.2.2).

5. The second suffix **-oy** is an added syllable which allows for the full syllable count to reach seven.

6. This parallel illustrates the disjunction between the tune and the semantic content. The **tanga'** interlude falls between lines 38 and 39 and between lines 40 and 41. Line 39 is composed of seven syllables but its parallel, line 41 is composed of only six because it is the first line of a three line stanza, which begins on a high note in this particular tune being sung.

The beginning of the section, lines 36 and 37, reiterate the discourse topic: the river **Migogling**. Grammatically it is the topic. Line 38 introduces the paragraph topic **sinu** 'whoever' which assumes, then, the topic role (reflected in the predicate affixes) in the following lines. The anaphora **dun** signals this change in topic attention (cf. also, chap. 3, note 8).

7. The tune consists of a register of four to five levels, depending upon the particular tune, with the beginning level somewhere around RE, then two or three levels ascending and the final level descending to a point below the beginning one.

8. The séance was recorded in 1967 in Tabayu', Reconella, Siocon, Zamboanga del Norte. The shaman is the late Tuantis Ma'is, male, and about 40 years old at the time of the recording.

9. Literally, "do not you yet truly (emphasis)" is considered untranslatable in the sense that there is no equivalent in English. However, it does have an interpretable analogue which appears here. The analogue may change slightly according to context. Generally in this work, as here, an attempt is made not only to render faithfully the Subanon meaning but also at the same time to preserve some semblance of the Subanon syntax. This may result at times in somewhat stilted English.

10. The second line of each verse usually ends in a prolonged nasal.

11. Literally, "a length of cloth measured in fathoms." Figurative speech will be interpreted in the English rendering.

12. At this point the elders who were gathered began to give their answer to the query raised by the spirit entity. The man addressed specifically (**Tumanggung**) was the one who gave the answer.

13. It has been expressed to me by Subanons that this is a result rather than a prerequisite of the shaman role.

14. The **moglokondawan** 'full moon ceremony' prayers were recorded in 1978 in Lintangan, Sibuco, Zamboanga del Norte. The prayers were made by the overseer of the ceremony. The prayer portion quoted here came in two parts. There were two prayers given during the ceremony. Between the prayers, ceremonial dancing took place (**mokpulin**).

15. The **mogoloba'a** 'act on Wednesday' is a religious occasion during which a prayer is given

The Patterns of Poetry

and ritual is performed. The recording was made in 1973 in Tabayu', Reconella, Siocon, Zamboanga del Norte.

16. This and the linear configuration of the verse were suggested to me by Dell Hymes. Following his suggestion for the linear configuration has helped to show the patterning very nicely.

17. The fixed structure of this kind of doublet was exemplified to me when I reversed the purely innocuous doublet **silung ditas** 'below above' to **ditas silung**. My Subanon companion, at once, corrected me and in the process plainly showed his near inability, in its apparent awkwardness, to repeat the doublet sequence as I had said it.

5 Poetic Patterns in Formal Speech

5.0 Introduction

In chapter 2, contexts for formal speech were presented in which speech occurred as the purpose of gatherings or the means through which at least part of the purpose of the gathering was achieved. Chapter 4 examined the major form of Subanon poetry, viz. parallelism. In the present chapter, the poetic forms of parallelism will be shown to occur in formal speech making.

The use of parallel structures in a speech within a formal context marks the speech as being formal. Parallelism functions as a rhetorical form in openings (as presented in chap. 3) and in presenting argument and persuasive speech. The Western Subanon places much importance upon how an argument is presented. The rhetoric of persuasive speech comes from and emulates tradition and precedent.[1] That is, the basis for truth and propriety may be seen as coming through past experience and traditional knowledge. The vehicle or means for dispensing and portraying this truth and propriety is through traditional poetic form and rhetorical forms that pattern very similarly to poetry.

Formal speech making is a form of verbal art just like any Subanon poetic form, including riddles, dueling, epic singing, or prayers. The parallel structures in speech making are elaborate.[2] It is this elaborateness which will be illustrated in the sections of this chapter.

5.1 Parallel structure in speech

Parallel structure has more than an esthetic function. Often parallelism consists of reiteration and/or repetition of a point of an argument. It promotes understanding. Obscure statements, or perhaps words not clearly heard, are understood when included in a parallel structure.[3]

The effect that parallel structure has on Subanon argument and persuasive speech is that of unhurriedness and careful reasoning. This effect exemplifies the actual decision making processes of the elders, that of unhurriedness and much deliberation.

The use of parallelism gives direct insight into the speaker's conception of grammatical equivalences (Jakobson 1968). As for grammatical categories utilized for parallels they include most of the parts of speech of the Subanon language.[4]

A reiterated or repeated grammatical concept often is used in the making of a point in an argument, giving an answer, and in explanation or teaching resulting in a rhetorical effect of highlighting. Parallels are frequently found in expressing conclusions.[5]

5.2 Parallelism and linguistic analysis

Hymes (1981:chap. 4) mentions in his discussion how the repetition of forms has aided in determining the segmentation of Chinookan narrative texts, as well as supplying internal cohesion.[6] Longacre (1968) discusses, within a tagmemic framework, the major kinds of discourse cohesive linkage which occur in Philippine languages. Depending upon the genre and the speaker, the linkage may be predominately grammatical or it may be predominately of lexical content. In Subanon, narrative discourse that is time oriented may utilize time aspectual words or an affix which translates into English as a gerund or a participle. There is often a reiteration or anadiplosis of lexical material with some of the time words and the gerund. Discourse genres that are not strictly narrative in nature may utilize, to a greater extent, the affixal system and deictic anaphora as grammatical means in tying the discourse together. Lexically, parallelism may occur by repeating central topics and of using pro-words and anaphora.

Parallels of grammatical clauses in Western Subanon have been described as a parallel sentence type (Longacre 1968, Hall 1973). Two subtypes of the Parallel sentence are posited in that analysis as the paraphrase and the amplification subtypes. The syntactic form of the sentences is composed of and includes parallel structures. The deep structure of the grammatical form distinguishes the subtypes. The amplification subtype expands the basic statement while the paraphrase subtype restates the basic statement. The problem with the positing of a sentence type such as this is that, as seen in chapter 4, a parallel can not be restricted to structural distinctions. The parallel may be based on semantic distinctions as well.

Another consideration in the analysis of parallels is that their use includes, in large part, the expressive function of language. Longacre's (1976:131–141) discussion of what he has posited as Paraphrase sentence types and the Subanon Parallel sentence are similar. Longacre's general analysis of sentence types is based upon deep structure criteria. He states, however, that in considering what he has posited as Paraphrase sentences, we leave basic deep structures of discourse " ... and begin the consideration of elaborative and rhetorical devices." He does not treat the elaborative aspects of this sentence type as is being done here.

In terms of a linguistic hierarchy, for Western Subanon there is, as Longacre states is the case for some other languages (ibid., 281), a sentencelike structure that blurs tight fitting distinctions of a well constructed paragraph as is analyzed for many Indo-European languages. One candidate for this sentencelike structure in Western Subanon is the sentence with numerous embedded parallels like those already described in chapter 4 and those which will be described in the following sections.

5.3 Parallels from formal speech

Many of the examples of parallels in the sentences of this section come from the texts in the Appendices. Some may be seen as being much more elaborate than others. There are, undoubtedly, factors associated with the use of speech, for example, social situations and linguistic competence, that result in differences in the use of these verbal art forms.

5.3.1 Linear patterns. Examples 1 and 2 are from the **piglimudan** 'caused to gather together' situation from the speech made by the middle-aged man mentioned in section 2.4.5. They both illustrate an elaborate sentence construction built on parallels. Like wheels within wheels, parallels occur between clauses within two parallel clauses.

Example 1.

1a Dadi da'idun na gustalan ku nog botad;
   so none now explain (1snt) (ntdet) custom

b   da'idun na gustalan ku nog gininisan
     none now explain (1snt) (ntdet) variety

               nog pangkat
               (ntdet) inheritance

2 po' mo'ana non inustal na. (CA103D4)
  because meaning (3snt) explained now

1a And so, I have no explaining of customs;
b   I have no explaining of the inherited ways
2 because, the meaning is (they are) explained already
        (by those who have already spoken).

Poetic Patterns in Formal Speech   89

The sentence structure is basically dualistic as seen in the **Dadi** 'And so' and **po'** 'because'. Semantically they function like an opening and closing: the "And so" being the opening and the "because" being the closing, or conclusion. Line 1b is an analogue of line 1a; it constitutes more than merely a restatement of 1a. It adds the fact that these are not just customs but their own inherited customs. There is repetition and cohesion in the use of the stem **ustal** in the nominals **gustalan** 'explain' in clause 1 and the verbal **inustal** 'explained' in clause 2.

Figures 6.1 and 6.2 show the clause constituents of the sentence of example 1.

In figure 6.2, the embedded structure of clause 1a is shown. Clause 1b may

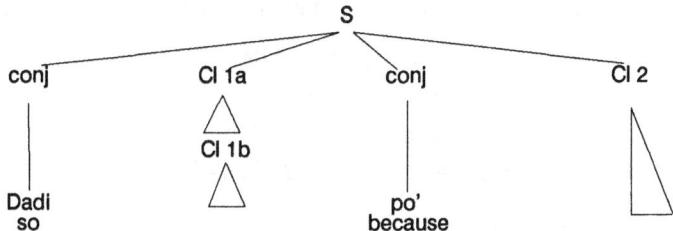

Figure 6.1 Parallel embedding

be similarly diagrammed.

In example 2 there is a contrast between lines a and b, where the com-

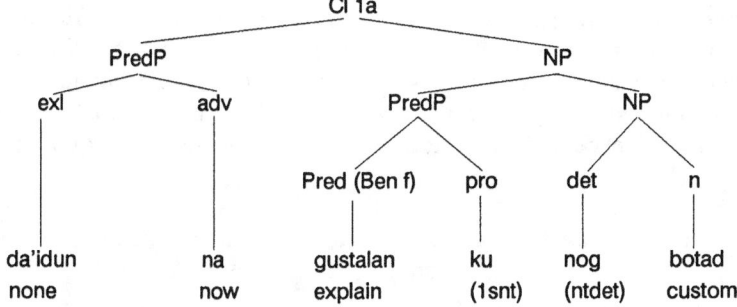

'I have no explaining of customs'.

Figure 6.2 Clause 1a structure

parison between **kilobotan** 'reminded' and **kitulikan** 'remember' is one of synonymity and lines c and d, where **mogipat** 'take care of' and **mogongkom** 'hold in hand' are analogous. This example illustrates that more than one variety of parallel may occur in a sentence.

Example 2.

a Ain   sog   kilobotan   ku,
  where (loc) reminded   (1snt)

b Ain   sog   kitulikan   ku,   Tobudan binogayan
  where (loc) remember   (1snt) Tobudan given

                         do   sop
                         (sta) also

c   nog   Mikpongon nog   mogipat   dun
      (ntdet) creator   (ntdet) take-care (ana)

d   mogongkom dun
                        hold-in-hand (ana)

e   sog   tubig nog   bawang   nog   Tobudan
      (loc) river (pos) habitation (rel) Tobudan   (CA013D4)

a Whatever I have reminded of,
b Whatever I have thought about, Tobudan has been
                                 also given
c   by the Creator, one to watch over it
d   one to care for it
e   the river of the place which is Tobudan.

In example 3 speaker A in the first speech act (which constitutes the introduction) of the **mogogoka'oy** 'explanation' event of the **polontu** 'death ceremony' makes his point (cf. Appendix C1). His point is made by way of a direct quote of one of the other participants. It is understood, however, that they are not necessarily the exact words of the speaker being quoted.

Example 3.

1a Dadi ma'   long non   dun,   "Ita   koni   momogilug
   so   like said (3snt) (ana)   (1ptin) this   brother

                              ma,
                              (emp)

b   mogusba[7] ma,
                              relative   (emp)

c   mogwaris   ma,
                              relative   (emp)

Poetic Patterns in Formal Speech

```
2a ion   poginuinuon   ta        kona'  sa'ot mona'ot;
   (3st) decide        (1pntin)  not    overtaking

b  ion   pogupokatan   ta        kona'  sikut monikut."
   (3st) decide        (1pntin)  not    narrow
```

1a And so, thus he said, "we here being brothers,
b   being relatives,
c   being relatives,
2a that which we are deciding is not just finding faults;
b that for which we have met is not to take revenge."

Both poetically and syntactically, the clauses parallel each other.[8] Syntactically, there is a pattern of duality between the preposed subject and the comment. For example,

Preposed subject	Comment
1a We here	are brothers,
b	are relatives,
c	are relatives,
2a that which we are deciding	is not finding fault
b that which we are deciding	is not taking revenge.

Lines 1a, 1b, and 1c are parallel in an analogous relationship as are also lines 2a and 2b. **gusba** and **gwaris** historically differentiated the matrilineal and patrilineal kin. This distinction is no longer made. The paralleled doublet structure of **sa'ot mona'ot** and **sikut monikut** in lines 2a and 2b (see example 3) both have the same meaning, that of finding fault for litigation purposes.

Example 4 is taken from a conversation that occurred between a shaman and a headman.[9] Poetic structure is illustrated in the parallels between clauses 1 and 2.

Example 4.

```
1a Ngon  gondow  gonsunoy  tumalu'  gina'    ta,
   (exl) day     happen    say      mother   (1pntin)

b                                   gama'    ta,
                                    father   (1pntin)

c                                   otawaka  bogolal  ta
                                    or       council  (1pntin)
```

2a long, "Dini ita poglumpuk,"
    say here (1ptin) gather

b long, "Dini ita kotimbul."
   say here (1ptin) bunch-together

1a There is a day coming when our mother,
b   our father,
c   or our council
2a says, "Here we will meet together,"
b says, "Here we will bunch up together."

Parallel structures include the associative parallel of lines 1a, 1b, and 1c and the synonymous parallel lines 2a and 2b. there is cohesion in the paralleled use of words of speaking, **tumalu'** 'say' in line 1a and **long** 'say' in lines 2a and 2b.

As seen above, sentences may be composed of a variety of parallels. These parallels may exist between numerous parts of the grammar as Example 5 below illustrates.[10] The parallels are centered under each other are lettered.

Example 5

1a Mongoni u nog ma'ak
plead 1st nt forgiveness

b   bu   gampun
        and pardon

c   songibu gampun
           1000   pardon

d   dianiu
          to-you

e   (sog) glam ta   koni
         loc   all   1ntin this

f   bata'
           child

g   mogulang
           elder

h   libun
           female

i   laki
           male

2a sabap
   reason

b bu   mo'ana
  and meaning

c   mokosun
     knowing

d   mogdoragyat
     proposing

3a Ita   koni, da' sunan   ta
  (1ptin) this not knowledge (1pntin)

b   dopot
         reach

c   kotalus ta
         wisdom (1pntin)

4a kabal   buta bongol ita   tokodoy sog dunya
  on-account-of blind deaf (1ptin) int   (loc) world

b sog   glupa'an
  (loc) earth

1a I am asking for forgiveness
b   and pardon,
c   one thousand pardons
d   to you,
e   to all of us here:
f   young,
g   old,
h   female,
i   male
2a the reason
b and the meaning is,
c   as far as to know,
d   to propose,
3a we here, we have no knowledge,
b   ability,
c   we have no wisdom
4a on account of we are ignorant of our surroundings
                           in the world,
b   on the earth.

The whole sentence is displayed first as three basic components in figure 6.3: the base sentence, a reason margin, and a cause margin. The relationship between the components is one of chaining, i.e., the cause margin refers to the content of the reason margin which refers to the content of the base sentence.

Base sentence	Reason margin	Cause margin
	sabap bu mo'ana ...	**kabal** ...
lines 1a-i	lines 2a-d, 3a-c	lines 4a, b

Figure 6.3 Sentence component display

The relationships that obtain between the members of the parallels are illustrated in figures 6.4, 6.5, and 6.6.[11]

The parallels in lines 2c and 2d in example 5 posed an identification problem. The speaker has used a non-Subanon word (**mogdoragyat** 'proposal') which is not well understood generally.[12] This illustrates the point made earlier that one result of parallels is understanding. The word need not be well understood because its mate (**mokosun** 'knowledge') is well understood and the sense of what is being said comes through clearly.

The poetic structure of example 5 may be seen by the lineation. There is a pattern of four "measures." Parallels between clauses 1 and 3 and between 2 and 4 are made apparent: the use of a 1st person singular pronoun in line 1a and a 1st person plural inclusive pronoun in line 3a, the use of a "reason" marker in line 2a and of a 'cause' marker in line 4a.

Syntactically, the elements paralleled in the sentence are predominantly the exponents of the NP. Another example, example 6, supports this.[13]

Example 6.

1a Dadi   sug   ita   sop   pomogilug
   so   (tmkr)   (1ptin) also brothers

b   pogbata'
                           youngster

c   pongmogulang,
                           elder

2 intoman   ku   dini,
  suppose (1snt)   here

3a   omba'is ta   olapon   nog   pondoga
      good   (1pntin) get   (nt)   example

b   molongas ta   imungon nog   glimbagan
      good   (1pntin) make   (nt)   image

Poetic Patterns in Formal Speech 95

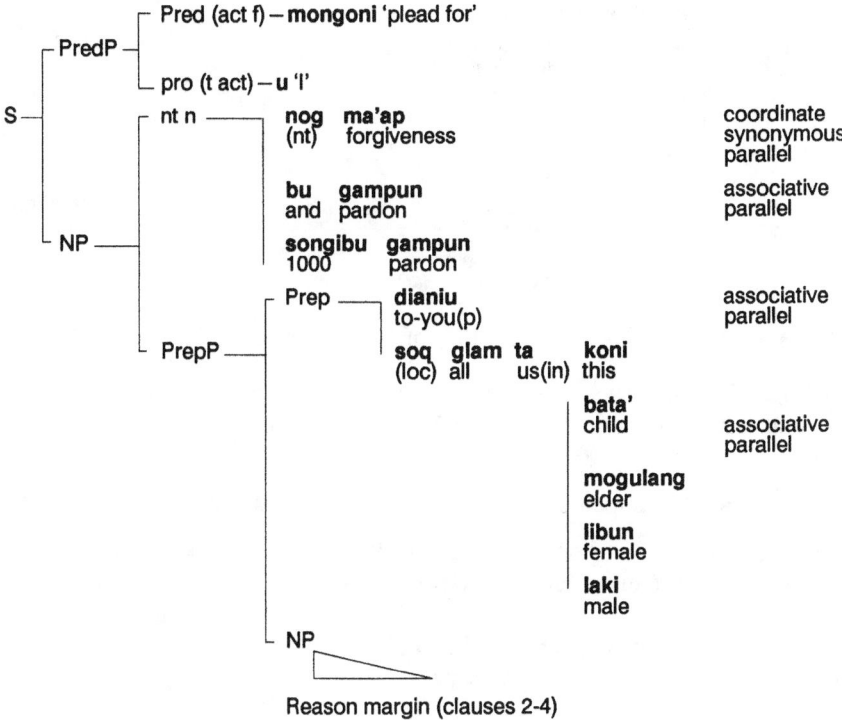

Figure 6.4 Display of Base sentence.

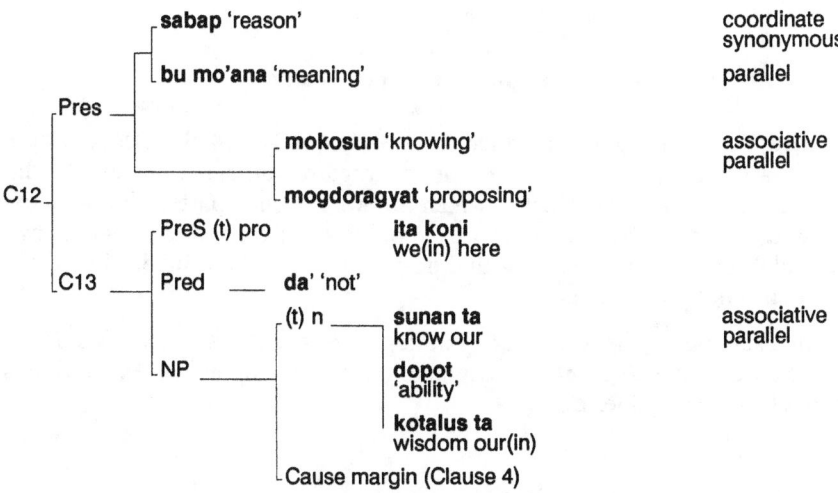

Figure 6.5 Display of Reason margin.

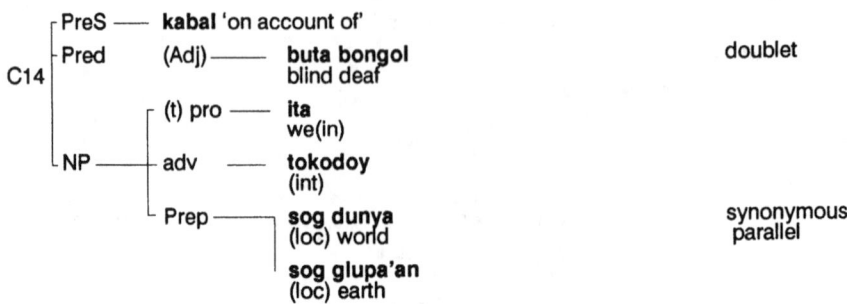

Figure 6.6 Display of Cause margin.

```
4a bog  olo   og  bayu'       nog   tanud   tumanud
   and  what  (t) appearance  (pos) belief  believe

 b      olo   og  bayu'       nog   tulik     nog   tumulik
        what  (t) appearance  (pos) religion  (rel) worship

5 sog   diwata nog  kogonat   sog   Mikpongon.   (CA012D)
  (loc) god    (rel) originate (loc) creator
```

1a And so, as for we who are also brothers
 b   youngsters
 c   elders,
2 I suppose here,
3a   it is to our benefit to take an example
 b   it is to our enhancement to make an image of
4a what is the appearance of a belief to believe in
 b what is the appearance of a religion with which to
                       be religious
5 towards the gods which originate with the Creator.

The parallels include embedded clauses, clauses 3 and 4. See also, example 1 for a similar occurrence. The poetic structure can again be seen in the three-lined parallel of clause 1, which follows the same pattern found in examples 3 and 4. The structure of example 6 shows a parallel in part 1, two parallels each in parts 3 and 4, and no parallel in parts 2 and 5. This whole sentence has poetic cadence.

In example 7, the staggered parallel pattern used as a conclusion by speaker C, in the **mogogoka'oy** 'explanation' event (Appendix C3), alternates lines b and e and lines c and f.

Example 7.

```
a Sinuksug  u     sog   glam  niu,
  related   (1snt) (loc) all   (2pnt)
```

b gondow   koni,
  day   this

c   milumpuk   ma   og   glam   nog   mokogulang   nami
    gathered   (emp) (t) all   (nt) elder   (2pntex)

d   pigilugan nami
                            brother   (2pntex)

e gondow   koni,
  day   this

f   milumpuk   ma
    gathered   (emp)

a I related it to all of you,
b today,
c   gathered together are all of our elders
d   our kin,
e today,
f   gathered together.

Highlighting may be achieved through variation in parallel form. In example 8,[14] the actual configuration of the parallel is like a doublet (chap. 4) where the parallel shares the same sentence element.

Example 8.

    Amu   tanan gapu' non   bogolal
    (2pt)   really owner (3snt) council

    You are, in fact its owner, the council.

Here, the two members of the parallel (lines a and c in example 8) share the same proposition in an equative sentence type, i.e., all elements equal each other.[15]

a Amu tanan
b   gapu' non
c bogolal.
You are its owner   a and b
Bogolal is its owner   c and b
(You are **Bogolal**)   a and c

This structural analysis may also be used in the following parallel sentence from the **piglimudan** 'caused to gather together' situation.

Example 9.

a Dadi sug mumun kitu'
   so (t) time that

b   mongoni ma   nog gustalan
       plead   (emp) (nt) explanation

c   gilug   ta   sog   sobuang bonua
           brother (1pntin) (loc) another land

d   dinumonggu' dinita
           made-port   to-us(in)

e monginongog ma   nog sosuku gupakat.   (CA012D)
  ask-to-hear   (emp) (nt) variety decision

a And so, as for right now,
b   pleads for an explanation
c   our brother from another land
d   has arrived here among us,
e asks to hear a variety of decisions.

The syntactic structure is: Adverb phrase (line a), PredP (line b), actor preposed NP of embedded sentence (line c), PredP of embedded sentence (line d), and paralleled PredP of main sentence (line e). The actor (topic) of the deep structure sentence (lines c and d) is also the actor for the two predicates which are paralleled (lines b and e). All verbal affixes are actor focus, i.e., they indicate that the actor of the action is the topic of discussion.

Other parallels may also be pointed out. Line a sets the time; in line b the verb shows incomplete aspect; line c introduces the topic; in line d the verb shows completed aspect; in line e the verb repeats the incomplete aspect. There is symmetry between lines a and c, and between lines b, d, and e. There is also a pattern of bracketing, where lines b and e bracket lines c and d, resulting in a four-part organization.

Parallels occur between clauses of two sentences, as in example 10. In the confrontation event of the **bisala** situation, the father makes the following point (cf. Appendix D). It is the central point of his whole defense against the accusation of the girl's mother.

Example 10.

a "po' bila bolu'an goiton mu   di' omba'is."
   (par) if   anger   carry (2snt) not good

b   Da' u   en   pogonggat moksuntuk dun.
     not (1snt) (3st) invite   fist-fight   (ana)

Poetic Patterns in Formal Speech 99

```
c    Lipas  tinalu'  u,
     but    said     (1snt)
```

```
d "Bila  bolu'an  goiton  mu       dini,  di'  ompia."
   if    anger    carry   (2snt)   here   not  good
```

a "If you carry anger it isn't good."
b I did not by this invite him to fist-fight.
c Rather, I said,
d "If you carry anger here, it isn't good."

Lines a and d are parallel in form and paraphrastic in meaning. In line d, the speaker adds the locative **dini** 'here' and the synonym **ompia** 'good' is substituted for **omba'is** 'good' in line a.[16] The pattern is a four-part pattern of lineation, like example 9. There is a chiastic relationship in the patterning of the lines.

5.3.2 Chiasmus. Parallel forms are often found in a chiastic relationship. Variability occurs in chiastic parallels depending upon the speaker and his personal speech styles in verbal art. The following examples illustrate chiastic parallels in Western Subanon. Again, all of the examples occur as a major point made within the speech content. It is obvious that chiasmus depends upon, at least, a four-part organization.

Example 11.

```
a Ondi'  ita      tokodoy  mogawid  nog   glimbung
  not    (1ptin)  (int)    hold     (nt)  deceit
```

```
b di'    ita      tokodoy  mogawid  nog   pogalap
  not    (1ptin)  (int)    hold     (nt)  obtain-by-craft
```

```
c po'      diwata  di'  mogalap
  because  god     not  obtain-by-craft
```

```
d diwata  di'  moglimbung. (RR003-2)
  god    not   deceive
```

a Let us not ever practice deceit;
b let us not ever practice avarice
c because god is not avaricious;
d god is not deceitful.

The parallel exists between lines a and b and between lines c and d. The first and last lines contain the stem **limbung** 'deceit' and the second and third lines contain the stem **alap** 'to get'. All of these together produce the typical chiastic configuration:

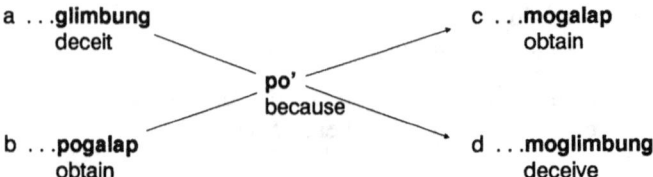

This parallel structure conforms basically to those discussed in chapter 4 where the syntax exhibits two clauses, the one functioning as a sentence margin. In some chiastic structures, the parallels are not synonymous but rather, are in the relationship where one is an analogue of the other. They may contain similar activities or items that may be semantically associated as are **limbung** 'deceit' and **pogalap** 'obtain by craft'.

Other structures are built around the same semantic referent. The following example, from the **mogogoka'oy** 'explanation' event, is the concluding argument of one of the participants.

Example 12.

a Olo nitu' o' ...inangon ta   mokpuli'
  what that (par) do   (1pntin) again

b otawa kitu' da   itu' imungon ta   nog dalan?
  or   that (sta) that make   (1pntin) (nt) trail

c Po'   bila di' ta   imungon nog dalan,
  because   if   not (1pntin) make   (nt) trail

d tobia', sopulu' tobia', di' ta   poginangon puli'.
  excuse ten   excuse not (1pntin) do   again

a What is that, huh? shall we do it again,
b or shall we make that one a precedent?
c Because, if we don't make it a precedent,
d excuse me, ten times excuse me, let's not do it again.

The 'or'[17] in line b highlights the parallel of lines a and b. Lines a and d and lines b and c produce the chiastic parallel that aids the argument with rhetorical force.

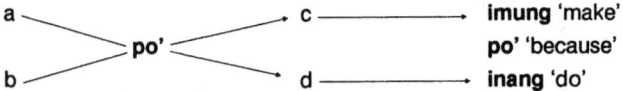

Example 13[18] illustrates the fact that both struc- ture and the underlying semantics may be paralleled in chiasmus. Here also, as was illustrated in chapter 4, there is an embedding of parallels. In example 13, what is paral-

Poetic Patterns in Formal Speech   101

leled is the positive versus negative aspect of **kopagun** 'strength' with **kotubu'** 'live' and **koguya'** 'weakness' with **patoy** 'death'.

Example 13.

a Dadi sumboy dion ita   kopagun sog botad,
  so   must   there (1ptin) strength (loc) custom

b   dion ita   koguya' sog botad;
              there (1ptin) weakness (loc) custom

c mo'ana non dion ita   sop patoy sog botad,
  meaning (3snt) there (1ptin) also death (loc) custom

d   dion ita   kotubu' sog botad.   (RR012B2)
              there (1ptin) life   (loc) custom

a And so, it must be that there is our strength in custom,
b   there is our weakness in custom;
c that means, there we also die in custom,
d   there we live in custom.

Chiasmus is one way of organizing parallel sentences. Very often they extend to include a number of parallel sentences. The following example illustrates a speaker's strategy in using two parallel sentences in a chiastic pattern based upon the nouns **mata** 'eye' and **tolinga** 'ear' in sentence 1 opposing the verbs **mokinongog** 'to hear' and **mogbantoy** 'to watch' in sentence 2.

Example 14.

1a Koyon loko,
   that I-say

b binogayan ita   nog mata ponontongon ta   nog omba'is;
  given   (1ptin) (nt) eye search-for (1pntin) (nt) good

c binogayan ita   nog tolinga ponginongog ta   nog omba'is.
  given   (1ptin) (nt) ear   listen-for (1pntin) (nt) good

2a Di' ita   mokinongog nog molaton
   not (1ptin) listen-to (nt) bad

b di' ita   mogbantoy nog molaton
    not (1ptin) watch   (nt) bad

  c po'   mo'ana non,   muli' sog gulu ta.   (RR003–2)
    because meaning (3snt) return (loc) head (1pntin)

1a As for that, I say,
  b we have been given eyes, let's look for goodness;
  c we have been given ears, let's listen for goodness.
2a Let's not listen to badness;
  b let's not watch badness
  c because, the reason is, that it will affect us unfavorably.

There is also a parallel between the opposites **omba'is** 'good' in sentence 1 and **molaton** 'bad' in sentence 2. Besides the chiasmus, then, there are also the parallels that link the two sentences into a somewhat expanded or embedding construction. The whole of sentences 1 and 2 form a parallel of positive and negative, while each sentence by itself also contains a parallel, the whole being tied together through chiasmus.

	Parallel	
Sentence 1	lines b and c	omba'is 'good'
Sentence 2	lines a and b	molaton 'bad'

The poetic pattern consists of part 1 having one line, parts 2 and 3 having two lines each and part 4 having one line. Line 1a functions as an introduction. Lines 1b and 1c are chiastically parallel to lines 2a and 2b as already illustrated. Line 2c functions as a conclusion to the whole. There is a bracketing of the inner structure of lines 1b to 2b by lines 1a and 2c.

Example 15 is a variation of the preceding example where the chiasmus is broken by an intervening sentence. Examples 14 and 15 are from the same speech. Here the parallels are again **mata** 'eye' and **tolinga** 'ear' and their respective functions. Sentence 3, example 15 also forms a conclusion to that which precedes it.

Example 15.

1a Dadi sop mata niu
     so   also eye (2pnt)

Poetic Patterns in Formal Speech

b   bila da' da   pokotongow mata niu,
      if   not (sta) can-see   eye (2pnt)

c   sagya da   midongog nog tolinga niu,
      just (sta) heard   (nt) ear   (2pnt)

d na' amu tokodoy monukpat dun.
  not (2pt) (int)   add-to   (ana)

2a Ingolanan ta   itu',
    called   (1pntin) that

b   somo' dianita sog   Sinubanon,
      (uc)   to-us(in) (loc) Subanon-language

c ingolanan ta   gyuba'.
  called   (1ptin) temptation

3a Dadi, bila midongog nog tolinga,
    so   if   heard   (nt) ear

b   da' kotongow nog mata,
      not seen   (nt) eye

c na' amu tumud nion. (RR003–2)
  not (2pt) believe that

1a And so also, as for your eyes,
b   if it has not been seen by your eyes,
c   only heard by your ears,
d don't you add to it!
2a We call that,
b   as for us speaking Subanon,
c we call it temptation.
3a And so, if it has been heard with the ear,
     b not seen with the eye,
c don't you believe it.

As in example 14, here also in example 15 there is a parallel between the sentences as well as the chiasmus that exists between them.

lines   1b   3a **tolinga** 'ear'

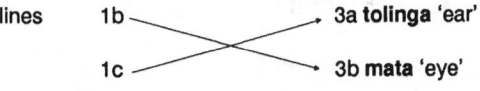

         1c   3b **mata** 'eye'

        1d **na' monukpat dun** 'don't add to it'

        3c **na' tumud nion** 'don't believe it'

The organization of the example is apparent, as it follows the same general pattern of example 14. It works from the two ends towards the middle. Line 1a functions as an introduction with the introducer **Dadi** 'so' and the preposed topic **mata niu** 'your (pl) eyes'. The introducer here and in line 3a parallel each other. Following that, the following lines are opposite each other: 1b and 3a, 1c and 3b, 1d and 3c, 2a and 2c. Line 2b functions as a parenthesis.

Another example where a chiasmus occurs as part of a larger parallel relationship is found in the **mogogoka'oy** 'explanation' event (Appendix C3, numbers 68–73). In example 16, the Subanon is arranged to make the chiasmus obvious. The English shows the actual form of the speech. The chiastic parallel comes in a formal argument to explain a certain action that was taken.

Example 16.

a Tibua koni og kilogon ta   nini da'idun langkap:
  but   this (t) hardship (1pntin) this none   provisions

        b da'idun bulinga   e og komanyan,
          none   egg   (t) incense

        c da'idun komanyan   g og bulinga
          none   incense   (t) egg

                d ain   ta   olapoy?
                  where (1pntin) obtain

                f ain   ta   gonti'oy?
                  where (1pntin) exchange

                h ain   ta   gonti'oy?
                  where (1pntin) exchange

a However, as for this, our hardship here is that
                            we do not have any provisions:
3 b   there are no eggs,
  c   there is no incense,
  d   where will we get it?
  e   the incense,
  f   with what shall we exchange it?
  g   the eggs,
  h   with what shall we exchange it?

Line a is the base statement. Lines b through h are an exposition of the base statement. Lines b and c are parallel as are lines e and g, all of which are

Poetic Patterns in Formal Speech   105

also in a chiastic relationship. The pattern seen in the English is that of the staggered line parallel mentioned in chapter 4.

There are a number of chiastic parallels which are based on a change of the grammatical status of elements from one sentence to another. Example 17 illustrates the change from being grammatically marked as topic in one sentence to being grammatically marked as nontopic in the next, while those elements marked as nontopic in the first sentence become marked as topic in the second.

Example 17.

1a Glam   nog   miongon sog   dunya   bulung   tokodoy:
   all   (pos)   created (loc)   earth   medicine (int)

b bulung   nog   glawas
  medicine (nt)   body

c bulung   nog   mosakit
  medicine (nt)   pain

2a Sosuku   nog   mosakit
   variety (pos) pain

b malap   ta   bosia   nog   bulung. (RR003-2)
  get   (1pntin)   (fru)   (nt)   medicine

1a Everything created on the earth is medicine!
 b medicine for the body,
 c medicine for pain/sickness.
2a Every kind of pain
 b should be able to be relieved by medicine.

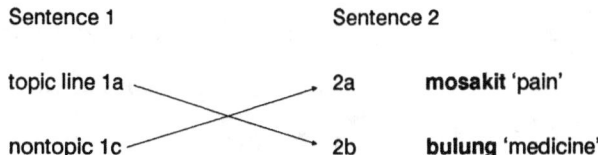

Sentences 1 and 2 are parallel. Sentence 1 begins with **bulung** 'medicine' as topic (line 1a) and it ends with the word **mosakit** 'pain' marked as nontopic. Sentence 2 begins with **mosakit** 'pain' being quantified by **sosuku** 'every kind' and functioning as the topic of the sentence. **Bulung** 'medicine' comes at the end of sentence 2 with the nontopic determiner **nog**. The parallel of lines 1b and 1c amplify the kinds of medicine. This parallel, both structurally and semantically, accomplishes what the quantifier **sosuku** accomplishes in line 2a. Also, the two quantifiers, **glam** 'all' and **sosuku'** 'every kind' each begin a sentence.

Elaboration in other types of grammatical shifts may also be illustrated. For example, in example 18[19] within a single sentence there is a change from marked topic going to a nontopic position within a prepositional phrase. The topic is the name of a small river called Tobudan. The predicate (**bogoy** 'give') is affixed for beneficiary focus, i.e., the topic is the beneficiary of the action.

Example 18.

a Tobudan binogayan do sop nog Mikpongon
   Tobudan given   (sta) also (nt) creator

b   nog mogipat dun
    (nt) take-care (ana)

c   mogongkom dun
       hold-in-palm (ana)

d sog tubig nog bawang nog Tobudan.   (CA013D)
  (loc) river (att) habitation (rel) Tobudan

a Tobudan has also been given by the Creator
b   one to watch over it
c   care for it
d that is, the river of the place that is Tobudan.

The parallel that exists between lines b and c is one of synonymy. The one statement is a paraphrase of the other. The name **Tobudan** occurs as the first word of line a and as the last word in line d.

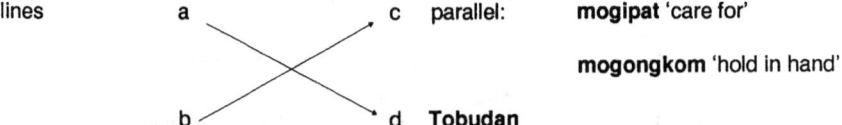

The switch of **Tobudan** from topic position to that of a locative phrase is not as abrupt as it would seem. The anaphoric **dun** in the parallel of lines b and c relegates to the nontopic position the previous topic, in this case **Tobudan**.[20] So **Tobudan**, in this sentence, is found explicitly as the topic, anaphorically referred to as nontopic and then again explicitly found in the location phrase.

The four-part organization is again evident where lines b and c are bracketed by lines a and d. They are also in a chiastic relationship (cf. example 10).

Poetic Patterns in Formal Speech 107

5.3.3 Verbatim repetition. Verbatim repetition of grammatical form as a verbal strategy infrequently occurs in formal speaking. It occurs after some sort of interruption. There is always the possibility of repetitions within the normal course and mechanism of speech production, e.g., hesitations and misunderstandings. Speaker C, in his first speech in the **mogogoka'oy** 'explanation' event makes the statement (see Appendix C3, number 45):

```
Dadi ...midopot na    pidangan og glungun...
so      reached  now  come-up   (t) coffin
```

And so, when it reached the time that the coffin
was brought into the house...

after which he is interrupted by speaker D agreeing with and reinforcing the argument. Speaker C then repeats verbatim what he had just said.

Besides interruption of this sort, another factor that bears on the use of verbatim repetition is the genre context. Reported speech occurs in discussions, teaching, explaining, and in other situations as a point of departure. However, the extended use of reported speech is common only in the genre of folktale telling and relating of incidents. In the **mogogoka'oy** 'explanation' event, speaker C relates the incidents surrounding the death of his neighbor. It is only in the reported speech, in this case direct discourse, where verbatim repetition occurs. The translation of the lines of Appendix C3 are reproduced in example 19.

Example 19.

49 Now, they said,"There are none, there are none."

53 "... let's take half of it;

54 this one also, let's take half of it..."

67 Now D said, "The custom is difficult to follow;
                                difficult to follow."

The variation in organizational strategy may be seen in the shifting and distribution of grammatical arrangements. Example 20 is taken from a speech that exhibited much poetic form (see also, examples 11, 14, 15, and 17 all of which are from the same speech).

Example 20.

```
1a Dadi  suksugon  ku
   so    relate    (1snt)
```

108   Aspects of Western Subanon Formal Speech

b   kpigbolianan   ku
        shamanistic-practice (1snt)

c   kpoktulikan   ku
        religious-belief (1snt)

d   og botad   nog diwata.
        (t) custom (nt) god

2 2a Dadi og botad   nog diwata
     so   (t) custom   (nt) god

b suksugon   ku
   relate   (1snt)

c   diniu
             to-you(p)

d   sog   glam nog   gombata u.
             (loc) all   (att) children (1snt)   (RR003–2)

1a And so, I'll relate
b   my shamanistic practice,
c   my religious belief,
d   the custom relating to god.
2a And so the custom relating to god
b I'll relate
c   to you,
d   to all of my children.

A graphic display of the sentences of example 20 in figure 7.1 shows how the speaker has arranged the syntax of the two sentences into a composite semantic unit. The predicate suffix **-on** highlights the goal of the action of the predicates.

Sentence	Predicate	Topic	Predicate	Ben/loc
1a	-on			
b		k-[21]		
c		k-		
d		og		
2a		og		
b			-on	
c				di(a)-
d				sog

Figure 7.1 Repetitive parallel sentences

Poetic Patterns in Formal Speech   109

Taken as a unit, there is a parallel of four elements (lines 1b–2a) marked as the topic. Lines 1d and 2a form an anadiplosis "of the custom of god." The markers **sog** and **di(a)-** indicate beneficiary or, in this case, the audience.

As two sentences, there is a chiastic structure between lines 1a and 2b and between lines 1d and 2a. There is no phonological reason to posit a major higher level grammatical break between sentence 1 and sentence 2. There would likely be some pause or characteristic intonation (which there are none) if this sentence marked the ending of one paragraph and the beginning of the next.[22]

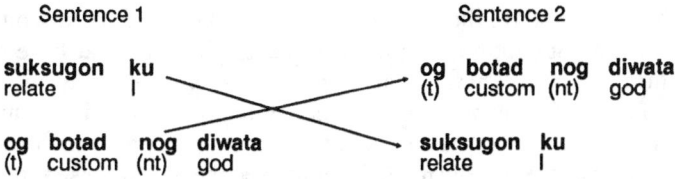

5.3.4 Word forms. Parallelism in repetition is found in the use of certain word bases. The word base is repeated in sequence first as a noun, i.e., in an unaffixed form, and then as a predicate or as an affixed form.

The forms appear to be taken as a formulaic repetition and are generally glossed as a semantic unit. The following examples are from the **mogogo-ka'oy** 'explanation' event:

sa'ot mona'ot (overtake) 'to find fault' from turn 1

sikut monikut (narrow) 'to take revenge' from turn 1

sulut monulut (agreement) 'to come to agreement' from turn 8

From the **piglimudan** 'cause to gather together':

tanud tumanud[23] (awaken) 'to believe in God'

tulik tumulik (think clearly) 'to believe in God'

From an old shaman:

sala' monala' (fault) 'to commit faults'

From a formal explanation:

sumpat monumpat 'to defeat in a contest'

These doublet forms have been found only in the speech of formal discussion and usually only in the speech of recognized speakers. They have not been found in the ritual speech described in chapter 4.

5.4 Conclusion

The marking of formal speech in Western Subanon is an important part of discourse analysis. To analyze discourse from the point of view of its social context tells us some things about discourse that analysis from a different point of view might not show. We can see that social context is necessary for some genre to even exist, e.g., the epic and seances. Prayers, as well, are a social event within the Western Subanon community. It is the social context that provides the stimulus for verbal art forms.

Some variations which exist in the syntax of the different discourse genres may be explained on the basis of the social context of the discourse. There are recorded Subanon examples of expository speech that have no parallel structures in them. Their social context is one of informality and consists of public face-to-face encounters between only two or three individuals. Public exposition, hortation, narratives and prayers with all the formal speech characteristics are usually made by noted speakers. But these same genres in a different, more private context, are not as replete with the poetic and rhetorical markings of formal speech.

Formal speech among the Western Subanon is not only used for political or persuasive purposes. As suggested in chapter 4, the character of formal speech is poetical and it is also for entertainment.

To try to persuade or teach in public to a Subanon audience and fail to use at least some of the recognized rhetorical characteristics of formal speech is to fail to be wholly effective. To know how to speak well in Subanon formal situations when the spotlight of public attention is on one, is to know how to talk in Western Subanon.

Poetic Patterns in Formal Speech

Notes

1. See Rosaldo (1973 Conclusion) for a statement regarding the relationship between the use of speech of persuasion and the social ideals of the Ilongot society. Like the Ilongot, the Subanon society is egalitarian. One basis for persuasion lies in the appeal to tradition.

2. Speech makers vary as to their use of lexical and structural parallelism. In 1980, I attended a conference of both Eastern Subanuns and Western Subanons, at which a number of community leaders who were chosen as representatives to national government, gave speeches. Each individual displayed his ability to the evident delight of the crowd.

3. In working with Subanon language assistants in transcribing and translating poetry and other formal speech material, obscure passages were often interpreted on the basis of parallels.

4. A systematic exhaustive analysis and count of all parts of speech that are paralleled has not been done yet. Evidence from studies in other languages suggests that the grammatical categories that may be used in parallelism are extensive (cf. Bricker 1974, Gossen 1974, Hymes 1981; 1982, Jakobson 1966; 1968, Rosaldo 1973; 1982).

5. "Some recent work in Mexican Indian languages has uncovered, in two languages, evidence of formal features of repetition and parallelism that characterize a denouement as opposed to an Episode." (Longacre 1968: xxiv)

6. For example, Hymes says (1981:177), "Parallelism between verses, and parts of verses, is obviously a major factor in recognizing lines."

7. In the nearby Sama languages these two terms (**gusba** and **gwaris**) distinguish matrilineal and patrilineal kin. However, for the Western Subanon there does not seem to be a semantic distinction between the terms. Both have the same equivalent meaning of "relative" or "kin."

8. Dell Hymes suggested the present scheme of display for this and several other examples. The same pattern may be seen in examples 3, 4, and 6. By displaying these by lines, the expressive function of the language is much more apparent.

9. The shaman and I had been travelling together on the way to visit this particular well-known headman. The speech took place at night with the participants sitting in a rough circle facing each other. Turn taking was the norm.

10. The example comes from the speech of speaker B in the summary of the **mogogoka'oy** 'explanation' event during the **polontu** 'death ceremony' situation. The sentence occurs in the opening of the speech act. The full text of the speech act has not been included.

11. The figures are 90 degree, flipped tree figures:

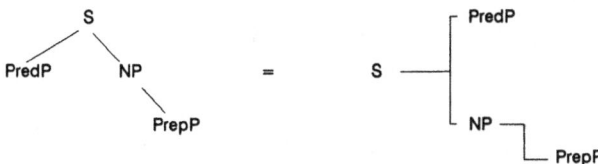

It will also be noticed that sometimes the main node of these constructions is labeled as Clause instead of Sentence, although the structure of the diagram is that of sentence in other contexts.

12. The word is glossed here from the Maranao Dictionary (McKaughan and Macaraya 1969). The Maranao are a Moslem people of north central Mindanao. The word appears in the recorded speech of this particular speaker at other times and always in this formulaic context.

13. The following is said by way of conclusion in the **piglimudan** 'caused to gather together' situation by the middle-aged man referred to in section 2.4.5.

14. From the **mogogoka'oy** 'explanation' event, turn 11. The full text is not included.

15. The interpretation of the sentence out of context would be ambiguous. The interpretation presented in the gloss is derived from the speech context.

16. These two words meaning "good" have different collocation restrictions. They are also used differently in different Western Subanon regions.

17. The word **otawa** (and its variant **otawaka**) may be either "or" or "and" showing its dual function, as far as English grammar is concerned. The word may function either as an alternative or as the coordinate concatenator "and". In this respect it is much like the Tagalog **o** 'or' (Schachter and Otanes 1972).

18. From the **mogogoka'oy** 'explanation' event, Appendix C2, number 9.

19. From the **piglimudan** 'caused to gather together' situation from the speech of the middle-aged man referred to in section 2.4.5.

20. See also, note 8, chapter 3.

21. The topic marker **og** often assimilates to the manner of articulation of the beginning consonant of the nominal following it. The consonant is then articulated as a double consonant, e.g., $\begin{bmatrix} k \\ p \end{bmatrix}$.

22. This type of construction illustrates the form of head-tail or summary paragraph linkage (Longacre 1968) but, in this case, it does not have the function of discourse linkage on a higher level.

23. The difference in these two forms and the other examples is that an **-um-** infix is used here. The other examples use an affix **moN-**, where the initial stem consonant of the word base assumes a nasal form at the same point of articulation. Here, all examples begin with an alveopalatal consonant so there is no contrast seen between them. For a discussion of Subanon verb classes and affix forms, see Hall (1969).

Appendix A

There are two sections to this text from the *polontu* 'death ceremony', the instruction and the prayer. They are spoken by the shaman. See section 2.4.1.1.

1. The instruction.

Ati le ma' ninia:... now friend like this	And now, friend, it's like this...
Mongoni u nog tobia' bu request (1st) (ntdet) pardon and busungbusung tokodoy... sog gilug excuse (int) (loc) kin gwarisgusba u... moloksang in-laws (1snt) large molintok lupa' baloy liu small ground house outside solod... po' ngon tolu'on inside because (exl) speech ku bu bisaraan ku... (1snt) and speech (1snt) atagan sog polontu... concerning (dir) death-ceremony	I request very much pardon and excuse from my kin and in-laws... those who are great and small, on the ground, in the house, outside and inside... because there is something I will say and speak about concerning the death ceremony...
/T: Mo'ana non gobi nog meaning (3snt) night (att)	(interruption by T) Its meaning is the night of

molimatoy./
ghost

La:lalan non gobi nog
  name (3snt) night (att)

molimatoy kotu' na ginobon
ghost that now time-span

non... sog kobon nitu' bila ngon
(3snt) (loc) long that if (exl)

polontuon... ngon pa gulang
polontu (exl) yet elder

bogolal ngon gulang glusadan
councilor (exl) elder shaman

motongow... gondow koni da'idun.
see day this none

(clears throat)

Ion do na motongow u
(3st) (sta) now see (1snt)

gondow koni og gina' u
day this (tdet) mother (1snt)

bu gama' u og ponugangan
and father (1snt) (tdet) in-law

ku motalu' mongina'
(1snt) called call-mother

mongama' u dun...
call-father (1st) (ana)

Tia tantu tantu nog gina' u
but real real (att) mother (1snt)

bu gama' u da' na tanan na.
and father (1snt) not now just now

Dadi mongoni u nog talus...
so request (1st) (ntdet) wisdom

mongoni u nog dopot labi
request (1st) (ntdet) reach more

kosunan...
knowledge

Ion goktob dopot... sog gina'
(3st) limit reach (loc) mother

ghosts.

(Speaker resents interruption thus making mistake *lalalan* instead of *ngalan*.) It's name being night of ghosts that one from its beginning... from long ago if there were those ceremonied by the *polontu*... (if) there were yet elder councilors; (if) there were elder shaman to be seen;... today there are none. (clears throat)

That being what it is, today I see my mother and my father (that is), my father-in-law whom I call mother and father...

However, my real mother and father are not here now (euphemism: dead).

And so, I request wisdom... I request ability, more so (I request) knowledge...

That which is the limit of ability is from my mother

Appendix A

u   bu gama' u   nog...
(1snt) and father (1snt) (rel)

linuwa' ... linumua' dinakon.
(mistake)   teared   to-me

Gondow koni paga...
day   this as-long-as

molimbata'   ami   ma...
present-generation (1ptex) (emp)

sog bata' mogulang libun laki
(dir) child elder   female male

dinami...   bu tantu non
to-us(ex) and real (3snt)

sinumindop no ma   gondow
go-under   now (emp) sun

ompalong   no ma   gunutan,...
extinguish now (emp) leader

Apu' ami   koni:...(clears
lord (1ptex) this

throat) sog mangoy na sog
        (loc) go   now (dir)

modolom... magow sog   kitu'
dark   wrestle (loc) that

og   gobi.
(tdet) night

Mondadi koni mongimunag u   na...
so   this sprinkling (1st) now

lagi'... og   mongugas na sog
indeed (tdet) cleanse   now (dir)

og   di' pia motalu' mokolaton
(tdet) not good called bad

mokosakit kitu' munsing munsing
pain   that dirty   dirty

nog og   gotow dialom lawas
(att) (hes) person inside body

ta   solod nog   tubu'on
(1pntin) inside (ntdet) life

ta   og   tubig da.
(1pntin) (tdet) water (sta)

and father who
suffered (in
bearing) me.

Today as long
as ... we are indeed
the younger
generation,
youngster, elder,
female, male,
among us and, in
fact, the sun has
set, the leader
has been
extinguished
(figure = sunset), ...
Lord, as for us
here...(clears
throat) where it
goes to
darkness...
wrestling with
that one, the
night.

And so, this one
I will now
sprinkle...
indeed... the
cleanser now for
the evil and pain
and filth of a
person inside
ourselves, inside
our life (breath)
is water.

Tantu ginimung ta   nog
real made   (1pntin) (ntdet)

bulung bu piulang tubig.
medicine and medicine water

Ndadi, sa' na dion, og   tantu
so   one now there (tdet) real

non,   gita   koni ngon po lual
(3snt) (1ptin) this (exl) yet other

og   gyokinon ta   sobion
(tdet) pray-for (1pntin) call-for

nog   tumabang sop dinita...
(ntdet) help   also to-us(in)

sog   kitu'...dini sog   dunya
(loc) that   here (loc) world

sog   glupa'an.
(loc) earth

Sogaga bu soga'id non   ma'
instead and instead (3snt) like

nini:... koni tuyung ku   og
this   this pour   (1snt) (tdet)

tubig... sog baloy koni bu
water   (loc) house this and

glupa' koni... ompisik na...
ground this   flick   now

(Su)ga'id non   bu sogaga non
instead   (3snt) and instead (3snt)

koni... sog   bino'... piglumpukan
this   (loc) (mis)   gathering

ta   koni... ondi' na ilan
(1pntin) this   not   now (3pt)

ita   bina'an moloksang molintok
(1ptin) punish large   small

dinita   libun laki bata'
to-us(in) female male child

mogulang... po'   koni mingimunag
elder   because this sprinkled

ita   na glam ta   sog
(1ptin) now all (1pntin) (loc)

The real medicine
and medicine (lit.
made old) is
water.

And so, that is
one point, the
real one, as for
us here, there is
another (one) our
prayer for calling
for help for us...
to that one...
here on the earth,
on the earth.

Instead and
instead it is like
this: this water I
am pouring on this
house and on this
ground, it is
being flicked
now.

Instead and
instead this
one... (false
start) this
gathering of ours,
they will not
punish us (all of
us) large and
small, child and
elder, female and
male... because
this one, we have
now sprinkled all
of us (false
start) all
in-laws/kin, child
and elder, female
and male...

Appendix A

sila:ag ... glam nog   gwaris
(mis)   all (ntdet) in-laws

gusba ... bata' mogulang libun
              child   elder   female

laki ...
male

15

Og   kolegan bu gomba'is
(tdet) desire   and good

ta   koni, di'   ita   ba'
(1pntin) this not (1ptin) suppose

nika   bina'an di'   ita   sila'on
(2snt) punish not (1ptin) accuse

nog   molimatoy kitu' nog
(ntdet) ghost   that (rel)

muna: muna   molimatoy, labi
previous previous ghost   more

ko... koni pinolontu koni; bagun
(hes) this ceremonied this so-that

ita   da   moksulut bagun
(1ptin) (sta) agree   so-that

ita   da   moksolabuk ilan
(1ptin) (sta) be-one   (3pt)

tanan tumabang kitu' mog... nog
just   help   that (mis) (ntdet)

pikilan nilan kotu' togu'on
thought (3pnt) that put-away

dianita   nog   molongas nog
to-us(in) (rel) good   (rel)

ko'iran mologdong nog   og
(mis)   straight (rel) (tdet)

pondoga ...
solution

Ion   labi tabang bila moglolat
(3st) more help   if   pity

dianita   bagun   ita   di'
to-us(in) so-that (1ptin) not

mogla'atla'at; bagun   ita ...
destroy   so-that (1ptin)

This is our desire and pleasure (that) we are not, imagine, punished, we are not accused by those ghosts that have preceded, the previous ghosts; even more, those being ceremonied at present; so that we will be in agreement, so that we will be unified, they will help by those thoughts of theirs put into us that are good, that are straight, that are solutions ...

It is more if (they) pity us so that we will not be destroyed; so that we will not be scattered;

ondi': mosiasia:
not   scatter

bagun ita   di' ba'   nika
so-that (1ptin) not suppose (2snt)

dun, mo: ... sagya ...
(ana) (hes)   just

/T: Sagboy./
    affliction

Mosagboy.
afflict

/Another: Mosagboy./
          afflict

Mindadi og   kini ... yokinon
so   (tdet) this   pray-for

ta   sog   koni gobi no   ma
(1pntin) (loc) this night now (emp)

o:' ... posungu'an ta ...
(par)   headed   (1ptin)

Ako:n na' amu mosobu'an.
(1st) not (2pt) surprised

Bila mosobu'an ainain ...
if   surprised whoever (false start)

ain da' non   kosunoy
who not (3snt) be-informed

kosobu'an; ain ... ain ...   og ...
surprised who   whoever   (hes)

kosunan non,   di' da   kosobu'an.
know   (3snt) not (sta) surprised

Po'   bila mogyakin u
because if   pray   (1st)

poksobion ku   kona' Sanag;
call-on   (1snt) not   Sanag

sogaga sobion ku   ingolanan
rather call-on (1snt) name

ku   si   Bata'Munglu'.
(1snt) (tper) Bata'Munglu'

so that we will
not, imagine,
uh ... just ...

Affliction from
the unseen world.

Be afflicted by
the unseen world.

Be afflicted by
the unseen world.

And so, as for
this, ... let's
pray to this one,
it is night
already, ... that
which faces us ...

Regarding me,
don't you all be
taken by
surprise.

If taken by
mistake
whoever ... (false
start) whoever has
not been informed
is surprised;
whoever ... whoever
uh ... is in the
know is not
surprised.

Because when I
pray the one I
call on is not
Sanag (a deity);
rather, I call on
whom I name Lord
Bata'Munglu' (lit.
young giant).

Appendix A

Indadi sobonal ah... so truth	And so, of a truth, ah....

2. The prayer.

Solamat tokodoy ina'ama'... bu thanks (int) mother-father and Apu' Bata'Munglu', Apu' Poktonudan, lord Bata'Munglu' lord Poktonudan Apu' Datu' Tulali, Apu' Dagbulawan lord Datu' Tulali, lord Dagbulawan Gotunow. Gotunow	Thank you very much mother and father... and lord Bata' Munglu', lord Poktonudan, lord Datu' Tulali, and lord Dagbulawan Gotunow.
Koni Apu' gobi na motalu' modolom this lord night now called dark na sinumindop na og gondow now go-under now (tdet) sun mipalong na gunutan. extinguished now leader	This one, Lord, is night now, is called dark now, the sun has set, the leader has been extinguished.
Apu' ami... sosuku gusip... koni lord (1ptex) all (mis) this gusiba'an nami koni atagan care-for (1pntex) this concerning sog polontu. (loc) death-ceremony	Lord, as for us...all (false start)...as for this one, this is our observance of the death ceremony.
Bila so' mokotigol ami da if (uc) persuade (1ptex) (sta) di' ami motulug... Mmmm. not (1ptex) sleep (assent)	If it was that we could stand it we would not sleep (tonight). Yes.
Mo'ana non moglokondawan meaning (3snt) ceremony-all-night ami... at... og... wan buan... (1ptex) (hesit) thing (emp) konia... konia og... this-one this-one (hesit)	The meaning is that we would observe all night the...uh...uh ...thing! this one this one...uh ...death ceremony! death ceremony...!

polontu   buan   pomuas...
death-ceremony (emp)   death-ceremony

Dadi di' tulugan.   And so, we will
so   not sleep   not sleep.

Domikian ba'   nika   mibantoy   Likewise,
likewise suppose (2snt) watch   imagine, we are
                                                    watched by
ami   nog   kitu' nog   those ... by those
(1ptex) (ntdet) that   (ntdet)   who are being
                                                    ceremonied by the
pinolontu   koen.   *polontu*.
ceremonied   that

Ndadi kolegan ku... bu   gomba'is   And so my
so   desire (1snt) and good   desire ... and my
                                                    pleasure (is that)
u...   bontayan,   ipaton   ami   we are watched
(1snt) watch-over care-for (1ptex)   over, cared for
                                                    very much lest
tokodoy bu kalu   ngon molaton   there be that
(int)   and perhaps (exl) bad   which is evil,
                                                    going to that
mangoy sog gondi' pia kosolag   which is not good,
go   (dir) not good biggest   the greatest being
                                                    that which is
non   mokoka'id   sog   molani   death-dealing
(3snt) death-dealing (loc) near   (comes) near us,
                                                    being called,
nami   motalu' pinunda ami...   curse ... lord,
(1pntex) call   curse   (1ptex)   clear it away,
                                                    remove it, take it
Apu' ilison   owa'on   poloyu'on   very far away.
lord clear-away remove   take-away

tokodoy.
(int)

Apu' Bata'Munglu' bu Apu'   Lord
lord Bata'Munglu' and lord   Bata'Munglu', lord
                                                    Poktonudan, lord
Poktonudan, Apu' Datu' Tulali, Apu'   Datu' Tulali, and
Poktonudan lord Datu' Tulali lord   lord Dagbulawan
                                                    Gotunow, the
Dagbulawan Gotunow og   sabap   reason and the
Dagbulawan Gotunow (tdet) reason   meaning, provide
                                                    knowledge and make
bu mo'ana mokosun   bu   proposal, lord, as
and meaning knowledge and   far as we Subanon
                                                    living in the
mogdaragyat Apu' ami   Subanon   west(?) (are
proposal   lord (1ptex) Subanon   concerned), we

Appendix A

moluntow sog sirupan, da' tokodoy
live(?)   (loc) west(?)   not (int)

sunan dopot labi og   talus; nda'
know reach more (tdet) wisdom not

tokodoy sunan nami
(int)   know   (1pntex)

kabal   buta bongol ami
on-account-of blind-deaf   (1ptex)

tokodoy Apu' sog dunya sog
(int)   lord (loc) world (loc)

glupa'an.
earth

(S)uga'id non   sogaga non
instead   (3snt) instead (3snt)

ni   Apu'... ion   Apu'...
(ntper) lord   (3st) lord

kolegan nami   bu gomba'is
desire (1pntex) and good

nami... sog bata' mogulang
(1pntex) (loc) child elder

libun laki dinami   sog
female male to-us(ex) (loc)

silangan sindopan lintu dibang
east   west   right left

nog   gondow bukid bu   dibaba'
(att) sun   inland and seaward

sog   molayu' molani Apu' molongas
(loc) far   near   lord good

bu gomba'is mologdong motintu
and good   straight sincere

baloy molonu' dasig   bu pagas
house clean   strength and strength

gugat bu gungud.
sinew and flesh

Dadi Apu' kolegan ku   omba'is
so   lord desire (1snt) good

just do not (have) knowledge, abilitiy, nor even wisdom; (we) just do not (have) knowledge on account of our being very ignorant, lord, of our earthly surroundings.

Instead and instead of lord (false start)... that lord... our desire and our pleasure (all) among us, child and elder female and male, in the east and west, on the right and the left of the sun (i.e., north and south), inland and seaward, those far and near, lord (grant us) blessing and goodness, straightness and sincerity, clean house, and strengthened sinews and flesh (i.e., health and strength).

And so, lord, my desire, my

u   Apu' Bata'Munglu' bu   Apu'
(1snt) lord   Bata'Munglu' and lord

Poktonudan, Apu' Datu' Tulali, Apu'
Poktonudan lord Datu' Tulali lord

Dagbulawan Gotunow amu   tokodoy
Dagbulawan Gotunow (2pt) (int)

koto   mokosampot bu mokpolatas
know-how make-reach   and pass-on

sog   mogaid nog   glupa'an
(loc) hold-on (ntdet) earth

mogaid nog   tubig, mogaid
hold-on (ntdet) water hold-on

nog   gapuy mogaid nog
(ntdet) fire hold-on (ntdet)

galu', mogaid nog
wind   hold-on (ntdet)

gumul   bu gongkom nog
length-of-life and palm   (ntdet)

kotubu' ma' ni   Apu' montoy
life   like (ntper) lord long-life

sog   dunya
(loc) earth

monolayun   sog
excellent-living-conditions (loc)

bawang   labi goktob solag si
habitation more limit large (tper)

Apu' mikpongon nog   dunya
lord creator   (ntdet) earth

dinumiun nog   glawas nami
molded   (ntdet) body (1pntex)

Apu' togu'an   nami.
lord container (1pntex)

Dadi Apu' pokisolamat u
so   lord ask-blessing (1snt)

tokodoy gyakin da' kopus   non
(int)   prayer not wear-out (3snt)

pleasure, lord
Bata'Munglu' lord
Poktonudan, lord
Datu' Tulali, and
lord Dagbulawan
Gotunow, you know
very much how to
reach to and pass
on to those who
control the earth,
those who control
the water, those
who control fire,
those who control
the wind, those
who control length
of life and who
hold life in their
palm, like lord
(Sanag) long life
on the earth...
excellent living
conditions in our
habitations, more
so, ultimately to
the lord Creator
of the earth, the
(one who) molded
our bodies, lord,
our containers.

And so, lord,
continually I ask
for blessing on my
prayer that lasts
forever, (my
prayer that)

Appendix A

mokulang sampoy Apu' tokodoy Apu'
lacking   even   lord (int)   lord

botad   bu tolitib   bu tingoban
custom and lucidity and complete

pa'at   bu guali   tintulu'
instruction and make-known teaching

pomali   piponog (p)ilusad sog
instruction descend appear   (loc)

milowlupa'an   Apu' Bata'Munglu' bu
unripe-earth   lord Bata'Munglu' and

Apu' Poktonudan, Apu' Datu' Tulali,
lord Poktonudan lord Datu' Tulali

Apu' Dagbulawan Gotunow.
lord Dagbulawan Gotunow

Ndadi so'   sog   bata' ion
so   first (dir) child (3st)

labi... gulang bata' mangoy
more   elder child go

gina'... o:'   gula... o...
mother   (hes) (mis)   (hes)

gina'ama'   solag non   mogulang
mother-father great (3snt) elder

nog   goktob non   bogolal   bu
(ntdet) limit (3snt) councilor and

glusadan, gondow koni mokotaksi'
shaman   day   this witness

mikodongog nog   talu' bu
heard   (ntdet) speech and

bitbitan   ku   og   gyakin
conversation (1snt) (tdet) prayer

bu   tulik   u   koni kosabi
and thought (1snt) this calling

nog   ngalan niu   Apu' gangyu'
(ntdet) name   (2pnt) lord nickname

niu.
(2pnt)

(Su)ga'id non   sogaga non
rather   (3snt) rather (3snt)

lacks, lord, very much, lord, custom and lucidity and completeness of instruction and what is common knowledge, teaching and instruction, cause these to descend, to appear from above on the earth, lord Bata'Munglu', lord Poktonudan lord Datu' Tulali, and lord Dagbulawan Gotunow.

And so, beginning with the children, on to the older siblings, going to the mother... uh... (false start) ...uh... parents, ultimately to the elders and the councilors and shaman, today (they) are witnessing and have heard my speech and conversation, these prayers and thoughts of mine, this calling on your names, lord, on your nicknames.

Rather, my desire, lord, (is

kolegan ku,   Apu', solomaton
desire   (1snt) lord   bless

tokodoy gyakin ku   koni Apu',
(int)   prayer (1snt) this Lord

solomaton tokodoy.
bless   (int)

(Su)ga'id non   sogaga non
rather   (3snt) rather (3snt)

le koni, koni Apu'... koni
friend this this lord   this

mipasad og   ginakon, suklian
settled (tdet) mine   exchange

mu.
(2snt)

'O!... suklian   mu   po'
yes   exchange (2snt) (par)

busison ku   mini na.   (RR012-D)
spray   (1snt) this now

that) this my
prayer is blessed
very much, lord,
is blessed very
much.

Rather, this one,
friend, this one,
lord, ... this one,
mine is finished,
you take over.

Here!... You take
over. I'll spray
this (water) now.

After saying this, the shaman took the container of water and flicked it about those present, the house, and outside.

Appendix B

This text is from the feast of **dakul** event (see sec. 2.4.1.2). There are three sections to this text, the formal preliminary dialogue, the instruction to the crowd, and the formal closing of the event.

1. The formal preliminary dialogue between ceremony initiator (Cer In) and **Timuoy** (Tim).

Cer In: ogog ... tolipunan ku
       uh   begin   (1snt)

Uh ... I'll begin ... okay?

ah ....
okay

Tim: 'O:.
     yes

Okay.

Cer In: Ponugangan ku.
       in-law   (1snt)

My father-in-law.

Tim: 'O:, si   bamba kotu'
     yes (tper) uncle   that

Yes, that (deceased) uncle.

Cer In: Tubus nitu' ogog gama'
       after   that (tdet) father

non   o:'   On og   Sol.
(3snt) (par) On (tdet) Sol

After that, the uh ... his father, you know, On (i.e., father who is) Sol.

Tim: Ah?
     huh

Huh?

Cer In: Sol kotu'.
       Sol that

That Sol.

Tim: 'O, og dipuntu Sol.
    yes (tdet) deceased Sol

Yes, the deceased Sol.

Cer In: 'O'o.
    yes

Yes.

Tim: 'O:?
    yes

Go on.

Cer In: Tubus nitu' bata' ni So.
    after that child (ntper) So

After that, the child of So.

Tim: So. ... konia 'o:. Sima pa?
    So this-one yes who yet

So ... that one, yes. Who else?

Cer In: Tubus nitu' og gina'
    after that (tdet) mother

ni lo'... At, ...si da' Mo.
(ntper) (par) At (tper) aunt Mo

After that, the mother of theirs ... At (i.e., the mother of At and his siblings) ... aunt Mo.

Tim: 'O:, og gilug nami.
    yes (tdet) cousin (1pntex)

Yes, our cousin.

Cer In: 'O'o. Ain dun si
    yes where (ana) (tper)

lo' Us, loko 'an?
(par) Us I-say thing

That's right. Where is Us, I say, what's-your-name?

Tim: Dini na ilan?
    here now (3pt)

Are they here now?

Cer In: Dini na.
    here now

(They are) here now.

Tim: Sogadan gilug nami
    never-mind cousin (1pntex)

kitu', dini da si...
that here (sta) (tper)

Nevermind that (deceased) cousin of ours, ... is here (did not name him).

Cer In: Ain ilan ban minangoy?
    where (3pt) (emp) went

Where did they go?!

Tim: Akon dini u na. Si
    (1st) here (1st) now (tper)

bamba Lu kitu' ma' itu' da.
uncle Lu that like that (sta)

As for me, I'm here. That uncle Lu, he also is here.

Uncle: Dini ami da.
    here (1ptex) (sta)

Here we are.

Tim: 'O. Bog sala kotow kotu' ma'
    yes if one person that like

Okay. If it's that other person,

Appendix B

nitu' do sop. Dadi olo ma
that (sta) also so what (emp)

ini, tutung na?
this burn now

he is like that also. And so, what is this, ready to burn the incense?

Another delivering the coals on which the incense is burned:

Olo botang nini... kobotang nini?
what place this place this

Where place this (mistake)... where is this to be placed?

Cer In: Olo nini Mon, tutung a
what this Mon burn (2st)

na?
now

What is this Mon, will you burn incense now?

Deliverer: 'O:.
yes

Yes.

Tim: Na tutungoy niu na.
now burn (2pnt) now

Now then, you burn incense now to the deceased.

2. The instruction to the crowd before the culminating 'soul send-off' prayer.

Cer In: Da'idun moktalu:! Ipus
none speak quiet

ipus mokinongog ita.
quiet listen (1ptin)

Nobody speak! Silence, let's listen.

Tim: Koni ma' ninia:
this like this

Now, it's like this:

Cer In: Hoy! Liu solod koni
hey outside inside this

di' ita pa niu moktalu'
not (1ptin) yet (2pnt) speak

po' bagun ta modongog
(par) so-that (1ptin) hear

ogo:g...
(hes)

Hey! You who are outside and inside, please don't be talking so that we can hear the uh...

Another: Gyakin.
prayer

Prayer.

Cer In: ...og gyakin koni nog
(tdet) prayer this (rel)

...this prayer which will deliver

moguakil nog go'o... nog deliver (ntdet) (mis) (ntdet)	the (false start)... the ghosts, the souls
molimatoy og glimukud nog ghost (tdet) soul (pos)	of the persons...
gotow... person	
Another: Bila moktulik ita if remember (1ptin)	If we indeed remember our customs)... that we
da... nog di' ita da... (sta) (ntdet) not (1ptin) (sta)	will not indeed.
Cer In: ...sog poguli'an pogoiton (loc) rest-place carry	...to the final rest (which) we carry here in the
ta dini sog kilawan. Dadi (1pntin) here (loc) seen-world so	seen world. And so, so that we, all together, may
magun ta samasama ta so-that (1pntin) all (1pntin)	hear...
modongog... hear	
Tim: Bila moktulik ita nog if remember (1ptin) (ntdet)	If we remember our custom, there is no one who
goidan ta, da'idun pa custom (1pntin) none yet	speaks (polite) because this one here, he will
moktalu' po' koni ion moktalu' speak (par) this (3st) speak	speak... the real one here who can speak, who is the
...og gultimul na ini nog (tdet) last now this (rel)	means by which...
mokopoktalu' nog pobian... can-talk (rel) pass	
Cer In: Ipus ipus! quiet quiet	Silence!
Tim: ...posungu' ditu' so:g... og headed there (loc) uh	...to head there to the unseen world called our
kodiwata motalu' sog gonita unseen-world called (dir) (1pntin)	belief. And so, to all of us gathered together, let us
nog poktulikan. Dadi sog glam (ntdet) belief so (dir) all	listen to the person whom we have designated,
ta bolohimpun mokinongog (1pntin) together listen	who will pray, (who) will reach

Appendix B

ita   sog   gotow nog
(1ptin) (dir) person (rel)

binogonan   ta   nog mogyakin
designated (1pntin) (rel) pray

mokposampot ditu'   so:g ... ginita
reach-to   there (loc)   (1ptin)

nog poktulikan. Dadi sa' ...
(rel) belief   so   reason

pongonion ku   da'idun pa
request (1snt) none   yet

moktalu'. Na sigi.
speak   now go-ahead

to there, to (what is) ours, that is, (our) belief. And so, that's why I am requesting (polite) that no one talk. Now, go ahead (said to the shaman).

After the shaman is finished speaking, the **Timuoy** makes the following remark which marks the end of the offering event.

3. The formal closing of the event.

Tim: (clears throat) Da'idun na
                     none   now

po'   solabuk da   ion
because one   (sta) (3st)

mogyakin. (Su)ga'id non   bog
pray   rather (3snt) if

mipasad ma' intu' na, konia
settled like that now this-one

koni og   gobi ban   nog
this (tdet) night (emp) (rel)

piksoluan.   Og   diadia
all-eat-together (tdet) everywhere

kotu' gusbawaris kuman nog ...
that in-laws   eat   (ntdet)

po'   koen 'o' piksoluan ....
because that (par) all-eat-together

Goktob nog misabut   u.
limit (rel) understand (1snt)

(RR012–E)

There is no one (else) now because just one will pray. Since it is finished like that now, as for this (ceremony?) here, this is the night which all eat together. Everyone of the relatives will eat ..., because that, I say, is what eating together is. That is what I understand about it.

Appendix C

These texts are from the **mogogoka'oy** 'reciprocally asking explanation' event (see sec.#2.4.2). The texts consist of six turns.

Turn 1, speaker A

1 Ati   BA ma' ninia:....
   now BA like this

1 Now then, BA,
it's like
this:....

2 Kini omba'is u   da: nog
   this good   (1snt) (sta) (com)

mikotua' amu po'   og
appear   (2pt) because (tdet)

mo'ana   non   omBa'is u   nog
meaning (3snt) good   (1snt) (com)

mikotua' amu...
appear   (2pt)

2 As for this, I
am just pleased
that you have
attended because
the meaning is
that I am pleased
that you have
attended...

3 Kini og   pogosuyon nog
   this (tdet) ceremony (ntdet)

gobi   koni nog   bombus gobi
night this (ntdet)   later   night

mangoy sog   dali' ondow asta
go   (loc)   near   sun   even

buloma'   sisolom gobi   nog
tomorrow morning night (att)

3 This ceremony
tonight, late this
evening lasting
until dawn, even
tomorrow morning,
is the night of
ghosts.

Appendix C

molimatoy.
ghost

4 Dadi gobi nog molimatoy sa'
  so night (att) ghost first

na sog mogulang ponugangan
now (loc) elder   in-law

ku; kodua' si   SO mangoy
(1snt) second (tper) SO go

sog kodumanan ni   KO tolu;
(loc) mate   (ntper) KO third

kopat bata' ni   SOL.
fourth child (ntper) SOL

5 Dadi: og   kini le   ini
  so (tdet) this friend this

ogog pigobitobitan nami   tidu
(tdet) conversation (1pntex) from

sog kolabung, asta komun
(loc) yesterday even earlier

sisolom, mikangoy og   Timuoy
morning came   (tdet) chief

ken dini, ion misobu'an.
that here (3st) surprised

6 Sa'an misobu'an, po'   og
  reason surprised because (tdet)

gilug non, mihilang dini sog
brother (3snt) bereaved here (loc)

dialom pigbogolalan.
under jurisdiction-of-council

7 Idu mitu' motolua' ma... /B: Ma'
  why that perform (emp)   like

antu'./ botad kitu' inangon ma
that   custom that do   (emp)

nog saka ion og   palin.
(rel) also (3st) (tdet) new-age

8 Ulaula inangon sog mama' nion
  result do   (loc) like that

nog di' pobolan   nog
(rel) not cause-smoke (ntdet)

4 And so, the
night of ghosts,
first now is for
my elder in-law;
second, SO, going
on to the mate of
KO, being the
third; the fourth
is the child of
SOL.

5 And so, as for
this one here,
friend, the
uh ... our
conversation from
yesterday up to
earlier this
morning, that
Timuoy came here
(and) he was
surprised.

6 The reason why
(he) was
surprised, is
because his
brother is breaved
here under the
jurisdiction of
the council.

7 Why indeed
observe passed
traditions ... /B:
It's like that./
accomplish that
custom indeed when
at the same he is
under the new
age.

8 The resulting
action like that
is not causing
incense to smoke.

komanyan.
incense

9 Di' tutungan ogog, uh... di'
  not burn (tdet) uh not

tolipunan, otawa di' dokulan,
begin or not placate

manggidanggid sog miapas.
similar (loc) still-born

9 Not burning the uh... (false start) not beginning it or not providing offerings resembles the death (ritual) of a still-born.

10 /B: M'm./ Po' minsan
  (assent) because even

kidanoy tutungan da.
old-way burn (sta)

10 /B: (assent)/ Because even with the old way (incense) was burned.

11 Dadi pogingalan dun, ma' long
  so named (ana) like said

su'usa nog gua... gusbawalis
(pity) (ntdet) (mis) relatives

nog motogas nog mama' nog
(rel) hard (rel) like (ntdet)

gamu manggidanggid sog
(2pt) similar (loc)

miapas.
still-born

11 And so, what it is called, thus say the kinsmen (pity marker) who are close kin, who are like you, it resembles one who is still-born.

12 Na tibua su'usa bog minangoy
  now but (pity) when came

dini, ion tinalu' ni Timuoy,
here (3st) said (ntper) chief

og gupakat bu gisun.
(tdet) discuss and discuss

12 Now, however, (pity marker) when he came here what the **Timuoy** said was to meet to discuss and to meet to arrive at a solution.

13 /B: Ma' antu'./ Po' sa'an
  like that because reason

gupakat bu gisun minsan sop
discuss and discuss even also

bogolal na, ainain nog
councilor now wherever (ntdet)

bogolal, mokosobola'
councilor on-the-other-side

mokosilangan, mokosindopan, solabuk
in-the-east in-the-west one

13 /B: It's like that./ Because the reason why to meet to discuss and to meet for solution, even though it is also now the councilors (here), no matter where the councilor, on the other side (of the peninsula), in the east, in the west, there is

Appendix C

da   koposadan.
(sta) solution

just one (i.e., the same) solution.

14 Dadi ma' long non   dun,
   so   like said (3snt) (ana)

"Ita   koni mo mogilug ma
 (1ptin) this (emp) brother (emp)

mogusba ma,   mogwaris ma,
relatives (emp) relatives (emp)

ion   poginuinuon ta   kona'
(3st) discuss   (1pntin) not

sa'otmona'ot; /B: Ma' antu'./
overtake   like that

ion   pogupokatan ta,   kona'
(3st) discuss   (1pntin) not

sikutmonikut."
narrow

14 And so, thus he said, "As for us here, we brothers indeed, are relatives indeed, what we are discussing is not simply finding fault; /B: It's like that./ what we meeting to discuss is not vengeance."

15 Dadi ma' long non   dun
   so   like said (3snt) (ana)

su'usa ... "Na' a," long,
(pity)   not (2st) said

"muba',   Ponglima, otagan
 take-offense   Ponglima concerning

sog   gombata' misiasia, og
(loc) children scattered (tdet)

gilug   u   nog   kopatoy
brother (1snt) (ntdet) death

non   sog   dialom pigbogolalan
(3snt) (loc) under jurisdiction

nika.
(2snt)

15 And so, thus he said, (pity marker) ... "Don't you," he said, "take offense, Ponglima, concerning those children who have scattered (not adhered to proper custom regarding) my brother, (i.e.), his death within your jurisdiction.

16 "Minsan   sop o'," ma' long
   even-though also (par) like said

non   dun, ... "gombata' na
(3snt) (ana)   children now

tolu'on kitu' kitu' si'
say   that that also

mikohinang," ma' long non   dun,
done   like said (3snt) (ana)

16 "Even though also, you see," thus he said, "it is the fault of the council."

"kulpa nog   bogolal.
fault (ntdet) council

17 Ngalan non,   da' kopomolioy
   name   (3snt) not instructed

nog   bogolal.
(ntdet) council

17 What it is is that (the children) were not properly advised by the council.'

18 Dadi gondow koni," ma' long
   so   day   this   like said

non   dun, "di' u
(3snt) (ana) not (1snt)

omponangkis sog   gombata' ken,
divert   (loc) children that

gombata' pa.
children yet

18 "And so, today," thus he said, "I will not accuse those children (because) they are yet children.

19 Suga'id taksil,"   ma' long
   rather evidence like said

non   dun, "mitaksil a
(3snt) (ana) accused (2st)

Ponglima."
Ponglima

19 Rather, (circumstantial) evidence says that," he said, "you are the one accused, Ponglima."

20 Dadi og   kotoksilan, una
   so   (tdet) accused-act then

u   pogbintingoy, ba'   nika
(1snt) study   suppose (2snt)

BA una u   poktima'anoy bog
BA then (1snt) observe   and

pogimutimut u   kotoksilan
examine   (1snt) accused-act

koulogisan bogolal. /B: Ma'
guilt   council   like

antu'./
that

20 And so, the accused act I then studied, imagine BA, I then observed and examined the accused act, the council is guilty of wrong doing. /B: It's like that./

21 Dadi og   koulogisan
   so   (tdet) guilt

bogolal... kolabung mipasad.
council   yesterday settled

21 And so, the councilor guilt was settled yesterday.

22 Ndadi da' kosunggud kolabung
   so   not pay-fine yesterday

22 And so, he has not paid the fine

Appendix C

po'   pokpopodotongon si
because just-waiting-for   (tper)

lo'   AT, si   lo'   o'   IG,
(par) AT   (tper) (par) (par) IG

si   lo' AL.
(tper) (par) AL

23 Sogadan   si   AL po'
   never-mind (tper) AL because

mimilin   na dunia sog   bamba
sent-word now here (loc) uncle

non   si'   IY.
(3snt) (tper) IY

24 Da' ilan ma   datong.
   not (3pt) (emp) arrive

25 Na sintak   non   bog da'
   now after-awhile (3snt) when not

datong miktalu' u   "Molumu da
arrive said   (1st) easy   (sta)

bog koin da ... po'   sogadan
if that (sta) because never-mind

non   gama' non   konia koen
(3snt) father (3snt) this that

somo' doda'   bosia di' ah ... kona'
(uc) indeed (fru) not ah   not

da   nog   misolot   a   nog
(sta) (com) hindered (2st) (com)

ion   pogupokatan koen mikodyadi
(3st) discussed   that can-be

o'   momasad, gombata' non
(par) settle   children (3snt)

da.
(sta)

26 Tibua, loko, kun ma   posadon
   but   I-say this (emp) settle

saka   si   bamba non
at-same-time (tper) uncle (3snt)

yesterday because
we were waiting in
futility for AT
and his party, IG
and his party, and
AL and his party.

23 Never mind AL
because he sent
word here through
his uncle IY.

24 They (i.e.,
the rest of them)
did not arrive.

25 Now after
awhile, when they
had not arrived, I
said, "It is easy
indeed, if that is
the
situation ... because
never mind that
father of his
here, if it was
indeed
(frustrative
marker) not uh ...
(false start) it
is not that you
are hindered by
the fact that he
is the one being
discussed, it can
be settled, you
see, because (they
are) indeed his
children.

26 "However," I
said, "this one
indeed is to be
settled, while at
the same time, his
uncle is right

dion ma.
there (emp)

27 Minsan di' ilan mokingkud
   even-though not (3snt) can-sit

posadon, loko, dun po'
settle   I-say (ana) because

mosabut   men posadon ken."
understand (emp) settlement that

28 Ati posadon ken minsan ain
   now settlement that even where

ta   liowoy   insan ain
(1pntin) circumvent even where

ta   libutoy ulagis da
(1sntin) go-around guilty (sta)

sabap   migyupayupa og
on-account-of wrong-action (tdet)

mihilang sog bonua.
bereaved (loc) land

29 Ain miktidu migyupayupa ken?
   where from wrong-action that

30 Motud da   gombata'
   true (sta) children

miglokohinangan.
performed

31 Tiba motaksil sog bogolal....
   but accuse (loc) councilor

32 Ma' nion....
   like that

33 Koni le   uli'on ku   ogog
   This friend return (1snt) (tdet)

mapa   u.
map(?) (1snt)

34 /B: Dadi mipasad a   le?/
       so   settled (2st) friend

there!

27 "Even though they are not seated (in council) to settle it," I say, "(it's alright) because they will understand indeed that settlement."

28 Now then, that solution even though however we might circumvent, even however we might go around it, the guilt (lies with the councilor) on account of not following the custom (when) there is bereavement in the land.

29 Whence came that wrong action?

30 It is true that children performed it.

31 However, the councilor is accused....

32 It's like that....

33 Here friend, I will return this uh,... map(?) (i.e., microphone).

34 /B: And so, are you finished, friend?/

Appendix C

35 Pasad.
　　settled

35 I am finished.

Turn 2, speaker B

1 Ati: atagan　le　dinakon　ma'nini:
　now　concerning　friend　to-me

1 Now then, friend, concerning what I have to say it's like this:

2 Ati　o'　(clears throat)
　now　(par)

2 Now then, I say, (clears throat)

3 Ati　sog　moidan　modiris　bila
　now　(dir)　hold　severe　if

sa'　binisara　dinika　sa'　moidan
first　speech　to-you　first　hold

modiris　kodua'... botad.
severe　second　custom

3 Now then, as for the severe observances, first it was explained to you, first the severe observances, also known as ... custom.

4 /Another: Botad./ Indadi　do
　　　　　　custom　so　(sta)

mo　doda'　ion　pokponontongon
(emp)　indeed　(3st)　looked-for

ta　　　sog　bonua... og
(pntin)　(loc)　land　　(tdet)

pangkat　bu　posaka'.
generation　and　inheritance

4 /Another: It is custom./ And so, indeed that which we look for in the land of the living are those things from of old and (our) inheritance. /Another: It's like that./

/Another: Ma' antu'./
　　　　like that

5 Olo　og　　pangkat　bu
　what　(tdet)　generation　and

posaka'?
inheritance

5 What is from of old and (our) inheritance?

6 Botad　bu　tukud　mangoy　sog
　custom　and　(?)　go　(loc)

tolitib　tingoban　pa'at
lucidity　complete　instruction

(cough)　tintulu'　bu　pomali.
　　　　teaching　and　teaching

6 It is custom and lucidity and completeness in teaching.

7 Di'　ta　　　tokodoy　bolongon;
　not　(1pntin)　(int)　forsake

7 Let's not forsake it; let's not scatter it.

ndi' ta   tokodoy siasiaon.
not (1pntin) (int)   scatter

8 Mo'ana   non   bila binolong
  meaning (3snt) if   forsaken

ta   posaka'... bu bolongoy
(1pntin) inheritance and forsake

ta   pangkat... da' na   tituk
(1pntin) generation not now memory

ta   sog mokogulang, motalu'
(1pntin) (loc) elder   call

munaotow. /A: Ma' antu'./
ancestor   like that

9 Dadi sumboy dion   ita
   so   must   there (1ptin)

kopagun sog botad; dion ita
strength (loc) custom there (1ptin)

koguya' sog og   botad.
weak   (loc) (tdet) custom

10 Mo'ana   non dion   ita
   meaning (3snt) there (1ptin)

sop patoy sog   botad dion
also death (loc) custom there

ita   kotubu' sog   botad.
(1ptin) life   (loc) custom

11 Dadi sumboy... gondow koni
    so   must   day   this

sumboy botad doda' ginangon
must   custom indeed do

ta.
(1pntin)

12 Po'   kona' tibua og
   because not just (tdet)

gulang bogolal, minsan bata'
elder councilor even   child

mika'an, bila mokotituk nog
small   if   remember (ntdet)

botad, ah na... bina'an ita.
custom ah now   reprimand (1ptin)

8 Meaning, if we forsake (our) inheritance ... and we forsake that which is of old ... there will be no memory of ours for our elders who are called (our) ancestors. /A: It's like that./

9 And so, it must be that there is our strength in custom; there is our weakness in the, uh, custom.

10 Meaning there also is our death in custom; there is our life in custom.

11 And so, it must be ... today it must be custom, indeed, that we perform.

12 Because it is not just the elder councilors, even a small child, if he can remember the custom, well now, we are reprimanded.

Appendix C

13 Ndadi gondow koni ... mipasad
   so   day   this   settled
amu na?
(2pt) now

14 /Another: Mipasad na./
              settled now

15 Ndadi bog mipasad amu na ...
   so   if   settled (2pt) now
ion   non   lo'   ion   poktolu'on
(3st) (3snt) (par) (3st) said
solamat no   lo'   ion   dinakon.
thanks now   (par) (3st) to-me

16 /Another: Solamat./ Mmm.
              thanks   (assent)

17 Dadi gondow koni minsan sop
   so   day   this   even   also
'koni moktalu'talu' u   na,   ah,
this just-talking (1st) now   ah
na   loklakoy   niu   bagun
now   disregard (2pnt) so-that
mokodongog tibua.
hear   just

18 Inana' kitu' sog momasad, abu!
   as-for that (loc) settle   wow
sanu   kali u   na posadoy?
how-many times (1snt) now settled

19 /A: tantu non   ma' long
        true (3snt) like said
nika   po   dun   gilug u
(2snt) yet (ana) brother (1snt)
koen dini na ma./
that here now (emp)

20 Dini na me   en   gulang
   here now (emp) (3st) elder
bata' dinami.
child to-us(ex)

13 And so today ... have you reached settlement now?

14 /Another: It is settled now./

15 And so, if you have made settlement now, then, friend, as it is said, thanks be from me, friend.

16 /Another: Thanks be./ Mmm (assent).

17 And so, today even though now I'm just jabbering, well now, don't take it seriously, so that you can just hear (i.e., listen very carefully).

18 As for settling cases, wow! how many times now have I been involved in settlements!

19 /A: It's really just as you say that brother of mine, he is indeed here now./

20 Here now indeed is our elder sibling.

21 Ion do   na   solabuk ma'
   (3st) (sta) now one   like

nini lo' bog midongogdongog
this (par) if kept-hearing

u...   kolabung...
(1snt) yesterday

22 Ati og   midongog u
   now (tdet) heard   (1snt)

kolabung ditu' mo   do   en
yesterday there (emp) (sta) (3st)

piksosa'an sog... minanga.
set-date   (loc)   river-mouth

23 Tianggi.
   market

24 Motud ta'   en   le
   true (que) (3st) friend

Ponglima?
Ponglima

25 /C: Doksu' nika   dion
       finish (2snt) there

piksambag u   kotu'./
answer   (1snt) that

26 'O'o.
   yes

27 Ndadi og   sosa' ditu' o'...
   so   (tdet) date there (par)

piksosa'an nog   polontu.
set-date   (ntdet) death-ceremony

28 Koni ginang bonua atagan
   this ginang bonua concerning

moga... mogaid... da' sosa'oy.
(mis)   hold   not set-date

29 Dadi ngon miktalu' solakotow,
   so   (exl) speak   one-person

"Idu mini   sosa'an ta   mo
 why (emp) set-date (1pntin) (emp)

21 Nevertheless, the point is like this, of a truth, when I overhear it,... previously (lit. yesterday)...

22 Now then, what I heard previously, there indeed the date was set at... the river mouth.

23 At the market.

24 Friend, is this true, Ponglima?

25 /C: Finish there that which I will answer./

26 Okay.

27 And so, that date setting there,... that was the setting of the death ceremony date.

28 As for this **ginang bonua** (ceremony) concerning (false start)... its observance... the date wasn't set.

29 And so, someone said, "What is this, do we set the date of the death ceremony

```
le       polontu          saka
friend   death-ceremony   at-same-time

ini    mogaid ion    ngon  ma    dion
here   hold   (3st)  (exl) (emp) there

sog    Globuk... og     ina...
(loc)  Globuk     (tdet) (mis)

mogaid... o'    go...  og     ginang
hold      (par) (mis)  (tdet) ginang

bonua  sog... /Molobok./ Molobok."
bonua  (loc)  Molobok    Molobok
```

30 Dadi dunon   ta   dun?
   so   solution (1pntin) (ana)

```
31 Dadi dion   da'   u       na    lo'
   so   there  not   (1snt)  now   (par)

ion    inongog... pokinongog
(3st)  (mis)      hear

kinongogoy sukpat      nion.
hear       connection  that
```

32 Da' lual ken mitalu' po'...
   not other that said   because

33 Ati mo'ana (clears throat)...
   now meaning

```
tiaptiap     ngon   og     pomoli
all-the-time (exl)  (tdet) bane

sog    dialom bonua... bu   ngon
(loc)  under  land     and  (exl)

mogaid momotuk  sog    dialom bonua
hold   ceremony (loc)  under  land

sumboy pogoidan... ah... pogunanon
must   hold        ah    precede

mo...  moginang... og
(mis)  perform     (tdet)

poglokonuon sog    bonua.
ceremony    (loc)  land
```

friend, while at the same time, as for this (other) observance, it is there at Globuk... the... uh, ... (false starts) the **ginang bonua** at... /Molobok./ Molobok."

30 And so, what are we to do about it?

31 And so, about that, I have not heard (the form should be **pokinongogoy**. He gets it in three tries but none of them are the complete form) the end of it.

32 Nothing else was said because...

33 And so, the meaning is (clears throat)... there is always some need for placating in the land... if there is the observance of the **ginang bonua** in the land, it must be observed... uh,... precede the uh, (false start) ... perform the yearly ceremony of the land.

34 /A: Ma' nion./ Mangka ta
    like that   then   (1pntin)

inangoy og polontu,
perform (tdet) death-ceremony

sumboy ompuas ogi o'...
must   pass   (mis) (par)

poglokonuon sog dialom bonua.
ceremony   (loc) under land

35 Tibua konia koen... minsan sop
    but this that   even   also

ma' antu' na,... da' do   men
like that now   not (sta) (emp)

inangoy ion do na sinosa'an.
perform (3st) (sta) now set-date

36 Mikuna sosa'oy polontu,
    ahead   set-date death-ceremony

mibinaya' og...   og   momotuk...
behind   (tdet) (tdet) ceremony

moginang bonua.
moginang bonua

37 Dadi og   koniaya.
    so (tdet) this-one

38 Koniaya.
    this-one-here

39 Akon koni sinumak tibua... bog
    (1st) this asked   just   if

tuman ta' olo.
realized (que) what

40 Bog tuma:an... da bagun
    if   realized   (sta) so-that

ku   da kosunan.
(1snt) (sta) know

41 Bog di', bagun ku   do
    if   not so-that (1snt) (sta)

sop kosunan.
also know

34 /A: It's like
that./ Before we
perform the death
ceremony it must
be that the, uh,
(false start) is
finished ... the
yearly ceremony
for the land.

35 However, as
for this now,
... even though
that's how it is
now, (the death
ceremony) was not
yet performed, it
was just the
setting of its
date.

36 The death
ceremony date was
set first,
followed by the,
uh ... ceremony,
the **ginang bonua**
ceremony.

37 And so, this
is the one.

38 Right here.

39 I have just
only asked ... if
it has come to
pass or not.

40 If it has come
to pass ... just
so that I will
know.

41 If it has not,
so that I also
will know that
too.

Appendix C

42 Sogaga dion ku pa
   rather there (1snt) yet

potomanoy.
cause-limit

42 Therefore, there I will put the boundary (i.e., stop)

43 /C: Dadi bila .../ Midoksu'.
       so   if   finished

43 /C: And so, if .../ I'm finished.

44 /C: Dadi, ginika ken, midoksu'
       so   yours that finished

na?/
now

44 /C: And so, is yours finished now?/

45 Midoksu' na.
   finished now

45 It is finished now.

Turn 3, speaker C

1 (inhales, clears throat) Koni
                           this

lo' en   ma' ninia:
(par) (3st) like this

1 Now then, it's like this:'

2 Moguksuguksug u.
  relate   (1st)

2 I will relate it.

3 Ha:?
  huh

3 Okay?

4 Sa'an moguksuksug u,
  reason relate   (1st)

'agun   ita   da: sog glam
so-that (1ptin) (sta) (dir) all

ta   koni modolag dianita.
(1pntin) this bright to-us(in)

4 The reason I will relate it is so that as for us, all of us here, it will be made plain to us.

/B: Ma' antu'./ /A: Ba'is da./
    like that   good (sta)

/B: It's like that.//A: Good!/

5 Po'   akon, ... sog kobata'
  because (1st)   (loc) birth

nog   pikilan ku,   nog
(ntdet) thought (1snt) (ntdet)

sa'an sinosa'an ku,   midongog
reason set-date (1snt) heard

u   na og   sosa', ... nog
(1snt) now (tdet) date   (ntdet)

5 Because, as for me ... my intentions (lit. from the birth of my thinking), regarding the reason I set the date, (because) I heard already the set date of the **ginang bonua** ceremony.

ginang bonua.
ginang bonua

6 Dadi, sa'an sinosa'an ku,
  so   reason set-date (1snt)

pomuas   koni gondow koni, ...
death-ceremony this day   this

ganta' u   dun, ompuas na
calculate (1snt) (ana) pass   now

gli'inan nog   ginang bonua. /B:
taboo (ntdet) ginang bonua

Ma' antu'./
like that

6 And so, that's why I set the date for this death ceremony on this date ... because I calculated that the taboo restrictions of the **ginang bonua** ceremony are past now. /B: It's like that./

7 Kona' og   mikuna og
  not (tdet) precede (tdet)

sinosa'an ku,   koni ogog ... gan
set-date (1snt) this (tdet)   thing

koni ... /A: pomoli/ pomoli koni.
this   bane   bane this

7 It is not that I went ahead and set the date of this ..., uh, ... /A: Bane ceremony./ this bane ceremony.

8 Mikuna da sosa'oy og
  preceded (sta) set-date (tdet)

ginang bonua. /B: Og   ginang
ginang bonua   (tdet) ginang

bonua./
bonua

8 The setting of the date of the **ginang bonua** ceremony preceded. /B: The **ginang bonua** ceremony./

9 Ma' antu'.
  like that

9 It's like that.

10 Dua' kopitu sosa' u   no:g
   two sevens date (1snt) (ntdet)

pomuas, ... og   ginilan hamis ...
pomuas   (tdet) (3pnt) Thursday

kososa' nilan dun.
date   (3pnt) (ana)

10 Two weeks after (the **ginang bonua** ceremony) I set the date for the death ceremony, ... theirs was Thursday (night) ... the date they had set.

11 O::g ... /A: Sala simana pa
   (tdet)   one week yet

gligat./ Sala simana pa gligat
interval one week yet interval

11 The, uh ... /A: One week yet is the interval./ One week yet is the interval. /B: It's like that./

Appendix C   145

non. /B: Ma' antu'./
(3snt)   like that

12 Ompayat pa nog   bigya'.
   long-time yet (ntdet) difference

12 The difference is great (i.e., the time span).

13 Dadi pigunauna u   sa'an
   so   reasoned   (1snt) reason

sinosa'an ku,   ganta' u
set-date (1snt) calculate (1snt)

dun   mipuas na   ginang bonua. /B:
(ana) pass   now ginang bonua

Ompuas na   gli'inan./
pass   now taboo

13 And so, I reasoned, the reason I set the date (for the time I did), I calculated that the **ginang bonua** ceremony is past already. /B: The taboo restrictions are past./

14 Ompuas na   gli'inan....
   pass   now taboo

14 The taboo restrictions are now past....

15 Dadi, ma' ninia:...
   so   like this

15 And so, it's like this:

16 Poguksuguksug dinika   le,...
   will-relate   to-you(s) friend

po'   ika   su'usa (clears
because (2st) (pity)

throat) ita   ba   ini mogilug.
        (1ptin) (emp) this brothers

/D: Mangka do ma
    then   (sta) (emp)

minginongogan u./
ask-for-info   (1st)

16 I will relate it to you friend,... because, as for you, (pity marker) (clears throat) we here are brothers, (i.e., kin). /D: Also, I asked to have the information./

17 Mangka do ma
   then (sta) (emp)

minginongogan. /B: Ma' antu'./
ask-for-info   like that

17 Also, the information was asked for. /B: It's like that./

18 Og   bianbian   nog...
   (tdet) experience (ntdet)

ogog... gilug   niu   kotu' ma'
(tdet) brother (2pnt) that like

ninia suksugan ku   dinika
this relate   (1snt) to-you(s)

18 As for the experience of..., uh,... that kin of yours it's like this, I will relate to you, even though, as for me I was

minsan nog akon kilikudan
even (ntdet) (1st) absence

ku nda' dini.
(1snt) not here

19 Kosuoy non nda' u
   separate (3snt) not (1snt)

dini.
here

20 Likud u sog tolunan.
   absent (1snt) (loc) forest

21 Tia minatong u modolomdolom.
   but arrived (1st) dark

22 Minatong u dini: miobonobon
   arrived (1st) here some-time

u mingku::d, miguksuguksug
(1st) sit   relating

kodumanan ku. /B: Ma' antu'./
mate   (1snt)   like that

23 "Olo dun poguksugan mu
   what (ana) related (2snt)

koen?"
that

24 "Ongon og longku'an
   (exl) (tdet) sick-unto-death

dio."
there

25 "Sima...?"
   who

26 Modali' ba akon og gan
   quick (emp) (1st) (tdet) thing

ku. /B: mhm./
(1snt) (assent)

27 "Koduma:n.../Another: ...ni
   mate   (ntper)

ba KO dow./ ni::... koni..../B:
uncle KO (hs) (ntper) this

absent, (I) was
not here.

19 When he
separated
(euphemism:
death), I was not
here.

20 I was absent
(being) in the
forest.

21 However, when
I arrived it was
early evening.

22 When I arrived
here, (while) I
was some time in
sitting, my wife
(respect) was
relating. /B: It's
like that./

23 "What is that
you are relating
there?"

24 "There is one
sick unto death
(i.e., died) over
there."

25 "Who...?"

26 I am abrupt in
my thing (i.e.,
questioning). /B:
(assent)/.

27 "The mate
of.../Another: of
uncle KO, it is
said./ of... this
one..../B:
(assent)/ the

Appendix C

Mmmm./ gulang bata' ni...
(assent) elder child (ntper)

dinita. /B: Ma' antu'./
to-us(in) like that

28 "Aba," loko /A: Mitokow mini./
   wow I-said sudden (emp)

"Mitokow mini.
sudden (emp)

29 Koni, loko, di' u mokangoy
   this I-said not (1st) can-go

ditu' nog gobi koni po'
there (ntdet) night this because

milupug u.
tired (1st)

30 Sogaga non buloma' u
   rather (3snt) tomorrow (1st)

angoy ditu' sisolom.
go there morning

31 Buloma' u angoy sisolom."
   tomorrow (1st) go morning

32 Miksisolom en minangoy u
   become-morn (3st) went (1st)

ditu'. /B: Ma' antu'./
there like that

33 Na modakol ami.
   now many (1ptex)

34 Mog... da'idun bogolal.
   (mis) none councilor

35 Sa'an tolu'on da'idun bogolal,
   reason say none councilor

koni glunsan gombata'.
this each-one children

36 Da'idun bogolal non. /B:
   none councilor (3snt)

Da'idun bogolal non./
none councilor (3snt)

elder sibling
of... of ours. /B:
It's like that./

28 "Wow," I said,
/A: That was
sudden./ "that was
sudden."

29 "Now then," I
said, "I can't go
over there tonight
because I am
weary.

30 Instead,
tomorrow I will go
over there in the
morning.

31 Tomorrow I
will go in the
morning."

32 When it was
the morning I went
over there. /B:
It's like that./

33 Now, we were
many.

34 (false start)
There were no
councilors.

35 The reason I
say there were no
councilors, these
were all young.

36 There were no
councilors
present. /B: There
were no councilors
present./

37 Sima pokinongogan?
   who listen-to

37 Who is there to listen to?

38 Da'idun ma. /B: Da'idun./
   none (emp) none

38 There is no one! /B: There is no one./

39 Dadi sug gla'... glam
   so (tmkr) (mis) all

nami kitu' ditu' miginuinu.
(1pntex) that there discuss

39 And so, all of us there, we counciled together.

40 "Da' ma bogolal ta.
   not (emp) councilor (1pntin)

40 "We have no councilors.

41 Hah...
   huh

41 Right?

42 Ita bogolal ita na
   (1ptin) councilor (1ptin) now

/B: Ma' antu'./ po'
like that because

piglogotowan ita nog
offering (1ptin) (pos)

bogolal. /B: Mmm./
councilor (assent)

42 As for us, we are now the councilors /B: It's like that./ because we are the offspring of the councilors. /B: (assent)/.

43 Dadi og glam nog
   so (tdet) all (ntdet)

pogupokatan, ita mongupakat."
discussion (1ptin) discuss

43 And so, all that needs to be discussed, let's council together."

44 ... Ma' nitu'.
     like that

44 It's like that.

45 Dadi, bog migupakat ami
   so when discussed (1ptex)

ini, ... midopot na pidangan og
here   reached now bring-up (tdet)

glungun /C: Motud talu'talu' non
coffin true speech (3snt)

hoen./ su'usa.
that (pity)

45 And so, when we were meeting there, it came to the time of bringing up the coffin (into the house for final ceremonies) /C: What he is saying is true./ (pity marker).

46 (clears throat) Midopot og
            reached (tdet)

46 It came to the time of bringing up the coffin.

Appendix C

pidangan og glungun.
bring-up (tdet) coffin

47 "Og   glangkap ta   ngon
   (tdet) tools   (1pntin) (excl)

da?"
(sta)

48 Tinalu' u   dinilan. /B:
   said   (1snt) to-them

Mmm./
(assent)

49 Na koni, "Da'idun...
   now this   none

da'idun..."
none

50 "Na, loko, koni mologon.
    now I-said this difficult

51 Sa'an, loko,   mologon gondow
   reason I-said difficult day

koni, og   ngon ma   og
this (tdet) (exl) (emp) (tdet)

tinagu'   nami...   nog   gama'
put-away (1pntex) (rel) father

nami   no:g ininonga' po'
(1pntex) (rel) halved   because

pomuasan   ma   posungu'.
death-ceremony (emp) headed

52 Koni si'   bosia ditu'
   this also (fru) there

podunutoy.   /B: Ma' antu'./
cause-to-accompany   like that

53 Inonga'an ta   pa.
   halve   (1pntin) yet

54 Koni si'oy inonga'an ta...
   this also halve   (1pntin)

po'   botad...nog
(par) custom   (ntdet)

47 There are the elements for the ritual, of course?"

48 I asked them. /B: (assent)/

49 Now, they said, "There are none, there are none."

50 "Now," I said, "this is difficult.

51 The reason, I said, this day it is hard, there is one we have placed in abeyance who is our father whose ritual is only half finished because we will hold the death ceremony in the near future.

52 This one also, if possible cause to accompany the other deceased. /B: It's like that./

53 Let's just take it half-way.

54 This one also, let's take it half way... under the custom of inclusion by circumstance

kisolokunan.
included-by-circumstance

55 Mologon nog   tipotan nog
   difficult (com) finish (ntdet)

mogunuyunuy tumipot saka ngon
go-ahead   finish same-time (exl)

sinama'. /B: Mm.//A: Saka
left-over   (assent)   same-time

sop mologon nog di' modunut./
also difficult (com) not follow

56 O'o, saka   sop mologon
   yes same-time also difficult

nog   di' modunut. /B: M'mmm./
(com) not follow   (assent)

57 Dadi su'usa:, sug ... doda' ...
   so   (pity) (tmkr)   indeed

mibabong no   ma   gombata'.
perplexed now (emp) children

58 Da' ilan pokosangkap ... "po'
   not (3pt) provide   because

sug   glam nitu:' ... sug
(tmkr) all that   (tmkr)

bulinga: soluyon da; ... sug
egg   buy   (sta)   (tmkr)

komanyan soluyon da;/A: Da'
incense buy   (sta)   not

bola'bola'oy./ sug   glam no
anticipate   (tmkr) all now

do   ma   itu' ... da' ita
(sta) (emp) that   not (1ptin)

pokosangkap po'   da' ta
provide   because not (1pntin)

bola'bola'oy og   patoy koni."
anticipate   (tdet) death this

(i.e., not to
finalize a ritual
for one if another
is pending).

55 It is
difficult to
complete, to go
ahead and complete
it when at the
same time there is
one left over. /B:
(assent)//A: At
the same time it
is difficult not
to accompany it./

56 Yes, at the
same time it is
difficult not to
accompany it. /B:
(assent)/

57 And so, (pity
marker), (false
start) indeed the
children
(descendants) are
in a state of
perplexity.

58 They were not
able to provide
the elements for
ritual ... "because
all of them:
... eggs must be
bought; incense
must be bought;
/A: (They) did not
anticipate./ just
everything
involved we were
not able to
provide because we
did not anticipate
this death."

Appendix C

59 Dadi: miktalu' ilan su'usa.
   so   spoke (3pt) (pity)

60 "Si Ina'," long non... long
   (tper) mother said (3snt) said

ni   IY... "Si   Ina'
(ntper) IY   (tper) mother

bila:... inonga'an sopolati
if   halved   for-example

non   di' ta' gostuan...?
(3snt) not (que) payment

61 Ha?
   huh

62 Di' ta' gostuan?"
   not (que) payment

63 Dadi miktalu' u, "Gostuan
   so   said   (1st) payment

batuk da   gastu non."
same (sta) pay   (3snt)

64 Dadi, long ni   IY,
   so   said (ntper) IY

"Pongonion ku   pa dianiu,
 request   (1snt) yet to-you(p)

amu ma... mimasad.
(2pt) (emp) case-settlers

65 Da'idun mini bogolal   ta.
   none   (emp) councilor (1pntin)

66 Amu ma   og   mimasad
   (2pt) (emp) (tdet) case-settler

gulang bata' dinami."
elder child to-us(ex)

67 Na:, miktalu' si   DA,
   now spoke   (tper) DA

"Mologon, og   botad; mologon."
 difficult (tdet) custom difficult

68 Tiba koni u,   "Sug... og
   but this (1st) (tmkr) (tdet)

59 And so, they spoke.

60 "As for mother," he said, ... IY said, ... "as for mother, if taken half way, for example ... will it not have to be paid for?

61 Huh?

62 Will it not have to be paid for?"

63 And so, I said, "What must be paid is the same price (i.e., no extra ritual)."

64 And so, IY said, "I will make a request yet to you, you are settlers of cases.

65 We have no councilor here.

66 You are the case settler, our older sibling."

67 Now, DA spoke, "The custom is difficult; it is difficult."

68 However, I said, "Our difficulty is

kilogon ta   nini, da'idun
difficult (1pntin) this none

langkap.
elements

69 Da'idun bulinga ta.
   none   egg   (1pntin)

70 Da'idun komanyan ta.
   none   incense (1pntin)

71 Ain   ta   ban   olapoy?
   where (1pntin) (emp) obtain

72 Og   komanyan, ain   ta
   (tdet) incense where (1pntin)

ma   gonti'oy?
(emp) substitute

73 Og   bulinga, ain   ta
   (tdet) egg   where (1ptin)

ma   gonti'oy?
(emp) substitute

74 Moganti'   gidoy   sog   bunga?
   substitute suppose (loc) betel

/A: Saka   kona'
    at-same-time not

kobolianan./
from-the-shaman

75 Saka   kona'
   at-same-time not

kobolianan...   koni kopatoy mini."
from-the-shaman this death   (emp)

76 Dadi, binogoy nami:... da
   so   gave   (1pntex) (sta)

ma' doma   nitu' nog   binogoy.
like indeed that (ntdet) given

77 Dadi, sa'an en   glona'   non
   so   reason (3st) result (3snt)

gondow koni, da' kotolipunoy, koyon
day   this not begun   that

bian ken...
way that

69 We have no
eggs.

70 We have no
incense.

71 Where will we
obtain them?

72 The incense,
with what will it
be substituted?

73 The eggs, with
what will they be
substituted?

74 Would they be
substituted, do
you suppose, with
betel nut? /A: At
the same time it
is not under the
jurisdiction of
the shaman./

75 At the same
time this death is
not under the
jurisdiction of
the shaman."

76 And so, we
allowed it ... like
that (the
situation) that
was given.

77 And so, that
is why the result
of today, it was
not begun (i.e.,
the death ritual),
that one, that
way ...'

this: there are no
elements for the
ritual.

Appendix C

78 Dadi, gondow koni, ... pada
   so   day   this   thus

minatong ma dini ... og
arrived (emp) here   (tdet)

gina'ama'   nilan koni,
mother-father   (3pnt) this

miksaksak ma   nog   bianbian
asking   (emp) (com) experience

koen ... nog   kobianbian ken
that   (rel) experience that

sinuksug u   dianon.
related (1snt) to-him

79 Ha?
   huh

80 Dadi, su'usa, sinumumba::g konia
   so   (pity) answered   this

gina'ama'   nilan konia koni ...
mother-father (3pnt) this this

og   bogolal   somo' ngon
(tdet) councilor (uc) (exl)

bogolal   dini, ... midunut ban
councilor here   follow (emp)

bogolal   langos. /B: M'm./
councilor mourn   (assent)

81 Hah?
   huh

82 Saka   bogolal   bosia ...
   at-same-time councilor (fru)

og   mongo'olobok nini. /A:
(tdet) responsible this

Mongingolog nog   botad koni./
take-charge (ntdet) custom this

83 Mongingolog nog   botad koni.
   take-charge (ntdet) custom this

84 Tibua minsan da'idun na
   but   even   none   now

bogolal, gondow koni, pagga
councilor day   this as-long-as

153

78 And so,
today, ... thus
arrived here
indeed ... these
parents of theirs,
asking about those
experiences ...
which experiences
I have related to
him ...

79 You see?

80 And so, (pity
marker), these
here, right here,
parents of theirs
answered (that)
the councilors, if
there were
councilors here,
(would have)
followed (the
custom) of the
mourning
councilors. /B:
Yes./

81 Right?

82 At the same
time the
councilors should
be the ones
responsible for
this. /A: The ones
in-charge of this
custom./

83 The ones
in-charge of this
custom.

84 However, even
though there are
no councilors,
today, as long as
you are now indeed

dinika   mo   na   loko le,
to-you(s) (emp) now   I-say friend

Ho' ponontong niu   botad ken.
hey! search-for (2pnt) custom that

/B: Ma' antu'./
    like that

85 Po'   akon bila loko
   because (1st) if I-say

botad,... da'idun lual bulung
custom   none   other medicine

nog   botad... og   botad
(ntdet) custom (tdet) custom

da. /B: Og   botad da./
(sta)   (tdet) custom (sta)

/Another: Ma' antu'. // B: Ma'
          like that   like

antu' ma./
that (emp)

86 Dadi, inuakil u   dianon...
   so   deliver (1snt) to-him

botang niu   dion... og
place (2pnt) there (tdet)

kosola'an ku,   bila ngon
fine   (1snt) if   (exl)

kotoksilan ku.
accusation (1snt)

87 Bila gulagis, botang niu
   if   guilty   place (2pnt)

dion, po'   ulogisoy niu   akon.
there because guilt   (2pnt) (1st)

/B: Mmmm./
    (assent)

88 Ma' nitu'.
   like that

89 Dadi, koni:... dinian ku   na
   so   this   here   (1snt) now

here friend..., I
say, you look for
that (proper)
custom. /B: It's
like that./

85 Because, as
for me, I say, as
for custom,...
there is no other
medicine for
custom...(except)
the custom itself.
/B: The custom
itself./ /Another:
It's like that./
/B: It's like
that!/

86 And so, I have
turned it over to
him...you place
there my fine, if
there is evidence
against me.

87 If there is
guilt, you place
it there because
you have
determined guilt.
/B: Yes./

88 It's like
that.

89 And so, as for
this... right here
now I will put a

Appendix C

potomanoy og   talu' u
limit   (tdet) talk (1snt)

po'   koin mingoktob na   dini
because that boundary now here

guksugan ku   diniu... /B: Bagun
story   (1snt) to-you(p)   so-that

ka   di' lumimbung nog   botad./
(2st) not deceive   (ntdet) custom

Agun   u   di' lumimbung nog
so-that (1st) not deceive   (ntdet)

botad sog glam nitu'. /B: Ma'
custom (loc) all that   like

antu'./
that

90 Sinuksug u   sog glam
   related   (1snt) (dir) all

niu,   gondow koni miglumpuk ma
(2pnt) day   this gathered (emp)

og   glam nog   mokogulang
(tdet) all (ntdet) elders

nami,   pigilugan nami   gondow
(1pntex) brothers (1pntex) day

koni, miglumpuk ma...
this gathered (emp)

91 Lilingliling   niu... gondow
   examine-closely (2pnt)   day

koni guksugan ku   diniu,   bog
this story   (1snt) to-you(p) if

glimbung u   ta'   diniu. /B:
deceive (1snt) (que) to-you(p)

Ma' antu'./
like that

Turn 4, Speaker D

1 Ati ma' nini...
  now like this

2 Motud da   binisara non.
  true (sta) speech (3snt)

limit to my speech
because this here
is the end of my
story to you.../B:
So that you will
not deceive the
custom./ so that I
will not deceive
the custom
regarding all of
that. /B: It's
like that./

90 I related it
to all of you
today, all our
kin, our elders
have met together
today, have indeed
met together...

91 You examine
closely... this my
story to you today
whether I have
deceived you. /B:
It's like that./

1 Now then, it's
like this:

2 What he has
said is true.

3 Olo og sabap non,
  what (tdet) reason (3snt)

inulogisan ku ilan ba'en
guilty (1snt) (3pt) result

sinungkud nilan...
pay-fine (3pnt)

4 Ion goli'anan ku moksak
  (3st) avoid (1snt) ask

lo' sog buloma'
(par) (dir) tomorrow

dinglag ain matong
day-after-tomorrow where arrive

nog gusbawaris... kosolag
(ntdet) relatives large

non bogolal, bog og ngon
(3snt) council (com) (tdet) (exl)

dalan non moguksug dianiran...
way (3snt) relate to-them

e'... dianilan, nog botad...
(hes) to-them (ntdet) custom

nog gininang nilan.
(rel) performed (3pnt)

5 Na po' ngon ponongowan
  now because (exl) look-for

niu dun duma: nog botad
(2pnt) (ana) other (rel) custom

ken... mokinongog u no sop
that listen (1st) now also

dianiu.
to-you(p)

6 Tibua, goktob midongog u
  but limit heard (1snt)

ma' nion.
like that

7 Po' akon gawoy u dini
  because (1st) purpose (1snt) here

kona' u moningkul.
not (1st) elbow-jab

3 What is the reason I found them guilty resulting in their paying a fine?

4 What I want to avoid, of a truth, is the relatives, more so the council, arriving and asking questions in the future (lit. tomorrow day-after-tomorrow), if there is a way to relate to them the custom which they have performed.

5 Now, if there is another way which you would look for, which is custom... I will also listen to you.

6 However, the extent of what I have heard is like that.

7 Because, as for me, my purpose here is not to disregard or go against custom.

Appendix C

8 Og   gawoy   bila da'
  (tdet) purpose if   not

pokotintu... dulu' og koniaya
make-reality (mis) (tdet) this-one

potintuon   dianilan. /B: Sumboy
make-reality to-them   must

potintuon./
make-reality

9 Bigya'   non   dalan non
  difference (3snt) way (3snt)

potintu...   sumboy sumboy botangan
make-reality must   must   place

ku   ilan. Ma' antu'.
(1snt) (3pt) like that

8 As for (my) purpose, if it is not made a reality (false start) this one I will make a reality to them. /B: It must be made a reality (to them)./

9 However, to make it a reality it must be that I fine them. It's like that.

Turn 5, Speaker B

1 Ati do   ma, D o', kotu' pa
  now (sta)(emp) D (par) that yet

og   talu' mu   bog miluksad
(tdet) speech (2snt) if finished

bu gonda'.
and not

1 Now then, D, excuse me, whether you are finished speaking or not.

2 Bila gilug   ta,   otawa
  if   brother (1pntin) or

mogulang ta,   goktob nog
elder   (1ptin) limit (ntdet)

bogoyon ta   dianon, og
give   (1pntin) to-him (tdet)

gomoy   sog baloy, sinandok.
cooked-rice (loc) house dished-out

/D: 'O'o./
    yes

2 If it is our brother, or our elder, the extent of what we will give to them is the cooked rice in the house, already dished out. /D: Right./

3 Bila og   botad, mologon
  if (tdet) custom difficult

nika   pogbolongon /D: Mologon
(2snt) forsake   difficult

ta   pogbolongon./
(1pntin) forsake

3 If it is the custom, it is difficult for you to forsake it. /D: It is difficult for us to forsake it./

4 Di' ompogbolong.
   not forsaken

5 Minsan bata' mu, ondi' nika
   even child (2snt) not (2snt)

ompogbogoy botad. /D: Ma' antu'./
give-away custom   like that

6 Dadi, koyon ma' nini ...
   so   that like this

paga   ma' antu' no ma,
as-long-as like that now (emp)

sogi ... kilala   u   nog
(mis) recognize (1st) (ntdet)

bitbitan koen, mipasad amu na?
speech that settled (2pt) now

/D: Mipasad na./
    settled now

7 Dadi, ah ... akon po ta'   ban
   so   (mis) (1st) yet (que) (emp)

di' ompasad ... ?
not settled

8 Ah: ika pa ma   gina'ama'.
   uh (2st) yet (emp) parents

9 Dadi, koen, ion pa og
   so   that (3st) yet (tdet)

tolu'on, mipasad ita   na.
say   settled (1ptin) now

Turn 6, speaker D

1 Mipasad ita   na.
   settled (1ptin) now

2 Bigya'   non   minsan ako:n ...
   difference (3snt) even   (1st)

akon mogulang bata' dianiu ...
(1st) elder   child to-you(p)

monginongogan   u   da ...
ask-for-information (1st) (sta)

4 It cannot be
forsaken.

5 Even your
child, you can not
give away custom
(i.e., each one
follows as he
wills). /D: It's
like that./

6 And so, that
one, it is like
this: as long as
it is like that
indeed, I
recognize from the
conversation, have
you reached
settlement now?
/D: Settlement has
been reached./

7 And so, (false
start) as for me,
mine is not yet
settled ... ?

8 Uh, you are
(polite) indeed
the parents (i.e.,
elder).

9 And so, as for
that, as it is
said, we have a
settlement now
(i.e., we are
finished now).

1 We have reached
settlement now.

2 Nevertheless,
even though I am
the elder among
you all ... I still
ask for
information.

Appendix C

3 /C: 'O   koni pa   potalu'
      yes this yet cause-to-speak

niu   pa   bosia mogulang pa
(2pnt) yet (fru) elder   yet

koni./
this

3 /C: Yes, this one here (polite), you cause this elder here to speak also./

4 Po'   sa'an   monginongogan
  because reason as-for-information

u...   di' u   do   sop   sunu'on
(1st) not (1st) (sta) also include

duma   u.
companion (1snt)

4 Because the reason I ask for information, I do not also falsely accuse my companion.

5 Diadia   og   talu'   non,
  everywhere (tdet) speech (3snt)

hah? ondi' u   do   sop
huh   not   (1st) (sta) also

malap...
get

5 His talk goes everywhere (not well presented), you know? I just do not understand it...

6 Tibua ngon   og   sinila'
  but   (exl) (tdet) complaint

nioyo, kioyo   ngon   do   sop,
there   that-one (exl) (sta) also

ba'   nika   dun,   kitu'
suppose (2snt) (ana) that

lidu'atoy   non.
bad-liver (3snt)

6 However, there are complaints over there, this one here, there is also, imagine!, that one there is very angry.

7 Huh! /A: Saka   sop   gusba
            at-same-time also kin

amu   doda'./
(2pt) indeed

7 You see! /A: At the same time you are indeed also kinsmen./

8 Saka   sop   gusma ma.
  at-same-time also kin   (emp)

8 At the same time (they are) also kinsmen!

9 Ondi' u   do   matas...
  not   (1st) (sta) endure

9 I could not endure it.'

10 Dadi, binisara u
   so   speech   (1snt)

10 And so, my accusations I couched in the

gotadan   ku   moguksug.
in-guise-of (1snt) relate

11 Bu bila o',   og   kitu'
   and if   (par) (tdet) that

dinakon... gustu   u   nog
to-me   pleasure (1snt) (com)

koposadan, hah?
settled   huh

12 Da'idun kuleke' ta.
   none   noise   (1pntin)

13 Na: po'   ngon pa kuleke'...
   now because (exl) yet noise

hah?... po'   tidu nitu' ngon
huh   because from that   (exl)

pa   og   dungagan, koin lo'
yet (tdet) added   that (par)

kopokan ku.
dislike (1snt)

14 Sa'an pinasad u,   sog
   reason settled (1snt) (loc)

kogobi   nog da' pa: poksudoy
last-night (rel) not yet   placed

glinubutan... po:k   u.
surrounding   dislike (1snt)

15 Pok   u   nog   ngon
   dislike (1snt) (ntdet) (exl)

poksiki'an.
quarrel

16 Na po'   gomon   sunoy   ondi'
   now because suddenly   not

u   tanan mampu', ma' lo'   nion
(1st) just mix   like (par) that

poduan ku. /C: 'O'o./
gall   (1snt) yes

17 Po'   ompok   u... nog
   because dislike (1snt) (com)

gobi   nog   molimatoy nog   gilug
night (att) ghost   (pos) brother

guise of relating
a story.

11 And if it is
up to me, I am
pleased with the
settlement, okay?

12 Let's not have
a lot of noise
about it.

13 Now, if there
is yet noise, you
see?... if from
that noise there
is added argument,
of a truth, that
is what I do not
like.

14 That's the
reason I settled
it, last night
when all seated
around were not
yet served (rice
wine)... I do not
like argument.

15 I do not like
that in which
there is
quarreling.

16 Now, if, of a
sudden I just do
not join in, of a
truth, that is the
reason for my
uncooperativeness.
/C: Okay./

17 Because I do
not like that this
being the night of
the ghost of my
brother, right?

Appendix C

u   ah?, nog kitu' sasow
(1snt) huh (rel) that turmoil

ta.
(1pntin)

18 Omba'is u   motinow motinow.
   good   (1snt) clear   clear

19 Da'idun samok. /B: Molonu'./
   none   bother   clean

20 Mmmm.
   (assent)

21 Da'idun moksusi.
   none   quarreling

22 Ma' lo' nion.
   like (par) that

is that which has us in turmoil.

18 I want clarity.

19 There is nothing to bother us. /B: It's clean./

20 Yes.

21 There is no quarreling.

22 It's really like that.

APPENDIX D

Confrontation event (see sec.#2.4.4) has been broken up into six ad hoc sections to facilitate presentation. They are 1) the council's decision, 2) the challenge, 3) the answer, 4) the argument, 5) the confrontation, and 6) the capitulation. The participants are the mother of the bride, the bride's uncle, the groom's father, the council representative of the bride's family (Council F), the council representative for the groom's family (Council M), and an elder (Elder). There are several germane comments from onlookers that have also been included.

1. The council decision not to annul the elopement.

Council F: Ma' ninia, ma' ninia,
          like this   like this

Im (= Council M): sa'an   o'
Im   reason (par)

da'idun mo   ita   poksusian
none   (emp) (1ptin) quarrel

ta   dun, ita   tidu sog
(1ptin) (ana) (1ptin) from (loc)

donsama', da'idun piksusian
before   none   quarrel

ta.
(1pntin)

Elder: (clears throat, sniffs)

It's like this,
it's like this,
Im: the reason, I
say, there is
nothing for us to
quarrel about is
because, as for
us, from long ago,
we have had no
quarrels.

Appendix D

Council F: Dadi gondow koni da'idun
        so   day   this   none

lual   en   towagon ta,
except (3st) called (1pntin)

og   guarisanan hen   moguna
(tdet) relatives   those go-ahead

ilan tolu'on nilan.
(3pt) speech (3pnt)

                              And so, today, there is none other that we shall call but the kin, they will proceed with what they have to say.

Elder: M'm.
      (assent)

                              Yes.

Council F: Dadi, po'   og...
        so   because (tdet)

guarisanan hen, sa'an ini
relatives   those reason this

towagon ta,   mokinongog ita
call   (1pntin) listen   (1ptin)

sop sog dua' ita.
also (dir) two (1ptin)

                              And so, (false start)... those kin, the reason now we'll call them, is so that we also will listen, the two of us.

Elder: Bog olo motalu' tolu'on
      if   what spoken speak

nilan.
(3pnt)

                              Whatever speech they will make.

Council F: Bog olo motalu' tolu'on
        if   what spoken speak

nilan.
(3pnt)

                              Whatever speech they will make.

Elder: Ma' antu' ma.
     like that (emp)

                              That's the way it is.

Council M: Na koen ma' nion ilan.
            now that like that (3pt)

Şogadan   bisala u   koni
as-expected speech (1snt) this

numun koni, po'   kona' nika
now this because not (2snt)

misala' dun, akon.
litigated (ana) (1st)

                              Now then, they are like that. As is expected, my defense is right now. It isn't you who is being litigated, it is I.

Elder: M'm.
      (assent)

                              Yes.

Council M: Po'   akon lo'
          because (1st) (par)

glaki.
male

Council F: 'O.
           yes.

Council M: Dadi, bila akon
           so   if   (1st)

glaki, ... ma' nion ma
male   like that (emp)

kohinangan nog gombata'anan koen,
deeds   (pos) children   those

ompok u   nog   ombutas.
dislike (1snt) (com) annul

Council F: Mmmm.
           (assent)

Council M: Koen poglogdong u
           that straight   (1snt)

dianika.   Ompok u   nog
to-you(s) dislike (1snt) (ntdet)

ombutas, basta   sog   botad.
annul   as-long-as (loc) custom

Onlooker: Sa'an   en   ma' nion
          reason (3st) like that

po'   botad.
because custom

Elder: 'O (chuckle).
       yes

Council M: Dadi bila ompok u
           so   if   dislike (1snt)

ma   ombutas motud da   gonika
(emp) annul   true (sta) yours

koen monaluy ita   no'   ogog...
that buy   (1ptin) (par) (hes)

og   sosuku gusba.
(tdet) every relative

Council F: 'O'o ma.
           yes (emp)

Because I am, in
truth, the male's
representative.

Yes.

And so, if I am
the male, ... the
deeds of those
children are
indeed like that,
I do not want that
they be annulled.

Yes.

That I will make
straight to you. I
do not want that
they be annulled,
as long as it's
according to
custom.

The reason for
the present
situation is
because of custom
(i.e., human nature
= a pun).

Yes (chuckle).

And so, if I do
not want that they
be annulled, what
you say is true,
let's buy (i.e.,
bring around to
our way of
thinking) the uh,
... all of the
kin.

Yes, indeed.

Appendix D

Council M: Na   dion. Si   In (=
         now there (tper) In

mother), ain   ma?   Si   In?
        where (emp) (tper) In

Now then: In, where is she!? Where is In?

Elder: Koyon
       there

There.

Council M: In, olo   ma' nion?
              In what like that

In, what do you say about the situation?

Council F: Po'   akon si'oy.
          because   (1st) also

Because I also am of the same mind.

Council M: Takun.
           let's-it

Let's have it.

Council F: Eh! di' le   kumboy
          well now friend allow

le   ombutas le.
friend annul   friend

Eh! They are not allowed to be annulled, friend.

Elder: 'O   ma.
       yes (emp)

Yes, indeed.

Council M: Olo   ma   glapal
          what (emp) argument

mu?
(2snt)

What is your argument?

Elder: Da'idun moleg momutas.
       none   desire annul

None of the council wants to annul.

Council F: Da'idun mini
          none   (emp)here

momutas le.
annul   friend

None here will annul, friend.

Council M: Ain   ma   si   Om
          where (emp) (tper) Om

(= bride's step-father)? Di' ita
                         not (1ptin)

tibua kosunan nog   ita   di'
just   know   (com) (1ptin) not

ita   momutas. Dadi, ilan koen,
(1ptin) annul   so   (3pt) that

Where indeed is Om? We just don't know that as for us we will not annul. And so, as for them, we don't know how they feel.

di' ta kosunan.
not (1ptin) know

Elder: 'O ma. Ma' antu' ma. yes (emp) like that (emp)	Yes, indeed. It's like that.

2. The challenge of the decision.

In this section, the mother's reaction was anticipated. She did not like the decision to proceed with the marriage. She wanted to "dig out" or "get all the details" (**lungkal**). (She used the word with dual meaning). She raised two questions of propriety. The first was that she felt she was not properly informed about her daughter's eloping. The second was a question regarding the price calculation.

Mother: Akon solabuk do ini (1st) one (sta) this da ko'anan ku koni. Koni da' (sta) thing (1snt) this this not u ini akon kosu'atoy sogaga (1st) here (1st) satisfied rather ma' nini si'oy... like this also	As for me, just one thing is my thing here. As for this, I just am not pleased; instead, even though it's like this...
Council F: 'O ma. yes (emp)	Yes, indeed.
Mother: Moglaglag le sog garbled friend (loc) ginongogan ku, le. Dongogan hearing (1snt) friend news ditu' nami. Dadi, koni takun there (1pntex) so this let's-it numun kotu' lumungkal u. now that pry-out (1st)	It is garbled in my hearing, ... friend. It was newsed there where we live (i.e., not explicitly stated regarding the elopement). And so, now, let's have it right now. I am asking for the details.
Elder: Ti' koni mini ha this (emp)here piglungkal ta... pried-out (1pntin)	What do you mean? Right now we are giving the details.
Onlooker: Konia ba! this-one (emp)	This one (i.e., the array of corn kernels).
Mother: Akon di' u ma (1st) not (1st) (emp)	As for me, that's not what I'm digging out. I'm

Appendix D

```
        lumungkal nion. Lungkalon ku          digging out my
        pry-out    that  pry-out    (1snt)    child. I will
                                              bring her away
        bata' u.    Oiton ku...               with me (i.e., try
        child (1snt) bring (1snt)             to annul the
                                              marriage).

Elder:  Eh!                                   Eh! (= what do you
        eh                                    want to do that
                                              for?)

Council F: Di::'  In (=mother),  ma'          Nooo, In, it's
           no     In             like         like this:

        ninia.
        this

Mother: po'      moglaglag                    Because it is
        because  garbled                      garbled in my
                                              hearing there.
        ginongogan ku     ditu'.
        hearing    (1snt) there

Elder:  Olo  moglaglag koni?                  What is this that
        what garbled   this                   is garbled?

Council F: Ogog...  og     bota:d...          Uh,... the
           (tdet)   (tdet) custom             custom...

Mother: Moglaplap                             It is unclear.
        unclear

Council F: gondow koni...                     today...
           day    this

Mother: Guksugan akon tiba                    Just relate to
        story    (1st) just                   me, I ask to be
                                              related to. Why am
        monginongogan.     Iduma akon         I considered as
        request-information why  (1st)        the male kin?

        pigbata' sog   glaki?
        kin      (loc) male

Council F: In, og     botad, bila             In, the custom,
           In  (tdet) custom if               if it's like
                                              today,... these
        gondow da    koni, koni na            are the details
        day    (sta) this  this  now          (i.e., what is
                                              shown in the corn
        poglungkal.                           kernel
        pried-out                             arrangement).

Council M: M'm.     Di'  na  en               Yes. It cannot be
           (assent) not  now (3st)            included in the
                                              fine.
```

ombotang.
place

| Mother: Ain | ban | en | botangoy | Where is that |
| where | (emp) | (3st) | place | fine of the male? |

sog glaki?
(loc) male

Uncle: Komun pa da' nilan ma   Since from
earlier yet not (3pnt) (emp)   earlier on they
                                      have not included
botangoy kolegan mu.   what you wanted.
place   desire   (2snt)

3. The answers of the council.

In this section the question raised by the mother were answered. The answers to the questions are in the reverse order from the order in which the questions were given by the mother. (See sec.#5.3.2 for other chiastic structures in Subanon.)

Council M: Ati o'   In (=mother),   Now then, you
          now (par) In   hear, In, the
                                              answer:... if that
tabalan:... bila binotang ma   one over there
answer   if   placed   (emp)   (one array of
                                              kernels) is
kioyo binotang mu na   kitu. Da'   included, that one
there placed   (2snt) now that not   now has your
                                              desire included.
a   ma,   da' a   ma   You have not, you
(2st) (emp) not (2st) (emp)   have not been
                                              fined for
pokolual.   Ion   non   lo'   displeasure. That
displeasure-fine (3st) (3snt) (par)   is the way it
                                              is,... And so, as
en   na... Dadi, konia di' nika   for this one here
(3st) now   so   this not (2snt)   (the other array
                                              of kernels), even
si' botangan dioyo na. Nion.   if your desire is
also placed   there now there   not included, it
                                              is already there
Bigya'   non gonika tolu   in the other one.
difference (3snt) yours three   It's like that.
                                              The difference is
pulu'. Ginakon sopulu' bu lima.   that what is yours
ten   mine   one-ten and five   is thirty **pesita**
                                              (**pesita** = 20
                                              centavos). Mine is
                                              fifteen **pesita**.

Onlooker: Da'idun gobokan ni   In has no
          none   recourse (ntper)   recourse. What
                                              indeed is your
In. Olo ban   gobokan nika   recourse when your
In what (emp) recourse (2snt)   child has decided

Appendix D

migbaya' na bata' mu?!
decided now child (2snt)

Council M: Na koen sop miglaglag,
now that also garbled

sulat nika minatong dini...
letter (2snt) arrived here

Mother: Akon tiba sulat u
(1st) just letter (1snt)

minatong. Amu, da'idun tanan
arrived (2pt) none just

guksugan niu dianakon ma' ninia
story (2pnt) to-me like this

ma' ninia.
like this

Council M: Sa'an en ngon
reason (3st) (exl)

sulat ditu' nika sabap non
letter there (2snt) reason (3snt)

gonat dini. Ma' nitu'. Da'idun
originate here like that none

sulat gomon sunoy nog kona'
letter of-a-sudden (rel) not

gonat sog gino'...
originate (loc) (hes)

ginolaolan.
of-an-action

Elder: M'm.
(assent)

Mother: Da'idun bu kotu' tanan.
none and that just

Elder: Dangku na tanan po'
disregard now just because

akon o' somo' en, somo' en
(1st) (par) (uc) (3st) (uc) (3st)

o' minangoy amu dini nakon
(par) came (2pt) here-to-me

moglandan,... ma 'o'o na botad
immediately (emp) yes now custom

already?

Now also, as for that confusion, your letter arrived here.

As for me only, my letter arrived. As for you all, there was just none of your story to me relating, "It's like this, it's like this."

The reason why there was a letter that arrived to you there is because it left from here. It's like that. There is no letter of a sudden which is not from the result of an action (i.e., from the house of and written by the elder).

Yes.

There is none if that one was it.

Never mind about that because, as for me, you hear, if it had been, if it had been, I say, from the first that yet it was spoken to me that uh, ... that, I say, ... you had come to my house

ken po'   ngon doda' botad
that because (exl) indeed custom

ken ma' nitu'. Tiba da' do
that like that but not (sta)

ban   doksu' numun. Da' doma.
(emp) finish present not (sta-emp)

Ugat   nika po ma   botangoy
only-now (2snt) yet (emp) place

numun kotu' saka koni no   mini
present that yet this now (emp)

mibotang.
here-placed

Council M: Binotang no   men   na.
           placed   now (emp)it now

Bila ko'   kolual   mu
if   (hes) displeasure-fine (2snt)

da   binotang na po'   da'
(sta) placed   now because not

a   dini.
(2st) here

Elder: Mmm.
       (assent)

Council M: Bigya'   non
           difference   (3snt)

binotang mu   tolu pulu' numun
placed   (2snt) three ten present

kotu'; binotang koni sopulu' bu
that   placed   this one-ten and

lima.
five

Elder: Mm.
       (assent)

Council M: Somo' tanan en   ma'
           (uc) just (3st) like

nog   duma di' lo'   tanan en
(ntdet) other not (par) just (3st)

botangon nog   gikam.
place   (ntdet) mat

here immediately, ... custom would be favored because there is indeed a custom like that. However, it has not been realized to this time. It has not. You have just now asked that the fine be included yet, at the same time, it is already included.

It has indeed already been included. If it is your displeasure fine, it is already included because you were not here.

Yes.

The difference is that your inclusion is right now thirty **pesita**; this inclusion here is fifteen **pesita**.

Yes.

Indeed, if it were like other cases it would not, of a truth, indeed, be included on the mat (i.e., considered at all).

Appendix D

Elder: Di' ma. Indeed not.
    not (emp)

4. The argument.
In this section the mother's strategy or ploy was to implicate the male's father in an unsettled fault. He allegedly challenged her to a fight which in Subanon custom is the sort of action that often is settled through litigation. However, the councilors began to reason with her again, continuing their patronizing tone, (e.g., they called her by a term generally used for a youngster, **nu'**).

Mother: Na, buka'oy mu pa
    now open-up (2snt) yet

ami diti'oyo. Inonggat ami
(1ptex) over-there invited (1ptex)

le ni D (= groom's father)
friend (ntper) D

le moksuntuk le. Na numun
friend box friend now present

kotu' akon gonggaton... akon
that (1st) invite (1st)

monggat dianon moksuntuk dianon.
invite to-him box to-him

Monog ami diti'o sog
go-down (1ptex) there (loc)

glupa'.
ground

    Now, you (polite) open us up a case (against someone) over there. We were invited, friend, by D to fist fight. Now, right now I am the one invited (mistake)... I am the one inviting him to fist fight. We will go down to the ground over there.

Council M: Di'. No.
    no

Elder: (laughing) Ah, poksuntukan
    Uh boxing-match

kini... kini poksuntukan. Koen
this this boxing-match that

lo' en na.
(par) (3st) now

    (laughing) Uh, the boxing match here... this is the boxing match (the array of corn kernels indicating the price and fines). That is what it is, friend.

Mother: Dadi, diti'a ami sog
    so there (1ptex) (loc)

glupa'. Di' ami dini sog
ground not (1ptex) here (loc)

    And so, we will be there on the ground. We will not fight up here in the house of uncle T.

baloy ni bamba T (= the elder)
house (ntper) uncle T

poksuntuk.
box

Council M: Na di' ma. Kini men
now not (emp) this (emp)

piksuntukan hen. Dadi, loko nu',
boxing-match that so I-say nu'

soupaya da di' moksuntuk koyon
so-that (sta) not box that

na.
now

Now, indeed, no!
This is the boxing
match here (array
of kernels). And
so, **nu'**, that's
there so there
will be no fist
fighting.

Elder: Ati, kolabung inonggat
now yesterday invited

a moksuntuk?
(2st) box

Now, yesterday
you were invited
to fist fight?

Mother: Di' non akon mo'an
not (3snt) (1st) thing

non...
(3snt)

He did not thing
me...

Elder: Mo'ana nog ginonggat
meaning (ntdet) invitation

a kotu' moksuntuk ion non
(2st) that box (3st) (3snt)

lo' ini da. Tontong niu
(par) this (sta) look (2pnt)

ini: kona' do ma moksuntuk
here not (sta) (emp) box

kodoksu'an non.
result (3snt)

The meaning of
that invitation of
yours to fist
fight, this is it
in truth, indeed
(the kernel
array). You all
look here; the
finish of this is
not a fist fight
but an amicable
negotiation.

Mother: (crying) Dadi, numun
so present

kotu' ditu' ami sog glupa'.
now there (1ptex) (loc) ground

(crying) And so,
right now, there
we will go to the
ground to fight.

Council F: Mioleg do ban
desired (sta) (emp)

bata' mu.
child (2snt)

This elopement is
the will of your
child!

Appendix D

The councilor for the male wanted to get to the bottom of the accusation. In confronting the father he used abrupt language. It put the father on the spot. The father's first reaction was to be noncommittal but then he denied the accusation. The elder, through the use of a figure, brought attention to the abruptness of Council M's question to the father. On the basis of the father's denial the councilors judged that the mother was not faulted.

Council M: Dangku   na. Ika,
      never-mind now (2st)

inonggat nika to' ban
invited (2snt) (que) (emp)

moksuntuk si   Lu (=friendship
box   (tper) Lu

name: bride's step-father)?

Never mind. You, did you invite Lu to fist fight?

Father: Da' u   sunoy. Da'
      not (1snt) know not

u.
(1snt)

I don't know. I did not.

Elder: (laughing) 'O   molok...
      (par) (hes)

molokas ma   gbolangoy mu   koen
fast   (emp) canoe   (2snt) that

le (laughing).
friend

(laughing) Wow! (false start) ...your canoe sure travels fast, friend, (laughing).

Mother: Bigya'   non akon,
      difference (3snt) (1st)

dini kitu' inuklakan   non
here that taken-advantage (3snt)

akon nog   botad, asta numun
(1st) (ntdet) custom until present

kotu' inuklakan   non akon
that taken-advantage (3snt) (1st)

nog   botad.
(ntdet) custom

The difference is, as for me, that, at an earlier date he took advantage of me in terms of the custom, even right now he has taken advantage of me in terms of the custom.

Council M: Da' a
      not (2st)

uklakoy.
taken-advantage

You have not been taken advantage of.

5. The confrontation between the bride's mother and the groom's father.

This section begins with an overt verbal insult made by the mother to the council. It is possibly triggered by Council M's last statement above. This begins the repartee between the mother of the bride and the father of the groom. The elopement **bisala** was sidetracked for a time and the whole proceedings seemed to leave the immediate control of the councilors.

The father asked the mother what his fault was. She answered that her second husband was challenged by him (the father) to a fist fight. The council knew now that it was not she after all who was threatened. The father answered that he was simply advising her second husband not to despise her because her second husband had not been aware that she was already married and yet she consented to live with him. The father related this in an attempt to answer the mother's accusation. It had no positive effect on her so he repeated his account but in "harder" speech.

Mother: Misinsala' bogolal. Gloput
        wasted   council liar

nog   bogolal.
(ntdet) council

You councilors
are ineffectual.
You councilors are
liars.

Council F: Og   gotow...
        (tdet) person

A person...

Father: Olo guklak   u
       what take-advantage (1snt)

dinika   nog   botad? Suksugoy
to-you(s) (ntdet) custom relate

nika   dow dinakon.
(2snt) (hs) to-me

With what custom
have I taken
advantage of you?
Please tell me'

Mother: Diti'oyo   ni   lo'   M.
       over-there (ntper) (par) M

Inonggat nika   akon monog
invited (2snt) (1st) go-down

moksuntuk si   Om.
box   (tper) Om

Over there at M's
house. You invited
me, that is Om (=
her second
husband) to go
down to fist
fight.

Council M: Te', kona' ba   ika.
        well   not (emp) (2st)

What do you mean!
It wasn't you
after all!

Father: Na ma' ninia: Pokinongog
      now like this   listen

a. Akon mogustal dinika.
   (2st) (1st)   explain to-you(s)

Now it's like
this: You listen!
I will explain it
to you.

Mother: Na' a   mogogan dun.
      not (2st) thing   (ana)

Don't you make
excuses.

Appendix D

Father: Sunan nika og tabang
       know (2snt) (tdet) help
pa dinika.
yet to-you(s)

    You know help that comes to you.

Mother: Ta:bang mu!
        help (2snt)

    What do you mean "your help"?!

Father: Kona' u migonggat
       not (1st) invite
miksuntuk po' si Om
box   because (tper) Om
(= mother's second husband), bila
                                if
moktalu' koyon nog ika, tobia'
say   that (com) (2st) excuse
dianika, kimud non dinika,
to-you(s) pick-up (3snt) to-you(s)
da' glaki mu. Da' poktulik nog
not male (2snt) not think (com)
ika togolaki a. Saka bila
(2st) have-male (2st) yet if
bogolal da koni miktalu', ika
council (sta) this said (2st)
togolaki a si Do (= first
have-male (2st) (tper) Do
husband). Ma' nitu'.
            like that

    I did not challenge to fist fight because as for Om, he was saying that, as for you, please excuse me, when he picked you up to live with you, you had no husband. He did not consider that as for you, you had a husband. On the other hand, if these councilors had spoken, as for you, you have a husband, namely Do. It's like that.

Mother: Dadi ma' nitu'?
        so   like that

    And so, it's like that?

Father: Ma' nitu' glam ta
       like that all (1pntin)
koni mikodongog dun.
this heard (ana)

    It's like that; all of us here have heard about it.

Mother: Monog ita sog
        go-down (1ptin) (loc)
glupa'.
ground

    Let's go down to the ground and fight.

Elder: Mm.
      (assent)

    Yes.

Father: Dadi, miktalu' u, o'
       so   said   (1st) (par)

"Akon", long "di' u   o'
(1st)   say not (1st) (par)

uh..."
(hes)

Mother: Numun kotu' akon piganan
        present that (1st) thing

nika   akon nog   botad.
(2snt) (1st) (ntdet) custom

Father: Pokinongog a   bagun
        listen   (2st) so-that

nika   modongog talu' u.
(2snt) hear   words (1snt)

"Dadi," long, "bila ma' antu',"
 so   say   if   like that

ma' long non   dun, "Akon,"
like say (3snt) (ana) (1st)

long, "og   glibun ku   koen
say   (tdet) female (1snt) that

mogilu'. 'O. Og   ngon og
deceive yes (tdet) (exl) (tdet)

glaki non.   Muli'   hog   glaki
male (3snt) go-home   (loc) male

non."   "Loko le,... na' a
(3snt)   I-say friend not (2st)

moginang nog   mama' nion,
do   (ntdet) like that

po'   bila bolu'an   goiton
because if   aggression bring

mu   di' omba'is." Da' u
(2snt) not good   not (1snt)

en   pogonggat moksuntuk dun.
(3st) invite   box   (ana)

Lipas tinalu' u,   "Bila bolu'an
rather said   (1snt) if   anger

goiton mu   dini, di' ompia."
bring (2snt) here not good

And so, I said, you hear, "As for me," I said, "I do not, uh..."

Right now, as for me, you are taking advantage of me through the custom.

You listen so that you can hear what I say. "And so," he said, "if it is like that," thus he said, "as for me," he said, "that woman of mine is deceitful. Yes. She has a husband. She can return to her husband." "I say friend, don't you act like that, because if you carry your anger it isn't good." I did not by this invite him to fist fight. Rather, I said, "If you bring anger here, it is not good."

Appendix D

Mother: Minonsing a   nog
         deny   (2st) (com)

inoit   nika   monog.
brought   (2snt) go-down

You deny that you brought him down to the ground to fight.

Elder: Mm'm
       (assent)

Yes.

Father: Da' le   poksak talu'
        not friend ask   say

dun   le   po'   koni   da
(ana) friend because this (sta)

og   taksi'   u   dun   ditu'.
(tdet) witness (1snt) (ana) there

There was nothing asked or said about it, friend, because this one here is my witness to it there.

Mother: Da'idun taksi'   taksi'
        none   witness witness

dun.
(ana)

There is no witness, witness to it.

Father: Omba'is moktalu' a.   Na'
        good   speak   (2st) not

amu   ba   imungon po'
(2snt) (emp) make-up because

akon...
(1st)

It would be good if you spoke straight! Don't you be making up stories because, as for me...

Mother: Da' gimungan dun.
        not made-up (ana)

There is no made up story.

Father: Soukat   nog   bata'
        even-though (ntdet) child

u   glaki, long niu   dun,
(1snt) male   say (2pnt) (ana)

akon o'   landu' na   pogamu'
(1st) (par) (int) now   respect

u   ain   da   og   botad.
(1snt) where (sta) (tdet) custom

Even though (=exasperation) my child is the male, as you all say, as for me, you hear, I have very great respect for whatever is custom.

Mother: Da' ita   hambug.
        not (1ptin) brag

We'll have no boasting.

Father: Po'   ken   nog   da'
        because that (rel) not

u   kohinang, da' u
(1snt)   do   not (1snt)

Because that which I have not done I have not said that I did do it; at the same time, it has been

poktalu' dun, saka poktolu'on
say   (ana) yet spoken

dinakon. Da' u   mini
to-me   not (1snt) (emp)this

sonsingoy og   talu' u
deny   (tdet) word (1snt)

mini.   Ma' nitu'. Dadi, olo
(emp)here like that so   what

mo   ban   talu' u   koen?
(emp) (emp) word (1snt) that

Kona' u   sugut   dinika.
not (1snt) take-side to-you(s)

Ika, inoit   a   ni   o',
(2st) brought (2st) (ntper) (par)

long ni   Om dun, ah... kimud
say (ntper) Om (ana) (hes) pick-up

non   dinika,... balu'   non
(3snt) to-you(s) thought (3snt)

da'idun glaki mu   po'
none   male (2snt) because

migbolongbolong amu buan po'
separated   (2pt) (emp) because

si   Do ki:tu' sogog...
(tper) Do that (loc)

Mother: Bulakan.
        Bulakan

Father: Bulakan. Ika   dioyoan
        Bulakan (2st) there

ka.   Ma' nitu' og   sabap
(2st) like that (tdet) reason

nion.
(that)

Mother: Bila og   bogolal koni
        if (tdet) council this

ngon og   glolat non.
(exl) (tdet) pity (3snt)

Father: Kitu'. Dadi, olo mo
        that   so   what (emp)

said about me that
I did do it. I am
not indeed here
denying what I
said. It's like
that. And so, what
indeed was what I
said? I am not
taking up your
cause. As for you,
you were uh . . .
picked up by . . . Om
said that, ah . . .
when he picked you
up, he thought
mistakenly that
you had no husband
because you both
indeed were
estranged because
Do was in uh . . .

Bulakan (place
name).

Bulakan. As for
you, you were away
over there
(opposite
direction). That's
the reason for
it.

If it is this
council, surely
they have pity.

That's right.
What else would it
be, uh . . .

Appendix D

buan   dun   ogog...
(emp) (ana) (tdet)

Mother: Tibua, ika   solabuk gan   However, your
         but (2st) one   thing   thing is
                                              another...

nika   mo...
(2snt) (hes)

Father: Onda', da' u   ma   I have not. I
         not   not (1snt) (emp)   have not
                                         discriminated
ika   dopigoy.   against you.
(2st) discriminate

Mother: Dapigdapig a.   You continually
          disriminate (2st)   discriminate.

Father: Tibua, olo   ma   og   However, what am
        but   what (emp) (tdet)   I going to do
                                         about it?!
dun   ku   dun?
(ana) (1snt) (ana)

6. The capitulation of the bride's mother.
    In this final section the councilors took control again and brought the talk back to the subject at hand, the elopement. Council M gave answer to the mother that her bringing up her affair with Om was inappropriate. (It was, in fact, the father who made the story explicit not the mother). The council did not wish to pursue the question raised by her because it would involve the discussion of another case (her second marriage) which had already been settled and would not be profitable. The mother's final act was to attempt, in frustration, to scatter the array of corn kernels on the mat close at hand.

Council F: Na'   amu na   mogan   Don't you all
          don't (2pt) now thing   thing it; instead
                                          this one...

en;   sogaga non   koni...
(3st) rather (3snt) this

Father: Botad ken motud mitu'   That custom, that
        custom that true   (emp)that is a true saying.

nog   talu'.
(rel) word

Elder: Mm.   Konia. Sungu'   Yes. This one.
      (assent) this   face   Let's face this
                                       one here (= the
ta   konia koni.   custom regarding
(1ptin) this   this   the settling of
                                     fines).

Council F: 'O'o. Konia.   Yes. This one.
           yes   this-one

Elder: Doksu' na   en   na.
       finish now (3st) now

That one (discussion) is finished now.

Council M: Koyon ah... loko In,
           that   ah   I-say In

That one, uh... I say, In, it's like this...

ma' ninia...
like this

Father: (aside) Poktolu'on buan
                spoken   (emp)

dinakon saka da'   u   tanan
to-me   yet   not   (1snt) just

pogonggat dinilan   moksuntuk. Lipas
invite   to-them   box   rather

ma' ninia mitalu' u,   "Akon,
like this said   (1snt) (1st)

bila bolu'an goiton..."
if   anger   bring

That was said about me but, at the same time, I just did not invite them to fist fight. But what I said was like this, "As for me, if anger is brought..."

Council M: Kini tabal   koen dia
           this answer that to

ni   D(= groom's father), ah...
(ntper) D   ah

na'   a   tumabal nog   ginika
don't (2st) answer (ntdet) yours

pa'ali   sog   gianiu   ni
concern (loc) yours(p) (ntper)

Om... bianbian niu   ombolong.
Om   happen   (2pnt) estrange

Na'   niu   na   sohobiton. Po'
don't (2pnt) now   relate   because

bila sohobiton niu   numun   kotu'
if   relate   (2pnt) present that

modakol magi.
many   gossip

As for this answer here to D, ... uh, ... don't you answer yourself regarding you and Om... your experiences in becoming estranged. Don't you now speak of it. Because, if you speak of it right now, there will be lots of gossip/discussion.

Father: Dungag   bila tolu'on
        increase if   speak

ku   inonggat non   akon
(1snt) invite (3snt) (1st)

monog.
go-down

There will be more so if I say/accuse that he invited me down to the ground to fight.

Appendix D

Council M: Modakol magi nion.
           many gossip that

Dadi, muli'muli' ngon lo' en
so   return-home (exl) (par) (3st)

kologonan dun.
difficulty (ana)

There will be lots of gossip from it. And so, to keep coming back, there is a difficulty about it.

Elder: Olo po dun.
      what yet (ana)

That's right.

Council M: Ngon kologonan nion.
           (exl) difficulty that

Po' sa'an ngon kologonan
because reason (exl) difficulty

nion, bu bila gonsunoy
that and if suddenly

...ponontongon numun kotu' og
look-for   present that (tdet)

golota' nog misunggud non
hardware (rel) paid   (3snt)

dinika   kologo'... ngon
to-you(s) (mis)   (exl)

kologonan dun.
difficulty (ana)

There is a difficulty there. The reason there is a difficulty there, because if, of a sudden, right now we look for the hardware of the bride price paid to you (false start)... there is a difficulty about it.

Mother: Iduma kologonan ma
       why   difficulty (emp)

dun?
(ana)

Why is it difficult?

Council M: Keen! Sa'an ini na'
           that reason this don't

mu   nion nog ion...
(2snt) that (rel) (3st)

Right there, the array of kernels! That's why you must not do that which...

Elder: Ma' nion ken potiang
      like that that disregard

mu   na.
(2snt) now

That sort of thing you never mind now.

Council M: Mangga' ita   nion.
           hinder (1ptin) that

Polokas mu na po'   koen
speed-up (2snt) now because that

We will waste time in it. Never mind it. Because that one, I heard about its

midongog u   da   og
heard   (1snt) (sta) (tdet)

koposadan nion. Mipasad na. Dadi,
settlement that settled now so

numun kotu' di' na ukadon
present that not now unwrap

boya'an su'usa monginloput.
result   (pity) lie

Monginloput a   na   nog
lie   (2st) now (ntdet)

bogolal. Sogaga, ma' ninia In,
council instead like this In

poktolu'on ku   koni, bila og
speech   (1nst) this if (tdet)

botang mu   da   konia,
place (2snt) (sta) this

kolabung nog kopokposabut
yesterday (rel) informed

dinika,   da' a   dini. Tibua,
to-you(s) not (2st) here but

inapa'   ni   T (= Elder) kitu'
ambushed   (ntper) T   that

da.   Kumolual   a   po'
(sta) displeasure (2st) because

kitu' sabap non. Hen. Ken
that reason (3snt) that that

sabap non.   Dadi, kini, bila
reason (3snt) so   this if

moleg amu nog   dan nog
desire (2pt) (ntdet) old (ntdet)

bolosi'an,   ion non   ini.
calculation (3st) (3snt) this

Elder: Gapus   mu!
       restrain (2snt)

Council M: Bila ompok   amu
           if   dislike (2pt)

settlement. It is
settled. And so,
right now don't
open it up, which
would result in
(pity) the telling
of lies. You have
already told lies
to the council.
Instead, it's like
this In, what I'm
saying here, as
for the inclusion
of your desired
fine here,
previously when
you were to be
informed, you were
not there.
However, you were
there when T
caught you at
home. You are paid
the fine of
displeasure
because of that
fact. There.
That's the reason.
And so, as for
this one, if you
all wish the old
way of counting
kernels, that is
the way this array
is counted here.

Restrain (her
from scattering
the arrays of
kernels)!'

If you all do not
want the uh . . .
because you all

Appendix D

no:g...	po'	kolegan	niu	bogu	want the new way
(ntdet)	because	desire	(2pnt)	new	of counting kernels, this is
bolosi'an,	kini.	Sogatus		bu	the one. One
calculation	this	one-hundred		and	hundred and twenty pesos.
dua'	pulu'. (CA022)				
two	ten				

The mother left the center of the proceedings and the **bisala** continued. This confrontation illustrates the strong influence of precedent on decision making. The interchange clearly shows interaction between male and female and their ploys and strategies in argument.

Appendix E

This is a polite request for a person to finish his speech. The councilor, Do, is making the request. The litigation overseer is Bu. This comes from an elopement **bisala**.

1) Ati, og guakil nika kotu'
now (tdet) delivery (2snt) that

motud mitu' nog guakil.
true that (ntdet) delivery

2) Tibua, na' a muba' nog tolu'on mu
but don't (2st) shame (com) say (2snt)

bog ika midoksu' na
(com) (2st) finish now

po' motud midoksu'.
because true finish

3) Tibua, da' nika kosuksugoy bianbian nog
but not (2snt) relate experience (rel)

gombata' midopot dini nika.
children arrived here (2snt)

4) Ion misuksug nika inuakil mu
(3st) related (2snt) deliver (2snt)

paga minatong na og bogolal
as-long-as arrived now (tdet) council

Appendix E

(somo' ngon bogolal)
(uc)   (exl) council

ngalan non   kotu' posadon na.
name (3snt) that settle   now

5) Dadi, sumboy lo' en   tolipunan mu   ditu'...
   so   must (par) (3st) begin   (2snt) there

bog   olo   ondowoy dun...
(com) what) day   (ana)

/Bu: Kibianbian non./
     experience (3snt)

...kodatong non dini;
   arrival (3snt) here

bog   olo: og   bobolapa   non.
(com) what (tdet) experience (3snt)

6) Ma' nitu'.
   like that

7) Dadi,...na' a   sop muba' dun   le.
   so   not (2st) also shame (ana) friend

8) Sumboy itu' kobolikan mu   og   guksugan kitu'
   must   that return (2snt) (tdet) story   that

po'   sumboy ma   ditu' tolipunoy...
because must   (emp) there begin

1) Now, that act of yours of handling over the proceedings, it was a true handing over of the proceedings.

2) However, don't take offense that you say that you that you are finished speaking now; it is true that it is finished.

3) However, you did not relate the experience which was how the children reached your place here.

4) What you related was that you handed it over after the council has now arrived, (if there is a council) which means it is ready to settle.

5) And so, you must begin there... on what day.../Bu: It happened./... did they arrive here; and what transpired?

6) It's like that.

7) And so, don't you take offense, friend.

8) It must be that you repeat your story because it must be that there is where it should begin.

Summary of the request:

Sentence 1. A positive statement is made by the councilor.

Sentence 2. An appeal is made that no offense be taken.

Sentence 3. **Do** defines the omitted part of the narrative.

Sentence 4. He reiterates what the speaker did narrate.

Sentence 5. He asks for specific points.

Sentence 6. **Do** concludes his request.

Sentence 7. He reiterates his appeal that no offense be taken and includes the term **le** 'friend'.

Sentence 8. He reiterates his request again using the term **sumboy** 'must' indicating necessity for compliance.

References

Austin, J. L. 1962. How to do things with words. London: Oxford University Press.

Blom, Jan-Petter and John J. Gumperz. 1972. Social meaning in linguistic structures: Code-switching in Norway. *In* Directions in sociolinguistics: the ethnography of communication, ed by John J. Gumperz and Dell Hymes. New York: Holt, Rinehart and Winston.

Bloomfield, Leonard. 1933. Language. New York: Henry Holt.

Bricker, Victoria R. 1974. The ethnographic context of some traditional Mayan speech genres. *In* Explorations in the ethnography of speaking, ed. by R. Bauman and J. Sherzer. London: Cambridge University Press.

Carroll, John B. 1953. The study of language. Cambridge: Harvard University Press.

Christie, Emerson Brewer. 1909. The Subanuns of Sindangan Bay. Bureau of Science Division of Ethnology Publications, VI.I. Manila: Manila Bureau of Printing.

Cole, Peter and J. L. Morgan, eds. 1975. Syntax and semantics, Vol. 3. New York: Academic Press.

Duncan, Starkey, Jr. 1974. On the structure of speaker-auditor interaction during speaking turns. Language in Society 3:161–80.

—— and Donald Fiske. 1977. Face to face interaction: Research, methods, and theory. Hillsdale, N.J.: Lawrence Erlbaum Associates. [Distributed by Halsted Press, New York.]

Edelsky, Carol. 1981. Who's got the floor? Language in Society 10:383–421.

Finley, John Park and William Churchill. 1913. The Subanu. Washington, D.C.: Carnegie Institution of Washington Publications. [Reprinted by Johnson Reprint Corporation, New York.]

Fox, James L. 1971. Semantic parallelism in Rotinese ritual language. Bijdragen tot de Taal-, Land- en Volkenkunde, DEEL 127:215–55.

──── . 1974. "Our ancestors spoke in pairs": Rotinese views of language, dialect, and code. *In* Explorations in the ethnography of speaking, ed. by R. Bauman and J. Sherzer. London: Cambridge University Press.

Frake, Charles O. 1960. The Eastern Subanun of Mindanao. *In* Social structure in Southeast Asia, ed. by G. Murdock. Chicago: Quadrangle Books. 51–64. [Viking Publications in Anthropology, Vol 29.]

──── . 1963. Litigation in Lipay: A study in Subanun law. [The proceedings of the Ninth Pacific Science Congress, 1957, Vol 3.] Bangkok.

──── . 1964a. A structural description of Subanun 'religious behavior'. *In* Explorations in cultural anthropology – Essays in honor of George Peter Murdock, ed. by W. Goodenough. New York: McGraw Hill.

──── . 1964b. How to ask for a drink in Subanun. *In* The ethnography of communication, ed. by John J. Gumperz and Dell Hymes. American Anthropologist 66:6, Part 2. 127–132.

──── . 1972. Struck by speech: The Yakan concept of litigation. *In* Directions in sociolinguistics: The ethnography of communication, ed by John J. Gumperz and Dell Hymes. New York: Holt, Rinehart and Winston.

Goffman, Erving. 1964. The neglected situation. *In* The ethnography of communication, ed by John J. Gumperz and Dell Hymes. American Anthropologist 66:6, Part 2. 133–136.

──── . 1967. Interaction ritual: Essays on face-to-face behavior. New York: Pantheon Books.

Gossen, Gary H. 1974. To speak with a heated heart: Chamula canons of style and good performance. *In* Explorations in the ethnography of speaking, ed. by R. Bauman and J. Sherzer. London: Cambridge University Press.

Grice, H. P. 1975. Logic and conversation. *In* Syntax and semantics, Vol 3, ed. by P. Cole and J. Morgan. New York: Academic Press.

Gumperz, John J. 1964. Linguistic and social interaction in two communities. *In* The ethnography of communication, ed. by J. Gumperz and D. Hymes. American Anthropologist 66:6, Part 2. 137–153. [Reprinted in J. Gumperz. 1971. Language in social groups. Stanford: Stanford University Press.]

Bibliography

—— . 1966. On the ethnology of linguistic change. *In* Sociolinguistics, ed. by W. Bright. The Hague: Mouton.

—— . 1967. The relations of linguistic to social categories. *In* A field manual for cross-cultural study of the acquisition of communicative competence, ed by D. Slobin. Berkeley: University of California Press. [Reprinted in J. Gumperz. 1971. Language in social groups. Stanford: Stanford University Press.]

—— and Dell Hymes, eds. 1972. Directions in sociolinguistics: The ethnography of communication. New York: Holt, Rinehart and Winston.

Hall, William C. 1969. A classification of Siocon Subanon verbs. Anthropological Linguistics 11.7:209–215.

—— . 1973. An outline of Siocon Subanon sentence structure. Philippine Journal of Linguistics 4–5.1–2:1–22.

Hymes, Dell. 1962. The ethnography of speaking. *In* Anthropology and human behavior, ed. by. T. Gladwin and W. Sturtevant Washington D. C.: Anthropological Society of Washington.

—— . 1964. Language in culture and society: A reader in linguistics and anthropology. New York: Harper and Row.

—— . 1972. Models of the interaction of language and social life. *In* Directions in sociolinguistics: The ethnography of communication, ed. by J. Gumperz and D. Hymes. New York: Holt, Rinehart and Winston.

—— . 1974. Foundations in sociolinguistics: An ethnographic approach. Philadelphia: University of Pennsylvania Press.

—— . 1981. "In vain I tried to tell you": Essays in Native American ethnopoetics. Philadelphia: University of Pennsylvania Press.

—— . 1982. Narrative form as a 'grammar' of experience: Native Americans and a glimpse of English. Journal of Education 164.2:121–142.

Irvine, Judith T. 1979. Formality and informality in communicative events. American Anthropologist 81:773–790.

Jakobson, Roman. 1963. Implications of language universals for linguistics. *In* Universals of language, by J. Greenberg. Cambridge: MIT Press. [2nd edition. 1966. Report of a conference held at Dobbs Ferry, New York, April 13–15, 1961.]

—— . 1966. Grammatical parallelism and its Russian facet. Language 42:399–429.

—— . 1968. Poetry of grammar and grammar of poetry. Lingua 21:597–609.

James, Deborah. 1978. The use of *oh, ah,* and *well* in relation to a number of grammatical phenomena. Papers in Linguistics 11:517–535.

Jefferson, Gail. 1972. Side sequences. *In* Studies in speech interaction, ed. by D. Sudnow. New York: Free Press.

Keenan, Elinor. 1974. Norm-makers, norm-breakers: Uses of speech by men and women in a Malagasy community. *In* Explorations in the ethnography of speaking, ed. by R. Bauman and J. Sherzer. London: Cambridge University Press.

———. 1975. A sliding sense of obligatoriness: The polystructure of Malagasy oratory. *In* Political language and oratory in traditional society, ed. by M. Block. New York: Academic Press.

———. 1977. The universality of conversational implicatures. *In* Studies in language variation, ed. by R. Fasold and R. Shuy. Washington, D.C.: Georgetown University Press.

Labov, William. 1966. The social stratification of English in New York City. Washington D.C.: Center for Applied Linguistics.

———. 1969. Contraction, deletion, and inherent variability of the English copula. Language 45:715–762.

———. 1970. The study of language in its social context. Studium Generale 23:30–87. [Reprinted in W. Labov. 1972. Sociolinguistic patterns. Philadelphia: University of Pennsylvania Press.]

———. 1972. Sociolinguistic patterns. Philadelphia: University of Pennsylvania Press.

Longacre, Robert E. 1968. Discourse, paragraph, and sentence structure in selected Philippine languages, Vol. 1. Santa Ana: Summer Institute of Linguistics.

———. 1976. An anatomy of speech notions. Lisse: Peter de Ridder Press.

Lynch, Frank. 1973. Social acceptance reconsidered. *In* Four readings on Philippine values, 4th edition, ed. by F. Lynch and A. deGuzman. Manila: Ateneo de Manila University Press.

Malkiel, Yakov. 1959. Studies in irreversible binomials. Lingua 8.2:113–160. [Reprinted in Y. Malkiel. 1968. Essays on linguistic themes. Berkeley: University of California Press.]

McKaughan, Howard and Batua Macaraya. 1967. A Maranao dictionary. Honolulu: University of Hawaii Press.

Pike, Kenneth L. 1967. Language in relation to a unified theory of the structure of human behavior, 2nd edition. The Hague: Mouton.

―――― and Evelyn Pike. 1977. Grammatical analysis. Dallas: Summer Institute of Linguistics. [Publication in Linguistics No. 53.]

Rosaldo, Michelle. 1973. I have nothing to hide: The language of Ilongot oratory. Language in Society 2:193–223.

――――. 1982. The things we do with words: Ilongot speech acts and speech act theory in philosophy. Language in Society 11:203–237.

Sankoff, Gillian. 1972. Language use in multilingual societies: Some alternative approaches. *In* Sociolinguistics, ed. by J. Pride and J. Holmes. Middlesex: Penguin Books.

Schachter, Paul and Fe Otanes. 1972. Tagalog reference grammar. Berkeley: University of California Press.

Schegloff, E., G. Jefferson, and H. Sacks. 1977. The preference for self-correction in the organization of repair in conversation. Language 53.2:361–382.

Searle, John R. 1969. Speech acts: An essay in the philosophy of language. London: Cambridge University Press.

――――, Ferenc Kiefer, and Manfred Bierwisch, eds. 1980. Speech act theory and pragmatics. Dordrecht: D. Reidel Publishing Company.

Trudgill, Peter. 1974. The social differentiation of English in Norwich. London: Cambridge University Press.

Walrod, Michael. 1977. Discourse grammar in Ga'dang. Dallas: Summer Institute of Linguistics and the University of Texas at Arlington. [Publication in Linguistics No. 63.]

Wolfram, Walt. 1974. Sociolinguistic aspects of assimilation. Washington, D.C.: Center for Urban Linguistics.

Wrigglesworth, Hazel. 1977a. Tulalang slays the dragon: A complete song from the Ilianen Manobo epic of Tulalang. Philippine Quarterly of Culture and Society 5:123–165.

――――. 1977b. Sociolinguistic features of narrative discourse in Ilianen Manobo. Lingua 41:101–124. xuOQrolaci57fcinikx

SUMMER INSTITUTE OF LINGUISTICS
Publications in Linguistics

(* = in microfiche only   ** = also in microfiche)

1. **Comanche Texts** by E. Canonge (1958) *
2. **Pocomchi Texts** by M. Mayers (1958) *
3. **Mixteco Texts** by A. Dyk (1959) *
4. **A Synopsis of English Syntax** by E. A. Nida (1960) *
5. **Mayan Studies I** by W. C. Townsend et al. (1960) *
6. **Sayula Popoluca Texts, with Grammatical Outline** by L. Clark (1961) *
7. **Studies in Ecuadorian Indian Languages I** by C. Peeke et al. (1962) *
8. **Totontepec Mixe Phonotagmemics** by J. C. Crawford (1963) *
9. **Studies in Peruvian Indian Languages I** by M. Larson et al. (1963) *
10. **Verb Studies in Five New Guinea Languages** by A. Pence et al. (1964) **
11. **Some Aspects of the Lexical Structure of a Mazatec Historical Text** by G. M. Cowan (1965) *
12. **Chatino Syntax** by K. Pride (1965) *
13. **Chol Texts on the Supernatural** by V. Warkentin (1965) *
14. **Phonemic Systems of Colombian Languages** by V. G. Waterhouse et al. (1967) *
15. **Bolivian Indian Tribes: Classification, Bibliography and Map of Present Language Distribution** by H. and M. Key (1967) **
16. **Bolivian Indian Grammars I and II** by E. Matteson et al. (1967) *
17. **Totonac: from Clause to Discourse** by A. Reid et al. (1968) *
18. **Tzotzil Grammar** by M. M. Cowan (1969) **
19. **Aztec Studies I: Phonological and Grammatical Studies in Modern Nahuatl Dialects** by D. F. Robinson et al. (1969) **
20. **The Phonology of Capanahua and its Grammatical Basis** by E. E. Loos (1969) **
21. **Philippine Languages: Discourse, Paragraph and Sentence Structure** by R. E. Longacre (1970) **
22. **Aztec Studies II: Sierra Nahuat Word Structure** by D. F. Robinson (1970) **
23. **Tagmemic and Matrix Linguistics Applied to Selected African Languages** by K. L. Pike (1970) **
24. **A Grammar of Lamani** by R. L. Trail (1970) **
25. **A Linguistic Sketch of Jicaltepec Mixtec** by H. C. Bradley (1970) **
26. **Major Grammatical Patterns of Western Bukidnon Manobo** by R. E. Elkins (1970) **
27. **Central Bontoc: Sentence, Paragraph and Discourse** by L. A. Reid (1970) **
28. **Identification of Participants in Discourse: A Study of Aspects of Form and Meaning in Nomatsiguenga** by M. R. Wise (1971) **
29. **Tupi Studies I** by D. Bendor-Samuel et al. (1971) **
30. **L'Enonce Toura (Côte d'Ivoire)** by R. Bearth (1971) **
31. **Instrumental Articulatory Phonetics: An Introduction to Techniques and Results** by K. C. Keller (1971) *
32. **According to Our ancestors: Folk Texts from Guatemala and Honduras** by M. Shaw et al. (1971) *
33. **Two Studies of the Lancandones of Mexico** by P. Baer and W. R. Merrifield (1971) **
34. **Toward a Generative Grammar of Blackfoot** by D. G. Frantz (1971) *
35. **Languages of the Guianas** by J. E. Grimes et al. (1972) *

36. **Tagmeme Sequences in the English Noun Phrase** by P. Fries (1972) **
37. **Hierarchial Structures in Guajajara** by D. Bendor-Samuel (1972) **
38. **Dialect Intelligibility Testing** by E. Casad (1974) **
39. **Preliminary Grammar of Auca** by M. C. Peeke (1973) **
40. **Clause, Sentence, and Discourse Patterns in Selected Languages of Nepal**, parts I, II, III, IV by A. Hale et al. (1973) **
41. **Patterns in Clause, Sentence, and Discourse in Selected Languages of India and Nepal**, parts I, II, III, IV by R. L. Trail et al. (1973) **
42. **A Generative Syntax of Peñoles Mixtec** by J. Daly (1973) **
43. **Daga Grammar** by E. Murane (1974) **
44. **A Hierarchical Sketch of Mixe** as spoken in San José El Paraíso by W. and J. Van Haitsma (1976) **
45. **Network Grammars** by J. E. Grimes et al. (1975) *
46. **A Description of Hiligaynon Syntax** by E. Wolfenden **
47. **A Grammar of Izi, an Igbo Language** by P. and I. Meier and J. Bendor-Samuel (1975) **
48. **Semantic Relationships of Gahuku Verbs** by E. Deibler (1976) **
49. **Sememic and Grammatical Structures in Gurung** by W. Glover (1974) **
50. **Korean Clause Structure** by Shin Ja Joo Hwang (1976) **
51. **Papers on Discourse** by J. E. Grimes et al. (1978) **
52. **Discourse Grammar: Studies in Indigenous Languages of Colombia, Panama, and Ecuador**, parts I, II, III by R. E. Longacre et al. (1976-77) **
53. **Grammatical Analysis** by K. L. and E. G. Pike (1980; revised 1982)   **Instructor's Guide for Grammatical Analysis** by K. L. and E. G. Pike (1976) **
54. **Studies in Otomanguean Phonology** by W. R. Merrifield et al. (1977) **
55. **Two Studies in Middle American Comparative Linguistics** by D. Oltrogge and C. Rensch (1977) **
56. **Studies in Uto-Aztecan Grammar**, parts I, II, III, IV by R. W. Langacker et al. (1977-84) **
57. **The Deep Structure of the Sentence in Sara-Ngambay Dialogues** by J. E. Thayer (1978) **
58. **Discourse Studies in Mesoamerican Languages**, parts I and II by L. K. Jones et al. (1979) **
59. **The Functions of Reported Speech in Discourse** by M. L. Larson (1978) **
60. **A Grammatical Description of the Engenni Language** by E. Thomas (1978) **
61. **Predicate and Argument in Rengao Grammar** by K. Gregerson (1979) **
62. **Nung Grammar** by J. E. Saul and N. F. Wilson (1980) **
63. **Discourse Grammar in Ga'dang** by M. R. Walrod (1979) **
64. **A Framework for Discourse Analysis** by W. Pickering (1980) **
65. **A Generative Grammar of Afar** by L. Bliese (1981) **
66. **The Phonology and Morphology of Axininca Campa** by D. L. Payne (1981) **
67. **Pragmatic Aspects of English Text Structure** by L. B. Jones (1983) **
68. **Syntactic Change and Syntactic Reconstruction** by J. R. Costello (1983) **
69. **Affix Positions and Cooccurrences** by J. E. Grimes (1983) **
70. **Babine and Carrier Phonology: A Historically Oriented Study** by G. Story (1984) **
71. **Workbook for Historical Linguistics** by W. P. Lehmann (1984) **
72. **Senoufo Phonology, Discourse to Syllable** by E. Mills (1984) **
73. **Pragmatics in Non-Western Perspective** by G. L. Huttar and K. J. Gregerson (1986) **
74. **English Phonetic Transcription** by Ch.-J. N. Bailey (1985) **
75. **Sentence-initial Devices** by J. E. Grimes et al. (1986) **

76. **Hixkaryana and Linguistic Typology** by D. C. Derbyshire (1985) **
77. **Discourse Features of Korean Narration** by S. J. Hwang (1987) **
78. **Tense/Aspect and the Development of Auxiliaries in Kru Languages** by L. Marchese (1986) **
79. **Modes in Dényá Discourse** by S. N. Abangma (1987) **
80. **Current Trends and Issues in Hispanic Linguistics** by L. Studerus**
81. **Aspects of Western Subanon Formal Speech** by W. Hall**

For further information or a catalog of all S.I.L. publications write to:

        Bookstore
        Summer Institute of Linguistics
        7500 W. Camp Wisdom Road
        Dallas, TX 75236

Errata for
Aspects of Western Subanon Formal Speech

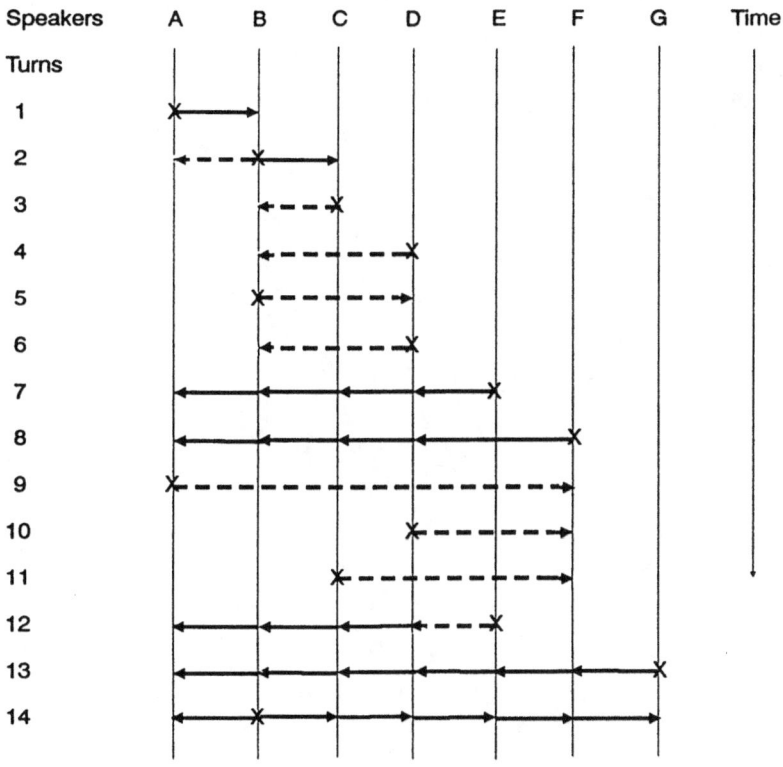

Figure 2.1 Speech sequencing

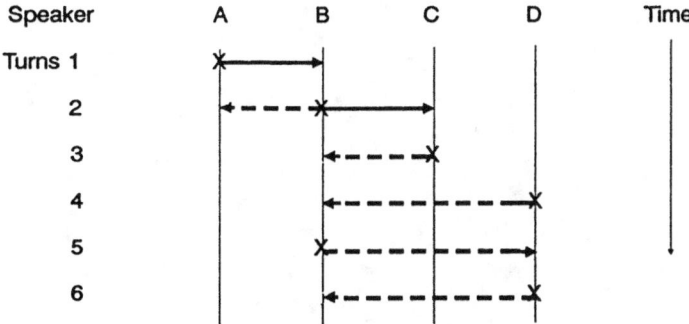

Figure 3.1 Dialogue embedding

Replacing Figure 2.1 on page 23 and Figure 3.1 on page 37 in *Aspects of Western Subanon Formal Speech*.

www.ingramcontent.com/pod-product-compliance
Lightning Source LLC
Chambersburg PA
CBHW051811230426
43672CB00012B/2693